D1132259

DEDICATION

To my wonderful, funny husband Keith.
And to my very first teacher, my mom Pat.

Simply

sim ply - simplē - adverb
1. in a straightforward or plain manner.
"speaking simply and from the heart"

When you decide to convert your work flow to the Google work flow, it doesn't have to be a complicated effort. It's just changing this for that. This being the work flow you are accustomed to, That being the Google Apps.

But what the Google work flow does for you, compared to the "this" work flow, it gives you Apps that have a natural language that talk to each other. Google Apps tie into the artificial intelligence of the Internet and gives it to their Apps.

My effort, in creating this book, is to help you with your transition to the Google interface, or even if you just want to learn Google. I try not to make it overly complicated. I laid the book out in a manner that I think takes you from start to finish. A natural flow, like reading a book, from upper left to lower right.

Within the book you will find various QR Codes that are used to scan and go to Google's Help sections for more in-depth explanations. If you need a QR Reader, go to the Google Play Store or the Apple App Store to download one.

All chapters display screen shots of the interface with easy explanations of what lies beneath the menu system. This is my way of building the application for you. Building any type of document is a mechanical process and the menus are the tools you need for your construction.

TABLE OF CONTENTS

TABLE OF CONTENTS

CHAPTER 3 – DOCS

CHAPTER 4 – SHEETS

TABLE OF CONTENTS

CHAPTER 5 – SLIDES

TABLE OF CONTENTS

CHAPTER 6 – FORMS

CHAPTER 7 – DRAWINGS

TABLE OF CONTENTS

CHAPTER 8 – SITES

GOOGLE

Let's start at the very beginning, it's a very good place to start!

Google was created in 1997 by American computer scientists Larry Page and Sergey Brin.

Since it's creation, it has become one of the most popular search engines in use. And there is good reason for it's popularity. The homepage is purposely left without the clutter of ads, adding to how fast it loads and how efficient it is.

As of the writing of this book, Google had 130 trillion individual pages and it is constantly growing.

How does Google do it?

Google navigates the web by crawling it's pages from the websites that the web designers/developers submit. It uses what are called Spiderbots. These Spiderbots crawl the web and find information and returns home with all the data it has found. And this data is than indexed.

On your computer, tablet or phone, access your account anyplace, online or offline!

And what gets indexed - links and text.

This is why, when a web page is designed and images are added, things like alt-text and alt descriptions are added.

Within these alt descriptions, keywords are used. It is a way of adding additional text for Google to index for it's algorithms.

What are algorithms?

A search engine algorithm - strings of keywords and operators - searches its associated database for relevant web pages, and returns results. These algorithms are clues given to Google to give you a better result in your search.

And based on the clues, you get the correct answer back!

WHAT NOW?

But Google isn't just about being the very best search engine, it has become so much more.

A suite of production apps that help make your life easier!
If you don't already have a Google account, you will want to get one.

Follow along in each chapter and get a better understanding of each App and how to use them. The Google products are great for personal or business use. Chapter One tells you about Chrome and how to get your account. Chapter two introduces the Drive and the following chapters give you a breakdown of the most popular production Apps.

1

Chrome – Not just a search engine but also a web browser that is used to access your applications (Apps).

2

Drive – Fifteen gigs of cloud-based storage that you can access from any device, and in just about any location that you can get onto the Internet.

3

Docs – Google Docs is a web-based editing program that allows users to create, share and edit documents through a secure networked system.

4

Sheets – A spreadsheet program with the ability to add, delete, and sort rows and columns, plus perform functions.

5

Slides – An on-line presentation program that can act as a layout program because of it's visual ability.

6

Forms – Easy-to-use survey / quiz creator tool that will export the answers to a Google Sheet.

7

Drawings – Diagramming program used to create flowcharts, organizational charts, website wire-frames, and other types of diagrams.

8

Sites – Create a website with this easy drag and drop platform. Great to use for an online portfolio.

① CHROME

The base of all things good!

Chrome is the base for all the Google Apps.
It is the house that they live in.

Chrome is both a web browser and a search engine. And yes, there is a difference. A **web browser** is graphical user interface for displaying HTML files, used to navigate the World Wide Web. A **search engine** uses keywords, as explained in the beginning of this book, to search the world wide web and bring back a result.

A web browser can exist without a search engine but a search engine needs a web browser to do it's searching. Chrome is that handy tool that does both jobs.

A. DOWNLOAD

Yes, you can access any Google App from the other browsers, but to have a nicer experience, it is recommended that you use Chrome. But Chrome does not come automatically installed on your device, you have to download this freeware.

FOR COMPUTER

1 To download Chrome, either scan the QR code on the right or go to the below website: **https://www.google.com/chrome/.**

2 Select **DOWNLOAD** from the top menu (1.1)

3 You will be prompted to either run or save, choose run. Chrome can be installed on the PC, Mac, Android, iPhone, iPad, and Linux.

Scan to download Chrome

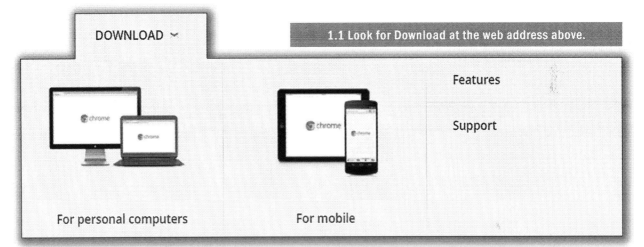

DOWNLOAD ⌄

1.1 Look for Download at the web address above.

Features

Support

For personal computers

For mobile

FOR ANDROID

1. On the Play Store, go to Chrome for Android.

2. Tap Install.

3. Tap Accept & Download.

4. To start browsing, go to the Home or All Apps page and tap the Chrome app

FOR IPHONE/IPAD

1. On your iPhone or iPad, download Chrome on the Apple App Store.

2. Tap Get.

3. Tap Install.

4. Enter your Apple ID Password and tap OK.

5. To start browsing, go to your home screen and tap the Chrome app

Google and the Google logo are registered trademarks of Google Inc., used with permission.

Simply Google | Page 15

B. CREATE AN ACCOUNT

You downloaded Chrome, now what?

You will want to create a Google account. With a Google account, you have access to their products such as Drive, Docs, Sheets, and Slides, plus a whole lot more. But, creating your account also allows you to sync your information across devices. This gives you the ability to access your synced data on any device, at any location. Some synced data includes your bookmarks, passwords, and browsing history. To keep your data safe, it is recommend you don't sign in if you're on a public computer. Only sign in to Chrome from trusted devices.

Create an account

To create your account. . .

1. Either scan the QR code on the top or go to: **https://accounts.google.com/signup**

2. You will be prompted to fill out a form as shown on the right (1.2). This is where you create your email address and set your password. Google request your personal information to keep your account secure and this will be used if you need to recover your account.

3. You will next be taken to a screen that will state Google's privacy and terms and you must agree to get your account. Google will ask for:

Name   Gender
User name   Mobile phone
Password   Current email address
Date of birth   Location

1.2 Account sign up form.

C. 2 WAYS TO ACCESS YOUR ACCOUNT

Now you have created an account, how do you access it?

Gmail   Images

1.3 Select Gmail

1. Load Chrome.
2. Upper right corner, select Gmail. (1.3)
3. Sign in screen will appear, enter email and select Next.(1.4)
4. Enter password.

1. At the top, right of the Chrome browser is a little person, click here (1.5).
2. A pop-up will open with a blue box that says "Sign in to Chrome".
3. Click there.
4. Enter your email.
5. Enter your password. Now your have access to your passwords, bookmarks, and your data can sync across devices.

1.4 Enter email

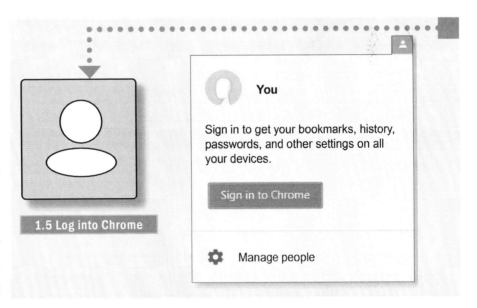

1.5 Log into Chrome

You

Sign in to get your bookmarks, history, passwords, and other settings on all your devices.

Sign in to Chrome

⚙ Manage people

D. MULTIPLE PEOPLE

You can have multiple people in the same device but with their own settings, bookmarks. Example of different people can be your work profile and your personal profile.

Anyone using Chrome can switch to any other Chrome profile added to that device. For example, if someone switches to your Chrome profile, they'll be able to see websites you visited. That's why it is recommend that you only share your device with people you trust.

Carol

You

Sign in to get your bookmarks, history, passwords, and other settings on all your devices.

Sign in to Chrome

Carol

⚙ Manage people

1.6 Add multiple people.

How to add multiple people?
1. On your computer, open Chrome.
2. At the top right, click the button that says either your name or People (1.6).
3. Select Manage people.
4. Click Add person.
5. Enter their email.
6. Enter their password.
7. Choose Save after your have chosen a name.

E. CHROME FEATURE OVERVIEW

1 **Forward / Backward Arrows** – Navigate back and forward to see pages you've already visited by going backward and forward in your browsing history.

2 **Reload this page** – Refreshes your page and helps restore it.

3 **Home** – The Home button does not show by default. You have to go to settings, scroll down to Appearance (1.7), and select Show Home Button. *(Number 14 will shows how to get to settings).*

1.7 Show Home Button

Appearance

Get themes Reset to default theme

☑ Show Home Button

New Tab page Change

☑ Always show the bookmarks bar

Search Box – The Google search box is where all things happen.

This is the area where you can enter the URL for the website your are looking for. When you enter your information into the search box, the Google algorithm will use the words and search to bring you results as close as possible to what you are looking for.

But the search box is just not to find websites, it can perform other task such as calculations.

You can also refine your search using a specific criteria such as placing your search words within quotations.

- **Use asterisks to specify unknown words:** imagine * * * living for today;

- **Limit search to one website:** Specify a particular website "Phillies site:si.com";

- **Find sites that are similar to others:** related: amazon.com;

- **Follow a song title** with the word 'lyrics';

- **Search within a Range of Numbers:** Use two consecutive dots to search within a range of numbers Nike $50..$85;

- **Use a - or + to include or exclude sites and words:** Civil War -Wikipedia;

- Find exact file types: .pdf, .ppt;

- Use it as a stopwatch and timer;

- Type 'Convert' and units for conversions;

- Type 'translate' and phrase. Choose language to translate From & to.

Apps Shortcut – In order for the Apps Shortcut to show, you first have to make sure your Bookmarks bar *(Number 8 will show how to access Bookmarks)* is showing.

Google Chrome Apps are web applications that run on the Google Chrome web browser. Chrome apps can be obtained from the Chrome Web Store where apps, extensions, and themes can be installed or bought.

The apps that I will review in this book are the productive word processing apps: Docs, Sheets, Slides, Drawings, Forms, plus Sites.

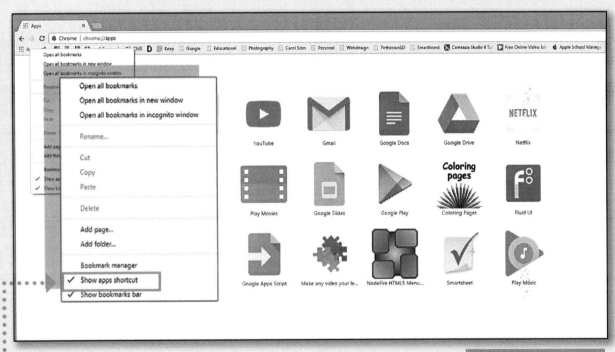

1.8 Show apps shortcut

1. From within the Bookmarks bar, right click. (1.8)

2. Select Show apps shortcut.

3. All apps you have installed from the Chrome Web Store will show in this area. To access the Chrome web store and get Apps, go to: **https://chrome.google.com/webstore**

4. Click on any of the installed apps for them to open.

You can also go to the Chrome Web Store to get extensions at: https://chrome.google.com/webstore

You can find apps, extensions, and browser themes for the Google Chrome browser in the Chrome Web Store. With these additions, you can do more with Chrome. Selecting "All" under Categories will show the full variety available.

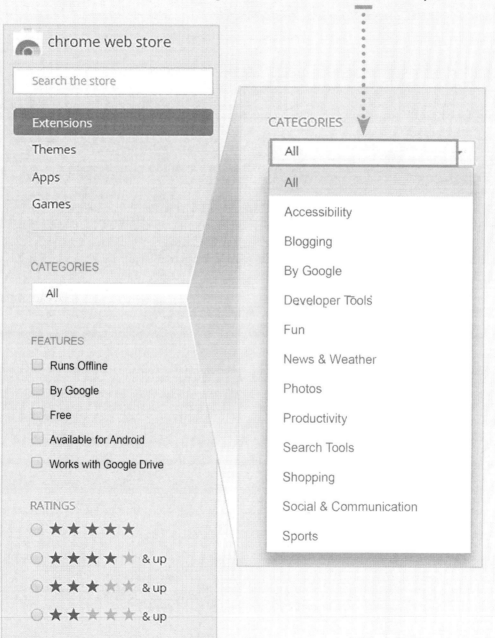

Tabs – When you open the Chrome browser, your first tab is open. Tabs can be pulled apart so that they are their own separate window by just grabbing it and pulling to the side.

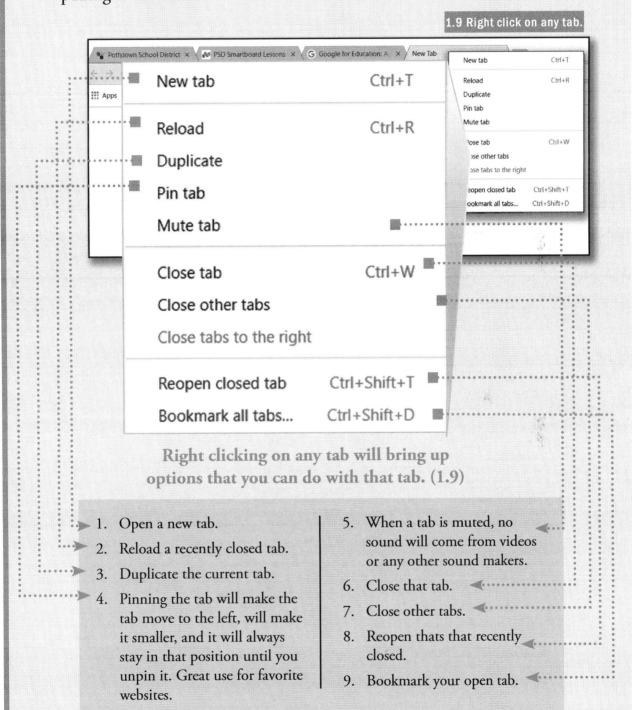

1.9 Right click on any tab.

Right clicking on any tab will bring up
options that you can do with that tab. (1.9)

1. Open a new tab.

2. Reload a recently closed tab.

3. Duplicate the current tab.

4. Pinning the tab will make the tab move to the left, will make it smaller, and it will always stay in that position until you unpin it. Great use for favorite websites.

5. When a tab is muted, no sound will come from videos or any other sound makers.

6. Close that tab.

7. Close other tabs.

8. Reopen thats that recently closed.

9. Bookmark your open tab.

7 **Open New Tab** – The small, gray parallelogram (1.10) to the right of your open tap will open a new tab when clicked.

1.10 Click to open new page.

8 **Bookmark Bar** – Bookmarks give you control of your browsing. You never have to lose a web page that you want to return to and read later. If you're using Chrome on a computer, you can have your bookmarks appear in a bar (1.11) at the top of every web page, just click Show bookmarks bar. You can also add, remove, or reorder items in the bookmarks bar at any time by choosing Bookmark manager. My favorite thing is to add folders and organize my bookmark bar. Bookmarks are not available on a mobile device.

1.11 Bookmark Bar

To access the Bookmark options:

1. Select 3 dots in upper right corner. (1.12)
2. Go down to Bookmarks.

   • **Bookmark this page** - when chosen, you can add current page to bookmarks bar, place it within a folder, edit name or remove.

   • **Bookmark open pages** - all open pages will be bookmarked. You can choose where they go by placing in folder or just on bar.

   1.12 How to get to bookmark bar

   • **Show bookmarks bar** - opens the bookmark bar.

   • **Bookmark manager** - add, remove, or reorder items

   • **Import bookmarks and settings** - Bookmarks from other browsers such as Internet Explorer, Firefox, Safari, can be imported.

⑨ Open Bookmark Star – An open star at the far right of the URL bar means that the webpage you are on is not a bookmarked page.

To bookmark your current page:

1. Select star.

2. Choose if you want to keep current page's name and if you want to place it in a folder. (1.13)

Blue Bookmark Star – A solid blue star indicates that the web page you are currently on is a bookmarked page.

1.13 Choices when you select star.

⑩ Your account – Selecting your name will take you to the area where you can sign into your Chrome browser and manage people.

⑪ Minimize – Selecting the minus symbol will hide the open window and place it on the bottom of your computer in your taskbar or the Dock in the Mac. Touching it will restore the window to the top.

⑫ Maximize – Selecting the rectangle symbol will fill the entire screen of your computer. Touching this symbol will release it from full screen.

⑬ Close – When you select the **X** the window will close.

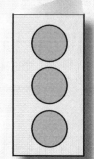

CUSTOMIZE AND CONTROL GOOGLE CHROME

Behind the three dots holds the internal workings and the ability to customize how your Chrome experience is. Let's look at some of the things that you can do:

14-1 Making Sure Your Chrome Is Up-To-Date:

It is important to Google to make sure that they are always improving their product.

There are a lot of developers who work at Google and their job is to improve the Google experience. So you don't want to miss out on any of the latest and greatest by being out-of-date!

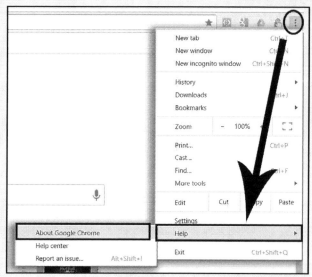

1. Click on the 3 dots.

2. Go down to **Help** > **About Google Chrome**. (1.14)

3. A new screen (1.15) will open and there will be a spinning dial checking to make sure your Chrome browser is at it's latest version.

4. You will be prompted to relaunch once updated.

1.14 Help > About

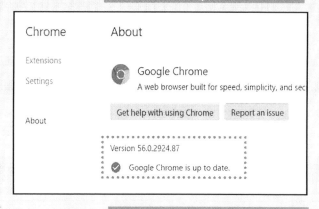

1.15 Up-to-date

14-2 Going Incognito:

If you don't want Google Chrome to save a record of what you visit and download, you can browse the web privately in **Incognito mode**.

Incognito mode only prevents Chrome from saving your site visit activity. It won't stop other sources from seeing what sites you've visited, including:

- Your Internet service provider

- Your employer (if you're using a work computer)

- The websites you visit themselves

- Chrome won't save a record of the files you download in Incognito mode. However, the downloaded files will be saved to your computer's Downloads folder, even after you close your Incognito tabs.

14-3 History

Chrome's history will keep a record of all the pages you have visited. Chrome will keep your history for three months.

By default, if you sign in to Chrome, your history is available across devices.

You can see your full history at: www.history.google.com

14-4 Settings

1. Select the three dots |••••▶
2. Go down to Settings.
3. A new window will open.

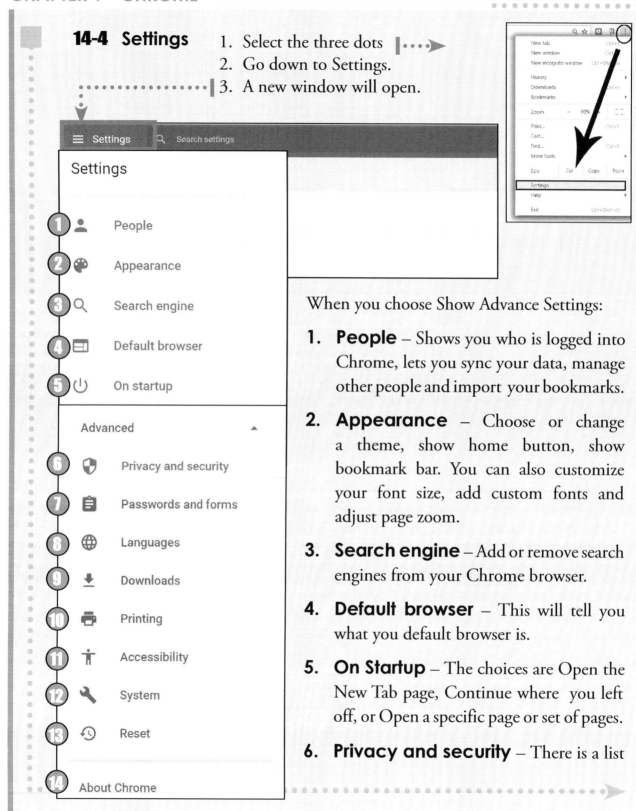

Settings

① 👤 People

② 🎨 Appearance

③ 🔍 Search engine

④ 🖥 Default browser

⑤ ⏻ On startup

Advanced ▲

⑥ 🛡 Privacy and security

⑦ 📋 Passwords and forms

⑧ 🌐 Languages

⑨ ⬇ Downloads

⑩ 🖨 Printing

⑪ 🧍 Accessibility

⑫ 🔧 System

⑬ 🕘 Reset

⑭ About Chrome

When you choose Show Advance Settings:

1. **People** – Shows you who is logged into Chrome, lets you sync your data, manage other people and import your bookmarks.

2. **Appearance** – Choose or change a theme, show home button, show bookmark bar. You can also customize your font size, add custom fonts and adjust page zoom.

3. **Search engine** – Add or remove search engines from your Chrome browser.

4. **Default browser** – This will tell you what you default browser is.

5. **On Startup** – The choices are Open the New Tab page, Continue where you left off, or Open a specific page or set of pages.

6. **Privacy and security** – There is a list

14-5 Advanced Settings

of 12 different options to choose from to tighten and control the privacy of your browser. It is a good idea to review these settings and customize your browser.

7. **Passwords and forms** – You can enable autofill of forms to save typing. You can also securely save often used passwords and if you forget them, you can come here to see what they are.

8. **Languages** – You can choose and set your default language here. This is also the area you set your spell check.

9. **Downloads** – Automatically set your download location so you never lose those downloaded files.

10. **Printing** – You can set up cloud printing devices here.

11. **Accessibility** – Clicking here will take you to the Chrome Web Store where you can choose extensions such as Color Enhancer, Long Descriptions, High Contrast.

12. **System** – Continue running background apps when Google Chrome is closed, Use hardware accelerations when available, or Open proxy settings.

13. **Reset** – Choosing to reset your browser will restore settings to their original defaults.

14. **About Chrome** – This is where you would go to see if your browser is up to date.

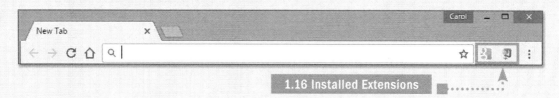

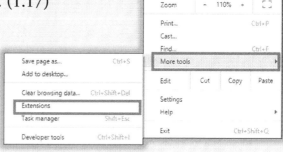

1.16 Installed Extensions

Extensions – Small software programs that can modify and enhance the functionality of the Chrome browser. An extension affects something global on your browser. Your installed extensions (1.16) can be viewed to the right of the URL box.

To access your installed extensions:

1. Select the 3 dots, scroll down and choose More tools.

2. From the flyout, choose Extensions

3. On the far left of this new window, upper corner, list down Extensions; Settings, About. (1.17)

4. Select Extensions and a new window will opens. You can see your installed extensions.

5. At the bottom of this window, you can choose Get More Extensions.

6. You can enable, disable or trash your extensions here.

1.17 Extensions Settings About

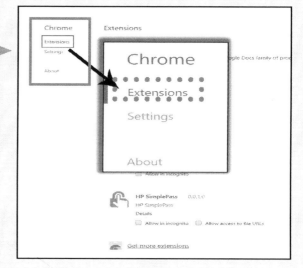

Gmail – Selecting Gmail will log you not only into your email account, it will also give your access to your apps.

You will be prompted to enter your Google Account user name and password.

If a user name is already filled in and you need to sign in to a different account, click Sign in with a different account.

Tip: If you're signing in to a public computer, make sure to sign out before leaving the computer.

I m a g e s – Selecting Images will load Google Images. From here, you can search for specific images by either:

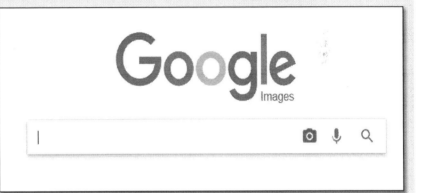

1. Typing in your request

2. Uploading an image (1.18). You can paste an image URL or upload an image. Uploading the image will return suggestions based your uploaded image.

1.18 Search by uploaded image

3. Voice request. You will have to have your microphone turned on and you can speak your request.

18

The Waffle – The 9-point grid at the upper right of your browser is called The Waffle. Depending on the type of account you have will determine which Google Apps are in your grid.

The icons can be dragged around to reorder them.

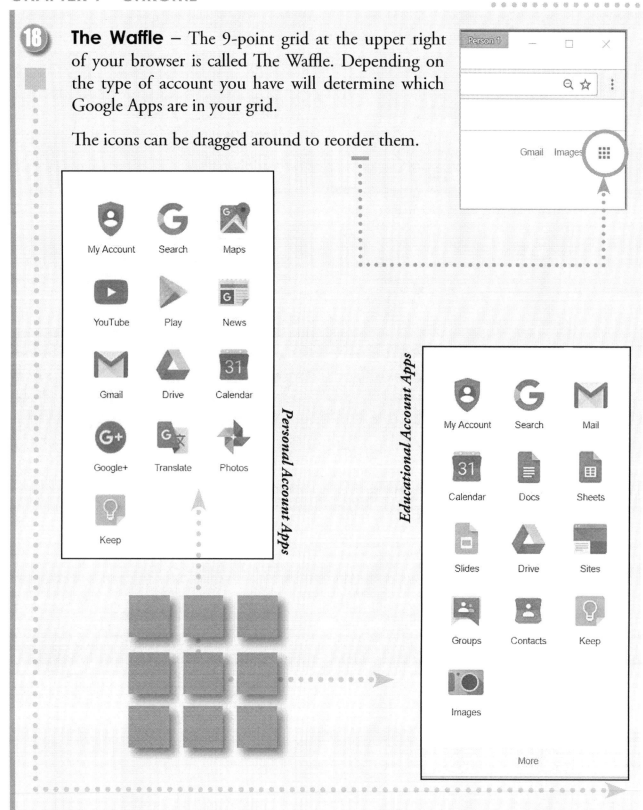

Personal Account Apps

Educational Account Apps

Notifications – If you have the settings turned on in Google + and Google Photos to receive notifications, you will get your alerts here.

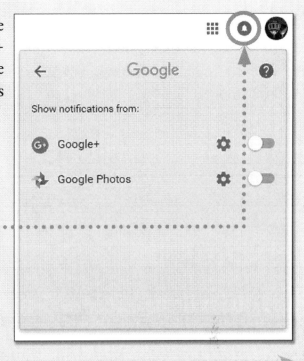

Google Account – Clicking at your icon will take you to:

- My Account information.

- Google + Profile

- Privacy

- Add an account

- Sign out

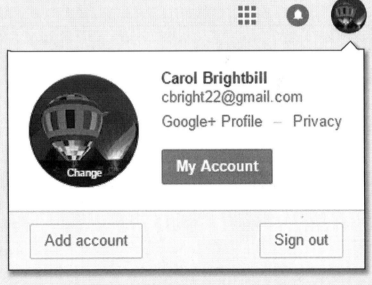

21 **Omnibox** – The search box in the center of the Chrome browser is called the Omnibox. When you start typing here, your question will jump to the top where the URL is. You can search by word, phase, and even image. The Omnibox can perform mathematical calculations and even answer questions such as "how many cups are in 2 liters?"

Google

Search Google or type URL

The Omnibox can be used to search the web or type in a question, but there are more functions it can perform for you!

Just by typing the word "define" followed by a colon and the word you would like defined, the Omnibox becomes a dictionary. Notice the dictionary includes an audio of the word, too.

How about a timer? Enter the word "timer" followed by the time period you want, and the Omnibox counts back the time. Or you can select the "Stopwatch" option. You can easily stop and reset the timer from the pop-up window and choose full-screen or not.

Use voice typing if you have your microphone turned on.

Tiles – The tiles that show in the middle of your Chrome browser are your most recently visited sites.

Your favorite web places will show up in a clean, colorful 8-grid within your Chrome browser.

When you hover over one, an X will appear in the upper right corner if you want to delete one.

After you delete one, at the bottom will appear, Thumbnail removed, Undo, Restore all.

② DRIVE

The activity hub for all your apps and files.

Cloud Storage and File Backup for Docs, Sheets, Slides, and Photos

What is the cloud? So if something is saved to the cloud, does that mean that it is just floating in the sky?

No! When you save to the cloud, your files actually are going to a server that is just off site. With the Internet becoming faster, this has enabled the ability to save large files with ease.

Saving to the cloud has created the ability to access your files, anytime, anywhere. You can be on someone else's computer. You can access your files on just about any device, from iPhone, iPad, Mac, PC, Android.

A. HOW TO GET TO YOUR DRIVE

①

After your have logged into your Chrome account, you can type in

https://drive.google.com

②

Go to the waffle and select the triangle icon.

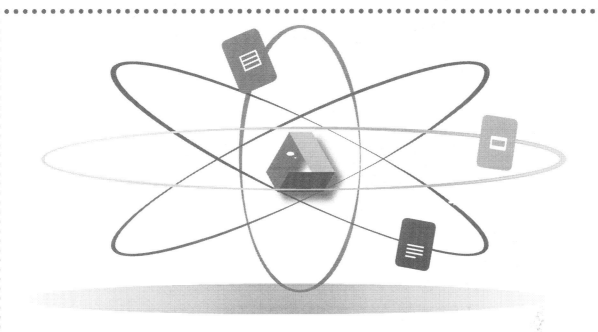

Nucleus

nu·cle·us - 'n(y)ooklēes - noun

The central and most important part of an object, movement, or group, forming the basis for its activity and growth.

This is why I call the Drive the nucleus, it is the HUB of all the activity. Not only does the Drive house all your files, it also houses the Google GSuite of applications.

Some of the features of the drive are:

- Creating a new Doc, Sheets, Slides, Form, and Drawing right from the drive.

- Download the Drive to your computer so you can always sync your files with your Cloud.

- A shared folder can be created in the drive to make for easy collaboration among team members.

B. HOW MUCH STORAGE DO YOU GET?

Account	Storage limit
G Suite Business	Unlimited storage 1TB if 4 or fewer users
G Suite Enterprise	Unlimited storage 1TB if 4 or fewer users
G Suite for Education	Unlimited storage 1 TB if 4 or fewer users
Google Apps Free edition (legacy)	Individual consumer accounts 15 GB

You can store files up to 5TB each.
Anything you create with Docs, Sheets, or Slides won't use up any of your storage.

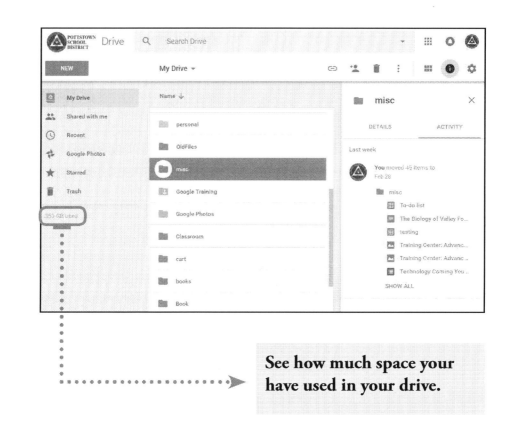

See how much space your have used in your drive.

C. WHAT ARE CLOUD-BASED APPS?

Google Docs is a free web based application.

What does that mean? It means that you don't have to install or download a program to work on your document. It is called an application now, not a program. Everything you do in that file, can be done on-line. You can access your files from any computer, or device with an Internet connection. And you can also choose to work off-line, in case you don't have Internet access. And yes, it is free.

When using Google Docs, you can share your file with your team and collaborate. Collaborators can view, comment, and make edits, depending on the privileges that you give them.

Working in this manner eliminates multiple versions of a document, eliminates attaching a file to an email so someone else can input their changes and than send it back.

D. WHAT IS **SHARING** ALL ABOUT?

Sharing

/SHer/- verb

have a portion of (something) with another or others.

"he shared the pie with her"

synonyms: split, divide, go halves on;

- give a portion of (something) to another or others.
- use, occupy, or enjoy (something) jointly with another or others.

What makes Google so powerful . . .

. . . is the ability to share documents, spreadsheets, and presentations with others, so you can collaboratively edit those documents together in real-time from anywhere on any devise. The people you share with will always see the most updated version. Let's dive deeper into what this is all about.

From education, to business, and even in your personal life, collaborating on a project enhances the likelihood of a successful outcome. It builds comradery and teamwork. It prepares students for an ever-changing digital future.

SHARING A FILE

SHARING A FOLDER

SHARING A LINK

So you want to share a file, let's break down the steps involved.

D-1 Sharing a File from the Drive

When you share a file from the Drive, you can either:
1. share it by adding people.
2. share it by link

1. Share by adding people

1. Select the file that you want to share.

2. Top menu appears. Select the icon at the upper right that has the person with the + symbol (2.1).

3. When you share a file, you are given three choices (2.2):
   - Can edit
   - Can comment
   - Can view

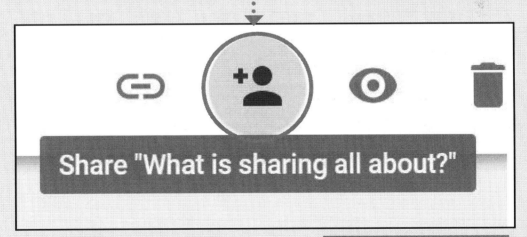

Share "What is sharing all about?"

2.1 Share with people

When you share a file, think about what you want the recipient to be able to do. . .

Share with others   Get shareable link

People

Enter names or email addresses...

✓ Get edit
Can comment
Can view

Done

2.2 Choose what they can do

D-2 Editing Rights in a Shared File

1. Can edit

Deliberate thought has to be put into the process of sharing a file. If you share the file with 50 people, giving all 50 the right to edit, that means that 50 people can be in that file editing at the same time.

When is it good to share with edit rights?

- If you are in a collaborative group who are working on the file together.

- A teacher sharing with the class, so that students can collaborative at the same time sharing their thoughts.

2. Can comment

Users who are given the "can comment" permission can not only view a doc, but they can also make and respond to comments, but they do not have editing rights.

When is it good to share with comment rights?

- You would like suggestions for others but you don't want them to be able to change the original.

- Student's can use this when sharing with a teacher to get their input on a project.

3. Can view

When you can only view a file, you can not comment or edit.

When is it good to share with view only rights?

- If you do not want the original document edited, you can force the views to make a copy of the file so they will have edit rights of their own file.

D-3 Advance Settings When Sharing

Select Advanced (2.3) at the bottom of the pop up window that appears after you select the icon to share. It takes you to ways that you can lock down and protect your file even further.

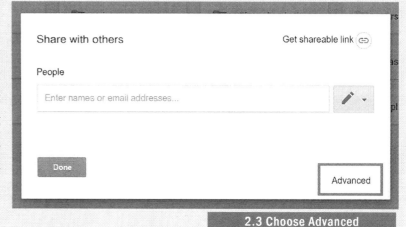

2.3 Choose Advanced

The two advanced selections are: (2.4)

- Prevent editors from changing access and adding new people

- Disable options to download, print, and copy for commenter and viewers.

These are great security options for teachers when they share with students or businesses sharing with clients.

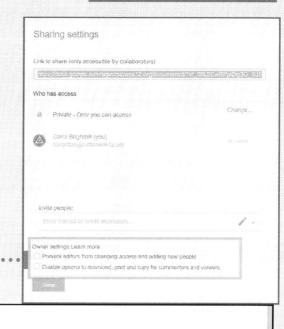

Owner settings Learn more

☐ Prevent editors from changing access and adding new people

☐ Disable options to download, print and copy for commenters and viewers

Done

2.4 Security Settings

D-4 Sharing a Link from the Drive

When you share a link from the Drive, you have to first turn link sharing on.

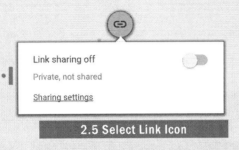

Link sharing off
Private, not shared
Sharing settings

2.5 Select Link Icon

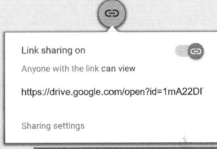

Link sharing on
Anyone with the link can view
https://drive.google.com/open?id=1mA22DI
Sharing settings

2.6 Slide button to turn sharing on

1. Select the file that you want to share.

2. Top menu appears. Select the link icon. (2.5)

3. Link sharing is off by default. You can select the slide button on the right to turn link sharing on. (2.6)

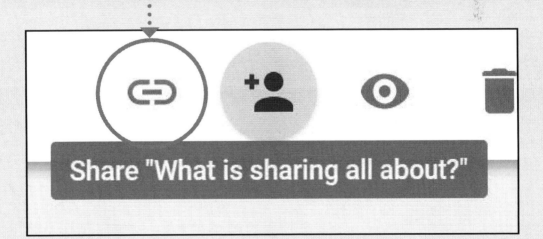

Share "What is sharing all about?"

4. Select Sharing settings (2.7)

5. Select drop down arrow beside Anyone with the link can view. (2.8)

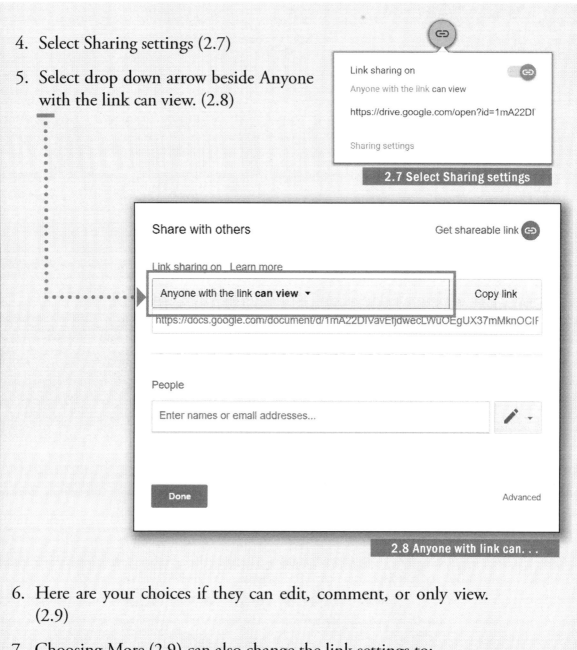

Link sharing on

Anyone with the link can view

https://drive.google.com/open?id=1mA22DI

Sharing settings

2.7 Select Sharing settings

Share with others   Get shareable link 🔗

Link sharing on   Learn more

Anyone with the link **can view** ▾   Copy link

https://docs.google.com/document/d/1mA22DIVavEfjdwecLWuOEgUX37mMknOCIF

People

Enter names or email addresses...   ✏ ▾

Done   Advanced

2.8 Anyone with link can. . .

6. Here are your choices if they can edit, comment, or only view. (2.9)

7. Choosing More (2.9) can also change the link settings to:
   - On-Public on the web(2.10)
   - On-Anyone with the link
   - Off-Specific people

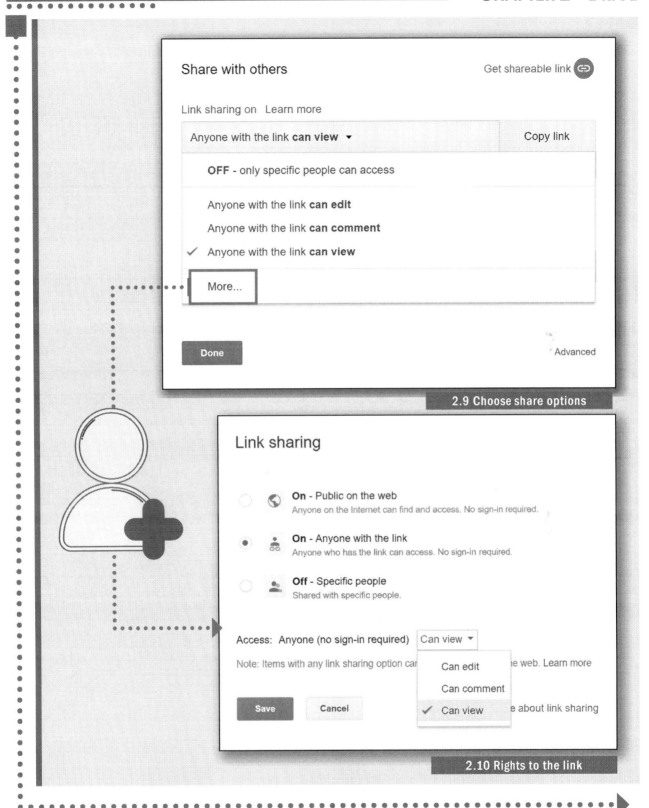

Share with others

Get shareable link 🔗

Link sharing on   Learn more

Anyone with the link **can view** ▾

Copy link

OFF - only specific people can access

Anyone with the link **can edit**

Anyone with the link **can comment**

✓ Anyone with the link **can view**

More...

Done

Advanced

2.9 Choose share options

Link sharing

🌐 **On** - Public on the web
Anyone on the Internet can find and access. No sign-in required.

👤 **On** - Anyone with the link
Anyone who has the link can access. No sign-in required.

👤 **Off** - Specific people
Shared with specific people.

Access: Anyone (no sign-in required)   Can view ▾

Note: Items with any link sharing option ca   e web. Learn more

Can edit

Can comment

Save   Cancel   ✓ Can view   about link sharing

2.10 Rights to the link

D-5 Sharing a Folder

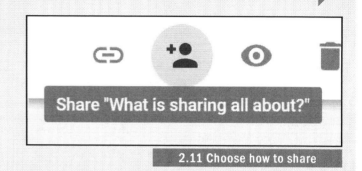

2.11 Choose how to share

1. Select the folder that you want to share, than select the icon at the upper right that has the person with the + symbol or choose the link icon. (2.11)

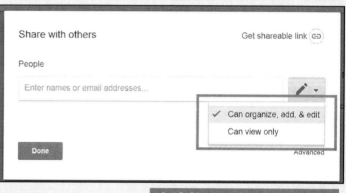

2.12 Choose what rights to give

2. A popup box will appear asking for the people you want to share with and what rights will you give them? (2.12) When you share a folder, you are given two choices:
   - Can organize, add & edit
   - Can view only.

When you share a folder, think about what you want the recipient to be able to do. . .

A folder is a great organized bin for all of a team's shared files. You can collect everything that you want others to have and place within this folder. The first thing you need to do to get started on your team sharing is to create a folder.

Create one by going to the New button on the upper left and then clicking on Folder from the drop-down menu.

1. Can organize, add, & edit

This is granting top level rights, you are allowing people to open, edit, delete, or move any files within the folder. People can also add files.

- If you remove a file from this shared folder, the people who you shared with will no longer see the file in their drive.

- Whatever permissions at the root of the folder will apply to everything within that folder but you can change individual documents to individual settings.

- A document moved into the shared folder will automatically show that it is shared with the same people.

When is it good to share with these rights?

- If you are in a collaborative group who are working on a project together.

- A teacher sharing with the class, so that students can collaborative at the same time sharing their thoughts.

2. Can view only

This level or rights say that people can see the folder and they can also open all the files within the folder, but not edit them.

When is it good to share with comment rights?

- You would like suggestions for others but you don't want them to be able to change the original.

- Student's can use this when sharing with a teacher to get their input on a project.

E. FEATURE OVERVIEW

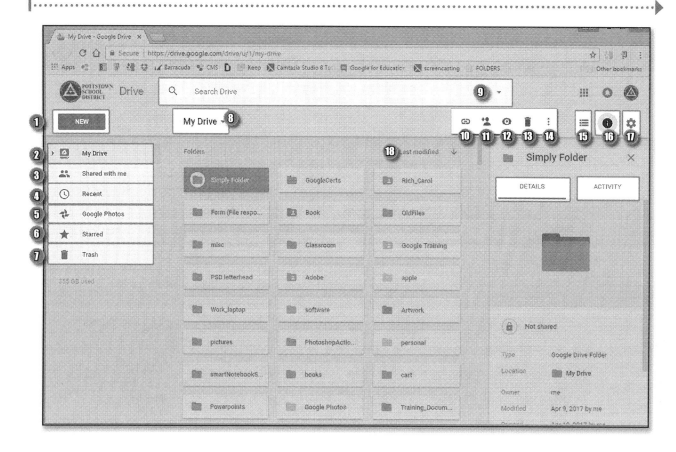

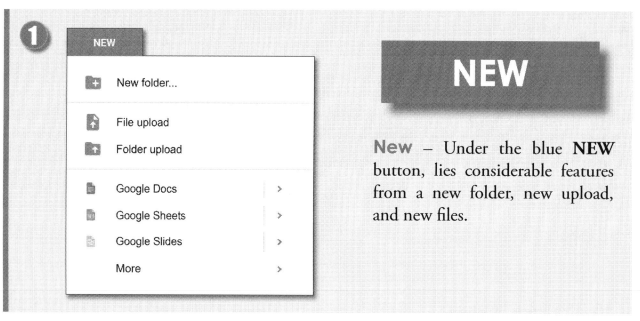

New – Under the blue **NEW** button, lies considerable features from a new folder, new upload, and new files.

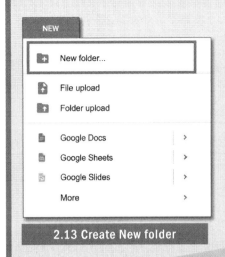

2.13 Create New folder

1-1 NEW FOLDER – The first option, when you select the blue **NEW** button is New Folder (2.13). A folder is a directory or catalog where you can organize your computer files. Many files can be kept in a folder. All your file types can be stored in a folder and you can even put folders within folders.

Right clicking (2.14) on the newly created folder will take you to a sub-menu where you can assign task to the selected folder:

- Creating a Shared Folder. Learn all about a shared folder in Section E.

- Get a Sharable link that can be sent via email.

- Moving the folder to another place within your drive.

- Adding a Star so that the folder is easier to find in a search.

- Color coding your files is a good way to organize. (2.15)

- Renaming to change the name.

- Viewing details show activity, ownership, creation date, modification date.

- When a folder is downloaded, it is zipped.

- Removing will move the file to the trash. Your file will stay there until you empty your trash.

2.14 Right clicking menu

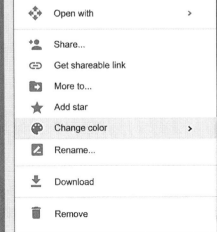

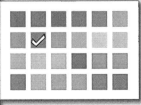

2.15 Color coding your folders

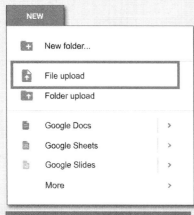

2.16 New File upload

1-2 NEW FILE UPLOAD – You can upload most any type of file up to your Drive. The list below comes from the Google Help menu. (2.16)

Your Microsoft files can be converted to the Google format. When you do this conversion, than they do not take up any space in the Drive. Plus when you convert the Microsoft files, you can edit them in the Google platform.

BELOW ARE THE FILE TYPES THAT YOU CAN UPLOAD TO YOUR DRIVE.

FILE SIZES

These are the documents, spreadsheets, and presentation sizes you can store in Google Drive.

- **Documents:** Up to 1.02 million characters. If you convert a text document to Google Docs format, it can be up to 50 MB.
- **Spreadsheets:** Up to 2 million cells for spreadsheets that are created in or converted to Google Sheets.
- **Presentations:** Up to 100 MB for presentations converted to Google Slides.
- **All other files:** Up to 5 TB.

SUPPORTED FILE TYPES

These are the most common file types you can view in Google Drive:

General Files

- Archive files (.ZIP, .RAR, tar, gzip)
- Audio formats (MP3, MPEG, WAV, .ogg)
- Image files (.JPEG, .PNG, .GIF, .BMP)
- Markup/Code (.CSS, .HTML, .PHP, .C, .CPP, .H, .HPP, .JS)
- Text files (.TXT)
- Video files (WebM, .MPEG4, .3GPP, .MOV, .AVI, .MPEGPS, .WMV, .FLV, .ogg)

Adobe files

- Autodesk AutoCad (.DXF)
- Illustrator (.AI)
- Photoshop (.PSD)
- Portable Document Format (.PDF)
- PostScript (.EPS, .PS)
- Scalable Vector Graphics (.SVG)
- Tagged Image File Format (.TIFF) - best with RGB .TIFF images
- TrueType (.TTF)

Microsoft files

- Excel (.XLS and .XLSX)
- PowerPoint (.PPT and .PPTX)
- Word (.DOC and .DOCX)
- XML Paper Specification (.XPS)

How to convert Microsoft files to the Google format

1. Select the Cog in the upper right corner of your drive (2.17)
2. Select Settings.
3. In settings, you can check the area that says: **Convert uploaded files to Google Docs editor format**. (2.18)

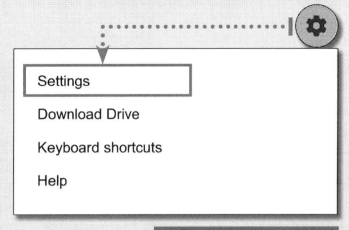

Settings

Download Drive

Keyboard shortcuts

Help

2.17 Select cog to access settings

Why would you want to do this? When files are converted, you will not take up space on your Google Drive. Also, you don't want to have multiple versions of your file in your drive, such as a Word version and a Docs version. When the file is converted, you can work on it in Docs and if you choose, download it back to the Microsoft format.

2.18 Select to convert files

Settings   DONE

Convert uploaded files to Google Docs editor format

General
Notificati
Manage Apps

Convert uploads   ☑ Convert uploaded files to Google Docs editor format

Language   Change language settings

Offline   ☐ Another user (cbright22@gmail.com) has already enabled offline access on this computer.
                       You can enable offline access on another computer, or use Chrome profiles to set up offline access for your account on this computer. Learn more

Density   Comfortable ▾

Create a Google Photos folder   ☑ Automatically put your Google Photos into a folder in My Drive

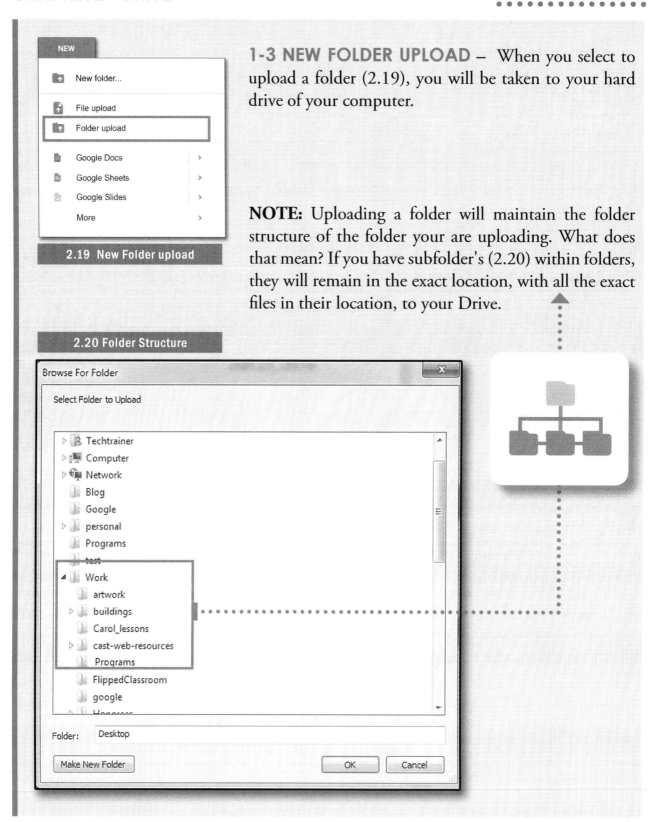

1-3 NEW FOLDER UPLOAD – When you select to upload a folder (2.19), you will be taken to your hard drive of your computer.

NOTE: Uploading a folder will maintain the folder structure of the folder your are uploading. What does that mean? If you have subfolder's (2.20) within folders, they will remain in the exact location, with all the exact files in their location, to your Drive.

NEW

New folder...

File upload

Folder upload

Google Docs   >
Google Sheets   >
Google Slides   >
More   >

2.19 New Folder upload

2.20 Folder Structure

Browse For Folder

Select Folder to Upload

▷ Techtrainer
▷ Computer
▷ Network
   Blog
   Google
▷ personal
   Programs
   test
▲ Work
   artwork
▷ buildings
   Carol_lessons
▷ cast-web-resources
   Programs
   FlippedClassroom
   google
   Honorees

Folder: Desktop

Make New Folder   OK   Cancel

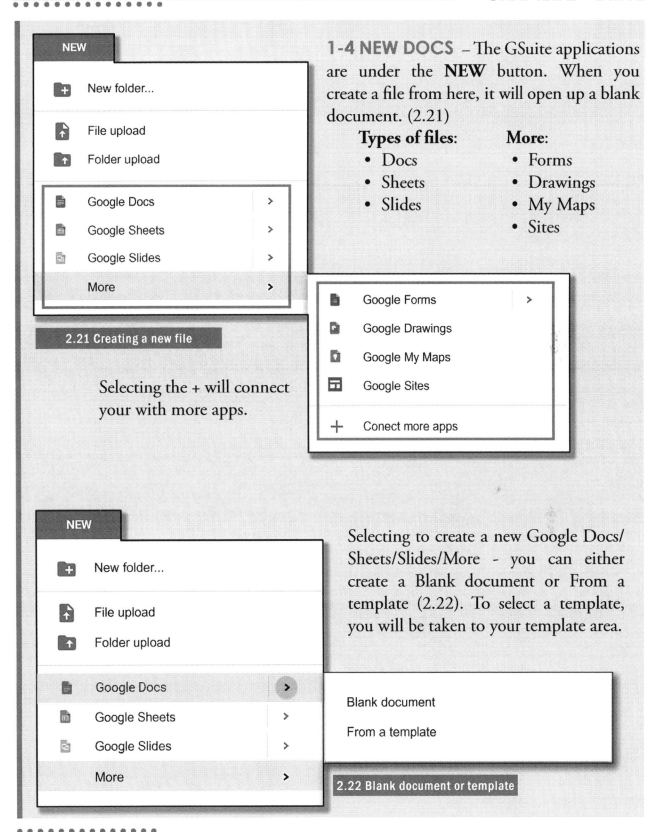

1-4 NEW DOCS – The GSuite applications are under the **NEW** button. When you create a file from here, it will open up a blank document. (2.21)

Types of files:
- Docs
- Sheets
- Slides

More:
- Forms
- Drawings
- My Maps
- Sites

2.21 Creating a new file

Selecting the + will connect your with more apps.

Selecting to create a new Google Docs/Sheets/Slides/More - you can either create a Blank document or From a template (2.22). To select a template, you will be taken to your template area.

2.22 Blank document or template

2 **My Drive** – Stored within your drive are all your files. Included in this are any files / folders you have uploaded. Also within your drive is where all the files you created are stored. You can create a folder structure in your drive to keep yourself organized.

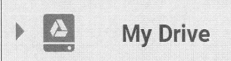

3 **Shared with me** – Anything that has been shared with you from anyone will show up here. If you move it to My Drive, it just makes a shortcut to the file, it does not make a copy of the file. Your rights to that file will depend on the privileges that the owner gave you. If you delete the file from your Shared with me, you are only deleting your access, not the original file. Only the owner can delete the original file.

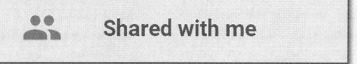

4 **Recent** – Just how it sounds. Anything that you just looked at or added. A quick way to access your file.

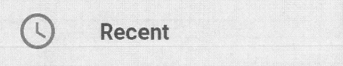

Google Photos – Google Photos is a way for your photos and videos to automatically be uploaded from your mobile device. Not only does it allow you to back up and organize photos from your different devices to a single place. Google Photos is also where your Google+ photos are stored. You can go to the Cog, go to Settings, and check to **Automatically put your Google Photos into a folder on your drive**.

> **Google Photos**

 Starred – Starring something gives it more importance is makes it easier to find in a search.

> ★ **Starred**

 Trash – Just how it sounds. Items will stay in the trash until you delete them. Once deleted they are gone for good. (Consumer accounts can contact Google for emergencies)

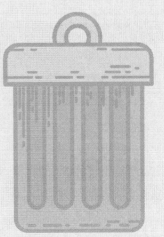

> 🗑 **Trash**

8

My Drive – Selecting My Drive is an exact replica of the NEW blue button.

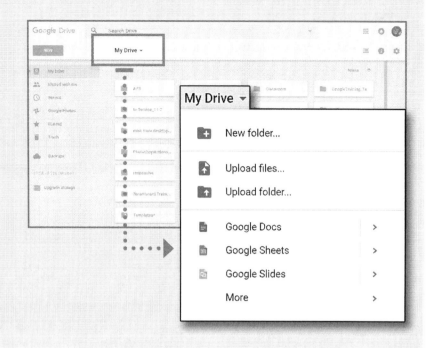

9

Search Drive – You can find files in your Google Drive such as Docs, Sheets, and Slides by searching for:

• File title

• File contents

You can also locate pictures, PDF files, or other files stored on your Drive.

You can also sort and filter search results.

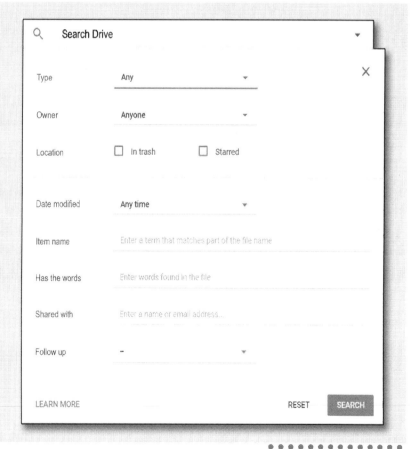

How to search the drive:

1. At the top, type a word or phrase into the search box.
2. To narrow your search, click the Down arrow.
3. Fill out any of the following sections:

Type: File types such as documents, images, or PDFs.(2.23)

Owner: The person the file belongs to. (2.24)

Location: Whether the file is in "Trash," or "Starred," for example.

Date modified: The date a file was last edited. (2.25)

Item name: Searches only for the title of the file.

Has the words: Searches for words and phrases within documents.

Shared with: Who can view, comment, or edit the file.

Follow up: If the file has action items assigned to you, or suggestions in files you own.

At the bottom, click Search.

2.23 Type of file you can search by

- Any
- Photos & images
- PDFs
- Text documents
- Spreadsheets
- Presentations
- Forms
- Audio
- Videos
- Archive (zip)
- Drawings
- Folders

2.24 Who is the owner of the file

- Anyone
- Owned by me
- Not owned by me
- Specific person...

2.25 Date file was modified

- Any time
- Today
- Yesterday
- Last 7 days
- Last 30 days
- Last 90 days
- Custom...

2.26 Drive menu icons

Numbers 10 to 14 are not visible when you first enter your Drive. You have to either select a file or select a folder for them to be come visible.

When you select any file or folder in your drive, icons will appear at the upper right of the drive. (2.26).

10

Link Sharing – Link sharing is a way to share your file/folder with someone else. For all the ins and outs of sharing a link, go to Section D-4 of this chapter.

11

Share – Selecting the Share icon will give you the ability to add the people who you want to share your file/folder with. You can select what rights you want to give them as explained in Section D-1.

12 *Google Drive lets you quickly preview a wide range of file types and you can quickly flip between files until you find the one you want.*

Preview – Two ways to preview a Google file, either right-click on the file name in your Drive and select "preview", or select the file and the "eye" icon will appear at the top menu and you can select this icon. Once the preview window is open, you can click on the arrows on either side to flip to other files (2.27). And right from within the preview, you can watch video files or scroll through multi-page documents such as a slide deck or Google doc (2.28).

Preview is not available when selecting a folder, but when you select a file, than select the preview icon, a new window will open and you can preview your file.

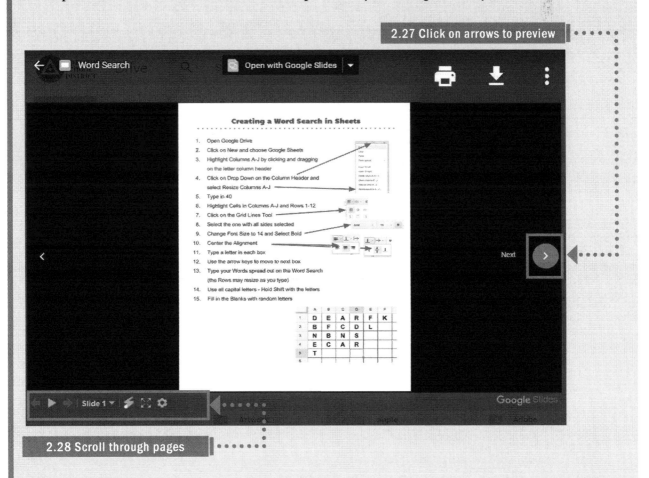

2.27 Click on arrows to preview

2.28 Scroll through pages

In the upper right corner of the preview, there are three icons (2.29).

Printer - Print your selected document.

Down Arrow - Download your selected previewed file.

Three Dots - (2.30) A sub-menu opens giving you the options to:

- Share your file with someone else.
- Move your file to a different place within your Google Drive.
- Add a star to your file, making it easier to find in a search result.
- Rename your file.
- All details regarding your file such as owner, date modified.
- Open in a new window.
- Report abuse.

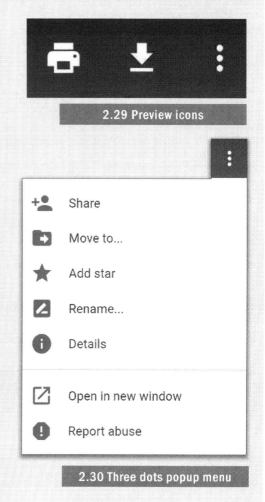

2.29 Preview icons

2.30 Three dots popup menu

13 **Remove** – Google does not empty the Drive trash by default. So, if you move something to the Trash in your Drive, it's going to stay there until you delete forever from inside the Trash.

14 **More Options** – When you select either a file or a folder, in the upper right corner, 3 dots will appear. When you select the 3 dots, a sub menu will appear depending on if you have chose a file (2.31) or a folder (2.32). From that menu, you can:

- Choose what to open it with.
- Move item to another area in your drive.
- Adding a Star so that the folder is easier to find in a search.
- Color coding your files is a good way to organize, (folder only).
- Renaming to change the name.
- Make a copy (file only).
- Download your file or folder. When a folder is downloaded, it is zipped.

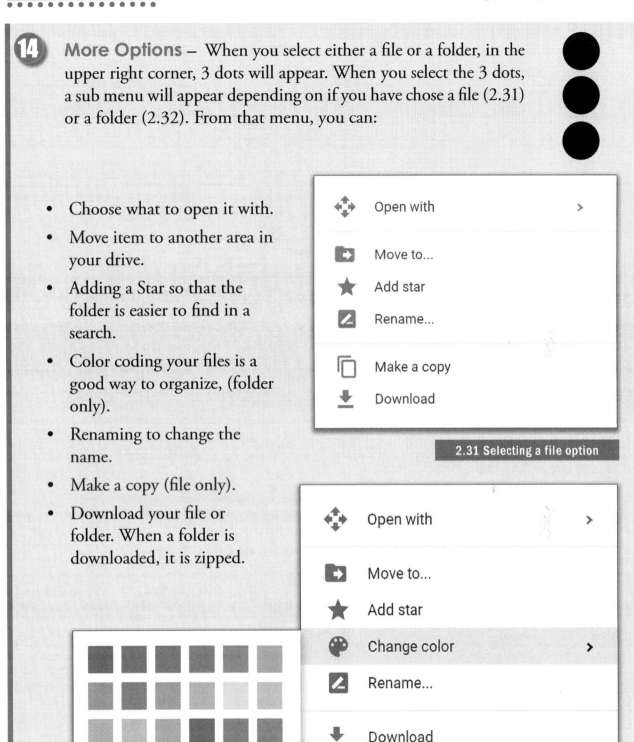

2.31 Selecting a file option

2.32 Selecting a folder option

15 **Grid Preview / List Preview** – Your Drive files are displayed in the center of your screen. They can be viewed either in Grid View (2.33) or List View (2.34).

2.33 Grid view of your folders/files

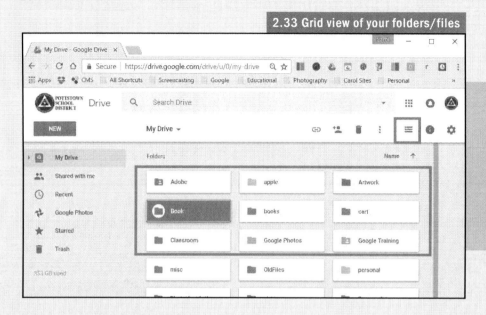

GRID VIEW

2.34 List view of your folders/files

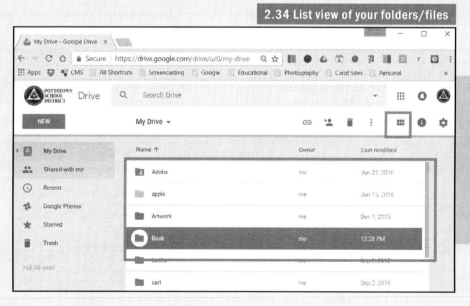

LIST VIEW

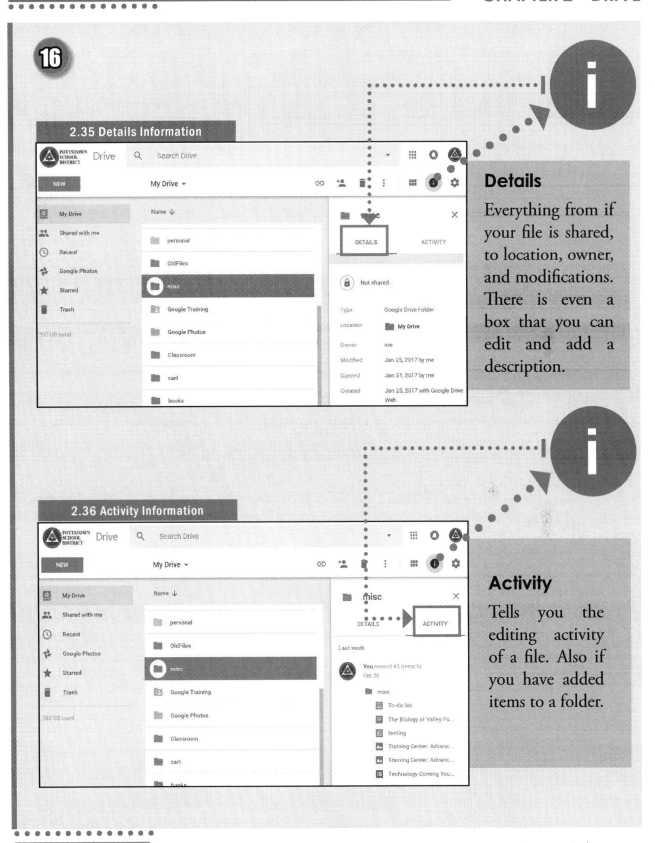

16

2.35 Details Information

Details

Everything from if your file is shared, to location, owner, and modifications. There is even a box that you can edit and add a description.

2.36 Activity Information

Activity

Tells you the editing activity of a file. Also if you have added items to a folder.

Cog – Some great features are available by choosing the gear icon. The two important ones are Settings (2.37) and Download Drive (2.38).

Top 3 Items in Settings:

1. Convert uploaded file to Google Docs editor format. Doing this not only saves you space on your drive, it also limits clutter by just give you the one format to work on.

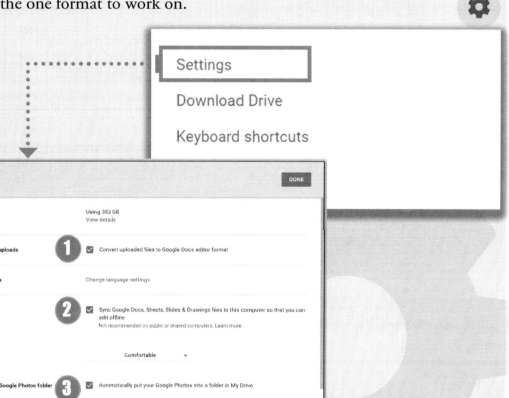

2.37 Setting options

2. Sync Google Docs, Sheets, Slides & Drawings files to the computer so that you can work off-line. No need to worry if you lose your Internet connection!

3. Automatically put your Google Photos in a folder in My Drive. Ensuring for backup of your important life moments.

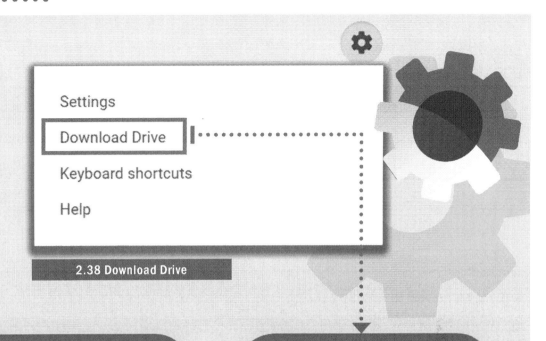

Settings

Download Drive

Keyboard shortcuts

Help

2.38 Download Drive

IN THE CLOUD

- Free storage

- All documents accessible with any Internet connection

- Search-able

- Automatically saves documents

- Ability to share files

LOCAL

- Files take up space on computer's hard drive

- Syncs to Cloud Drive

- Not search-able

- Extra steps

③ DOCS

Created, Edited And Stored Online

Create a new file and share collaboratively - available on or offline.

Google Docs is a web-based editing program that allows users to create, share and edit documents through a secure networked system. With Docs you can upload a Word document to your Google Drive and convert it to the Docs format. Multiple users can work on the same document at the same time, adjusting margins, adding pictures, editing content and putting the finishing touches on documents from any location with internet access.

A. HOW TO GET TO YOUR DOCS

1

After your have logged into your Chrome account, type in

https://docs.google.com

2

Go to the waffle and select the blue rectangle icon.

3

From your Drive, select **BLUE NEW** button and go down to Docs.

Repository

repäzetôrē/

noun;

- a central location in which data is stored and managed.

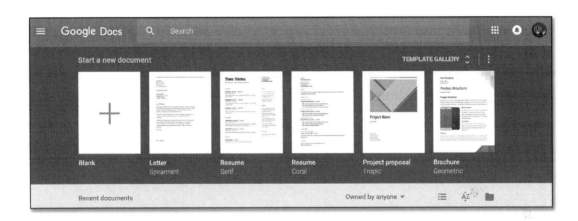

Selecting the Waffle Icon or typing into the Omnibox docs.google.com, will take you to the repository of all your docs.

- From within this area, you can create a blank document.
- Choose one of the templates that are provided in the Template Gallery.
- Sort by owner of document.
- List or Grid view
- Sort A to Z or Z to A.
- Go to file picker.

B. FEATURES OVERVIEW

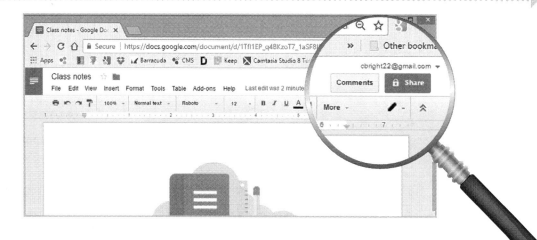

With revision history, multiple versions of documents to be stored, allowing users to roll them back to previous versions without losing any information.

Docs also allows the document owner to determine what privileges are given to each user. This means that you can have multiple viewers, editors and commenters on a single project. When complete, your file can be downloaded as a Word, OpenOffice, RTF, PDF or HTML format along with the option to zip the file.

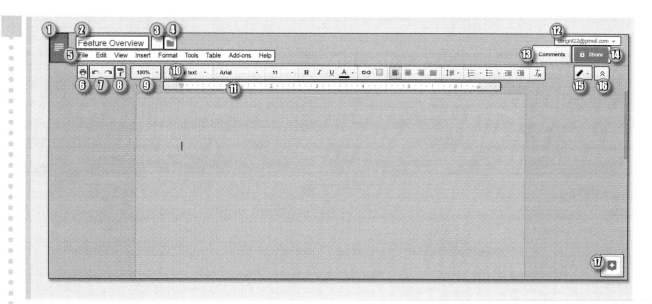

Home – Selecting the blue rectangle with white lines in the upper left corner of your window will return you to your Docs Repository. It is a quick, easy navigation tool. From here, you can start a new blank Doc, use a template or open a previously created Doc.

Title – After you have created your first blank doc, it will be an Untitled document. You will want to give your new document a title right away because, one of Doc's powerful features is that it auto-saves.

Star – Starring a document gives it importance and makes your file easier to search for.

Move to – Selecting the folder icon will give you the option to move your document to another location. Moving a file to a folder is good file management.

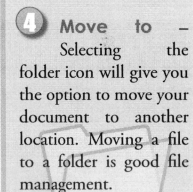

Text Menu – The next chapter in this section will give you an in-depth overview of the entire Text Menu.

Print – Brings up your print menu and if your have print drivers installed and a printer, you can print. If not, print to PDF and save your file.

Undo/Redo – Go back one step to your last move in your files and go forward.

Paint Format – This handy tool will copy the formatting of text, cells, or an object with the paint format tool.

1. Open a Google file.
2. Select the text, range of cells, or object you want to copy it's formatting.
3. In the toolbar, click Paint format .
4. Select what you want to paste the formatting onto.

 Zoom – Change the view of your document from Fit to view, all the way up to 200%

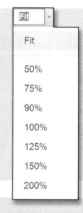

Fit
Fit
50%
75%
90%
100%
125%
150%
200%

 Icon Menu – Adding style to your document is how you make your file stand out from the competition. This is called formatting. Various ways to format is to change fonts, font sizes, bold, colorize and adding a bullet list. The Style menu is located below the drop-down menus.

- Text Style
- Font
- Font Size
- Bold
- Italics
- Underline
- Font Color

- Insert Link
- Add Comment
- Left Align
- Center
- Right Align
- Justify
- Line Spacing

- Numbered List
- Bulleted List
- Decrease Indent
- Increase Indent
- Clear Formatting
- Keyboard

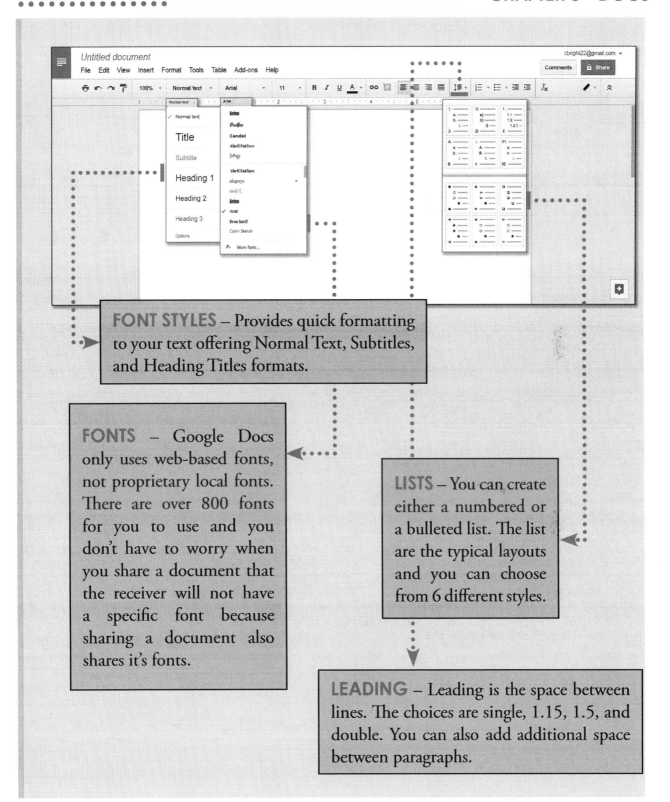

FONT STYLES – Provides quick formatting to your text offering Normal Text, Subtitles, and Heading Titles formats.

FONTS – Google Docs only uses web-based fonts, not proprietary local fonts. There are over 800 fonts for you to use and you don't have to worry when you share a document that the receiver will not have a specific font because sharing a document also shares it's fonts.

LISTS – You can create either a numbered or a bulleted list. The list are the typical layouts and you can choose from 6 different styles.

LEADING – Leading is the space between lines. The choices are single, 1.15, 1.5, and double. You can also add additional space between paragraphs.

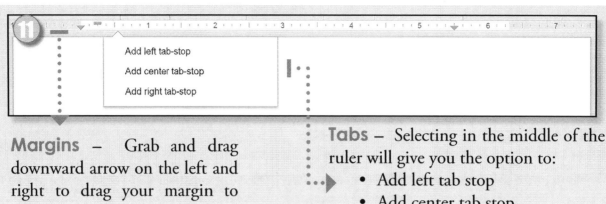

Margins – Grab and drag downward arrow on the left and right to drag your margin to where you want it to be.

Tabs – Selecting in the middle of the ruler will give you the option to:
- Add left tab stop
- Add center tab stop
- Add right tab stop

Account – When you select your email address, a box will open showing your My Account button to go see an overview of your account settings. You can also add an account, Go to Google +, Privacy settings, and Sign out of your Google account.

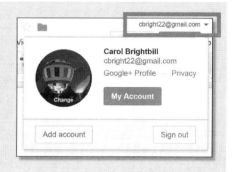

Comment – You must first add a comment to the side of your Google Doc. Now when you select Comment, at the top, you can see your comment and any additional comments that are added throughout the document, even a multiple page document, will show as a running text stream at the top of the page.

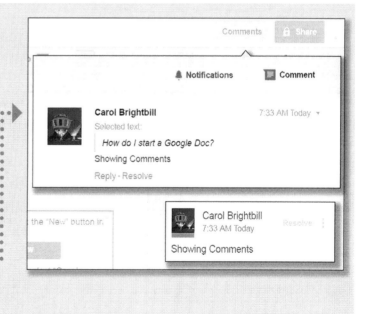

Share – All about sharing on pages 40-49 of this book.

 Editing Mode – There are three options:

1. **Editing** – Gives full rights to whoever the Doc is shared with.

2. **Suggesting** – This is a great mode for collaborators. When you are reviewing a document, but do not want to change things without the consent of someone else on the team, Suggesting mode is great to use because you will not affect the original information. When you are in this mode, you can just start to type where you want the changes, and your suggestions will appear as a new color and the original text will be crossed out. The original owner will receive an email and they will than either accept or reject your suggestions.

3. **Viewing** – You can only read or print the final document, you can not edit or suggest edits.

 Show your menu – Clicking the double arrow will hide the menus and clicking the arrows again will show the menu.

 Explore – Located at the bottom right of every Doc that is opened. When you select it, the Explore panel will open.

When you select this tool, without any words selected, the **artificial intelligence** of **Google** will scan your document and present suggestions based on different words in the document.

C. TEXT MENU OVERVIEW

When learning a new application, or if you want to become more efficient, than familiarize yourself with what lies within the menu system.

TEXT MENU

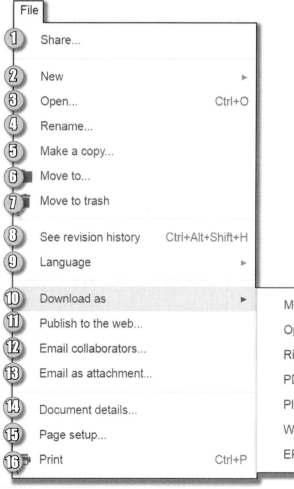

	File	
①	Share...	
②	New	▶
③	Open...	Ctrl+O
④	Rename...	
⑤	Make a copy...	
⑥	Move to...	
⑦	Move to trash	
⑧	See revision history	Ctrl+Alt+Shift+H
⑨	Language	▶
⑩	Download as	▶
⑪	Publish to the web...	
⑫	Email collaborators...	
⑬	Email as attachment...	
⑭	Document details...	
⑮	Page setup...	
⑯	Print	Ctrl+P

Microsoft Word (.docx)
OpenDocument Format (.odt)
Rich Text Format (.rtf)
PDF Document (.pdf)
Plain Text (.txt)
Web Page (.html, zipped)
EPUB Publication (.epub)

Here lies the life of the program. You will be amazed at the capabilities that Google Docs has under the hood of it's menus.

C-1 Text Menu - FILE

 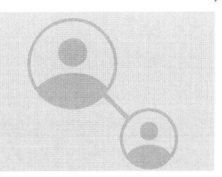

 Share – The first thing under the file menu is one of the most important things about Google Apps, the ability to **Share** your file, covered intensively in the Drive section, pages 40-49.

New – Clicking New shows how dynamic Google Apps are. From the New, you can create any one of the Google core apps. Additionally, you can select to create a new Doc from a template.

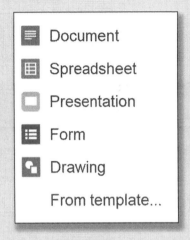

- Document
- Spreadsheet
- Presentation
- Form
- Drawing
- From template...

 Open – Selecting **Open** gives you the choices of going to:

- My Drive
- Shared with Me
- Starred
- Recent
- Upload

Selecting the dropdown arrow will let you open by a file type in the expanded list.

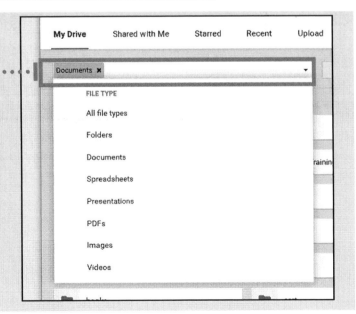

My Drive   Shared with Me   Starred   Recent   Upload

Documents ✕

FILE TYPE

All file types

Folders

Documents

Spreadsheets

Presentations

PDFs

Images

Videos

Rename – When you select Rename, your cursor will instantly pop up to where your file has it's existing name and it will be highlighted. Renaming does not make an additional file, it just gives your existing file a new name.

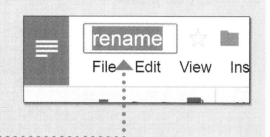

Make A Copy – There are two reasons to make a copy of your file:

1. When a file is shared and the rights are **View Only**, you can not edit the file. This is a smart practice to maintain the integrity of your file. If you select **Make a Copy**, you can rename it, now it is yours to go into and edit.

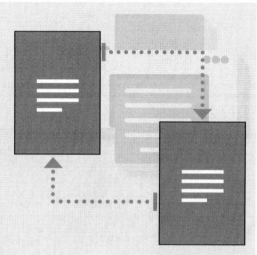

2. You want to update a file with new information but you want to keep the original file. This is another reason to make a copy of your original, so you can have a different version with the new information and keep your old version.

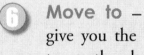

Move to – Selecting the folder icon will give you the option to move your document to another location. When you create a file, directly in the Drive, that file is not placed in a folder, it is placed in your Drive.

Folder structure is a good organizational skill to master and use.

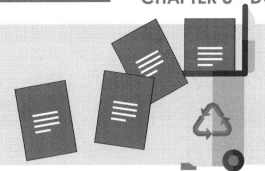

7. Move to trash – This will delete your file from your drive but it is not permanently deleted until you delete it from your trash.

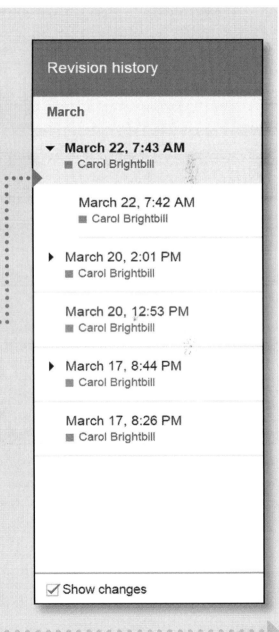

8. See Revision History – Gone are the days of paper drafts that teachers reviewed to see the thought process of their student. This is where Revision History comes in handy. It is also a great way to keep students, working on teams collaborating honest! You can see who has done what in the file.

When you choose **File > See Revision History**, another window opens showing the document, and a side bar will appear that details all the changes within the document.

You can select various dates or times and see the changes that occurred. You can also restore a previous version from this area.

When you restore a previous version, you do not loose any of the other versions, the restored version just jumps to the top.

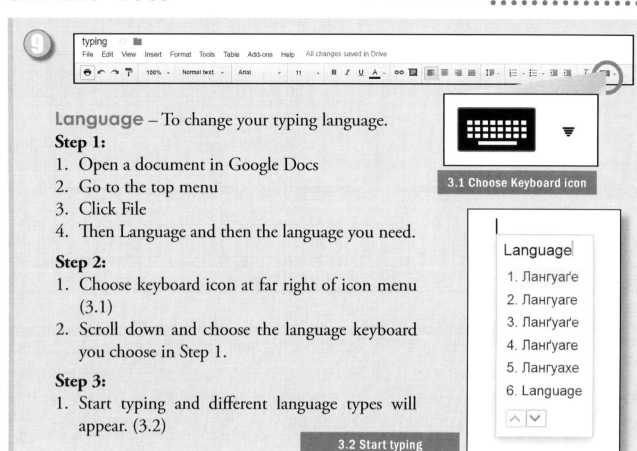

⑨

Language – To change your typing language.

Step 1:
1. Open a document in Google Docs
2. Go to the top menu
3. Click File
4. Then Language and then the language you need.

3.1 Choose Keyboard icon

Step 2:
1. Choose keyboard icon at far right of icon menu (3.1)
2. Scroll down and choose the language keyboard you choose in Step 1.

Step 3:
1. Start typing and different language types will appear. (3.2)

3.2 Start typing

Language|
1. Лангуаѓе
2. Лангуаге
3. Ланѓуаѓе
4. Ланѓуаге
5. Лангуахе
6. Language

⑩ **Download As** – You still have the ability to download your Docs as other programs versions such as Microsoft Word, in case you are sending the file to someone who only uses that program.

Also downloading the file as a PDF will maintain the layout and embed the fonts enabling the file to be sent via email.

Saving as a Web Page or EPUB allows the file to be uploaded and viewed online.

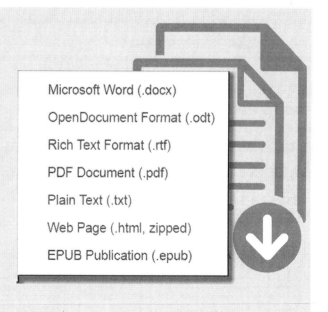

Microsoft Word (.docx)

OpenDocument Format (.odt)

Rich Text Format (.rtf)

PDF Document (.pdf)

Plain Text (.txt)

Web Page (.html, zipped)

EPUB Publication (.epub)

Publish to the web – Publishing to the web creates a webpage where anyone with the link can view your document. A URL is created for your Doc.

When a file is published, a copy of the original file

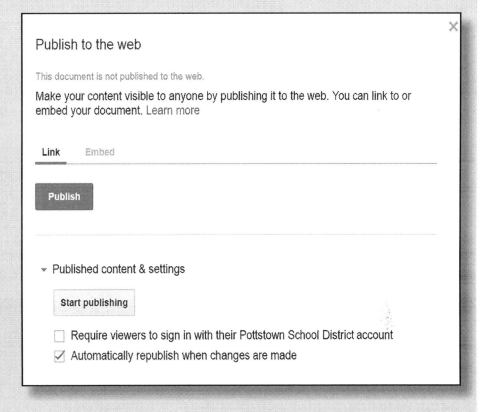

is made. The copy is the file that people see when they visit your website. It doesn't carry over sharing permissions, so anyone will be able to see it.

When you publish, you can do the following:

- Create an embeddable HTML version of a doc. The HTML version can be embedded in blogs, Google Sites, and more.

- Show your doc to large web audiences. Only 50 people can view a shared doc at a time, but a lightweight webpage can be opened to the public.

- Provide quick access to file downloads.

- Publish a one-time snapshot of a your document. To create such a snapshot, make sure you un-check "Automatically republish" when you publish your doc.

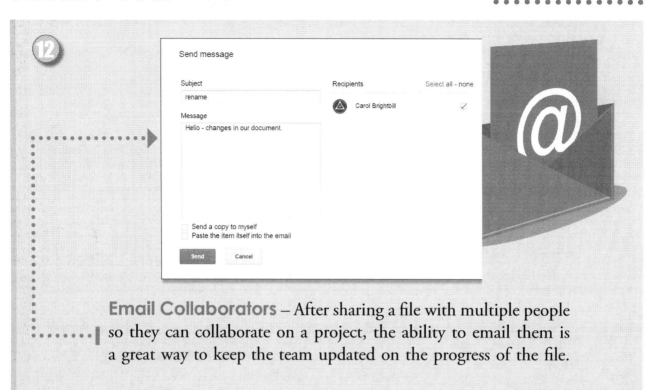

Email Collaborators – After sharing a file with multiple people so they can collaborate on a project, the ability to email them is a great way to keep the team updated on the progress of the file.

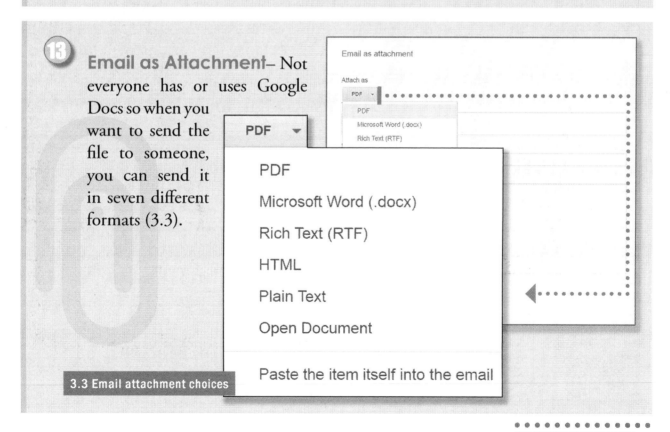

Email as Attachment– Not everyone has or uses Google Docs so when you want to send the file to someone, you can send it in seven different formats (3.3).

3.3 Email attachment choices

14 **Document details** – The details of the document provides useful information, especially if you don't know what folder your file is located or who the owner is.

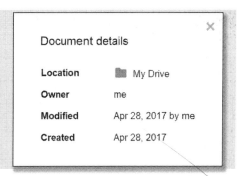

Document details ✕

Location	📁 My Drive
Owner	me
Modified	Apr 28, 2017 by me
Created	Apr 28, 2017

15 **Page setup** – Going into page setup, change orientation, you can change your document's margins, paper size, and document's background color. (3.4)

Page setup ✕

Orientation

● Portrait   ○ Landscape

Paper size

Letter (8.5" x 11") ⇕

Page color

☐ ▾

Margins (inches)

Top 1

Bottom 1

Left 1

Right 1

OK   Cancel   Set as default

3.4 Change background color

✓

Custom...

16 **Print** – Your printer will appear and you can print your document.

C-2 Text Menu - EDIT

KEYBOARD SHORTCUTS –
The **edit** menu has some of the must useful shortcuts that will boost your productivity.

The above shortcuts are cross platform and used in multiple programs.

Where would word processing be without cut, copy, paste! And Control Z!! The best ever! Let's go down the menu:

1. **Undo** – action that takes you back one step in your editing (ctrl+Z).

2. **Redo** – action that jumps you back to where your were before your Undo (ctrl+Y).

3. **Cut** – places what you cut onto the computer clipboard and removes it from your file (ctrl+X).

4. **Copy** – places what you copy onto the computer clipboard and leaves it in your file. Your computer clipboard only holds one item, the last thing you either copied or cut (ctrl+C).

5. **Paste** – pasting will put whatever you cut or copied, from the computer's clipboard onto your file (ctrl+V).

6. **Paste without formatting** – existing formatting from what your cut or copied will be stripped away when you paste and your content will take on the existing format where it is being pasted into (ctrl+Shift+V).

7

Web clipboard – Copying to the Web clipboard is different than just copying to your computer's clipboard.

This clipboard can hold multiple items at once, across different apps. And since your are signed into your Google account, it also syncs. Items will clear after 30 days.

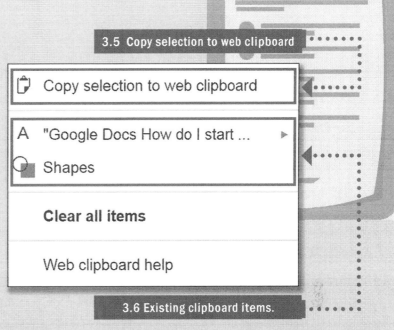

3.5 Copy selection to web clipboard

Copy selection to web clipboard

A "Google Docs How do I start ... ▶

Shapes

Clear all items

Web clipboard help

3.6 Existing clipboard items.

1. Select what you want to copy.
2. Choose Edit > scroll down to Web clipboard.
3. Choose Copy selection to web clipboard. (3.5)

Under where you select Copy selection to web clipboard, your existing items on the clipboard will list down (3.6). The next list item is Clear all items.

8

Select all – Depending on if you are in a text box, all your type will be selected, or if you are just on the page, all the objects on the page will be selected.

9

Select none – This will deselect what your have selected, weather text or object.

10

Find and replace – Great time saving way to find specific words to replace.

C-3 Text Menu - VIEW

Let's see what can be viewed!

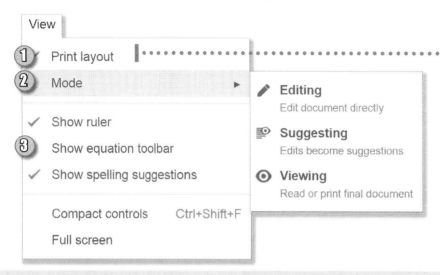

View

① Print layout

② Mode ▶

    ✏ **Editing**
    Edit document directly

    🖼 **Suggesting**
    Edits become suggestions

    ◎ **Viewing**
    Read or print final document

✓ Show ruler

③ Show equation toolbar

✓ Show spelling suggestions

Compact controls   Ctrl+Shift+F

Full screen

Print layout on – Breaks into individual pages.

Print layout off – Looks like one continuous page.

2 Mode – There are three options under Mode (3.7):

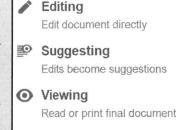

1. **Editing** – In editing, the document is edited directly by anyone who has edit rights.

2. **Suggesting** – When you are reviewing a document, but do not want to change things without the consent of someone else on the team, Suggesting mode is great to use because you will not affect the original data. When you are in this mode, you can just start to type where you want the changes (3.8), and your suggestions will appear as a new color and the original text will be crossed out. The original owner will receive an email and they will than either accept or reject your suggestions.

3.7 Three Modes

3.8 Suggesting edits mode

3. **Viewing** – In Viewing mode, you can only read or print the final document, you can not edit or suggest edits.

3 Show Equation Toolbar – When you show the equation toolbar, you can insert the symbols you want to add from one of these menus: Greek letters. Miscellaneous operations. Relations. Math operators. Arrows.

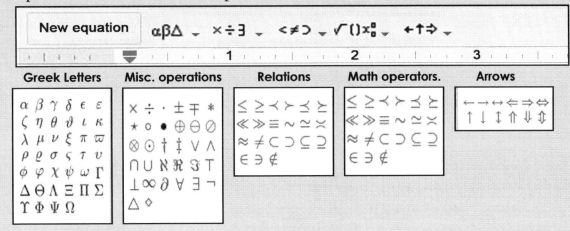

C-4 Text Menu - INSERT

Inserting in a Google Doc opens so many possibilities!

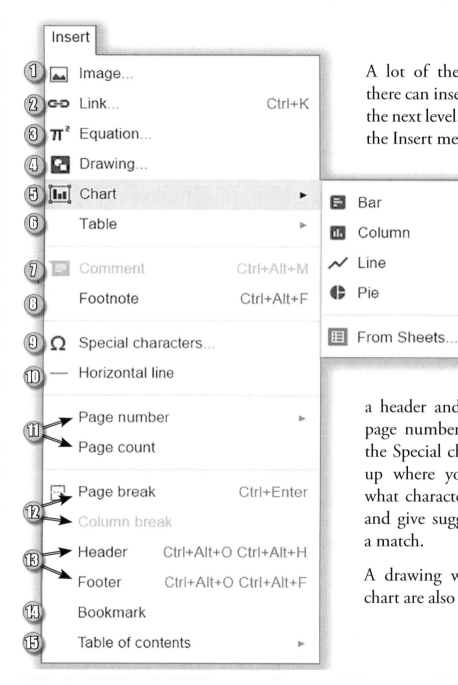

A lot of the word processors out there can insert, but Docs takes it to the next level. And what lies beneath the Insert menu is the beginnings of your digital worksheet. You just insert a table and build your worksheet by inserting links or images. You can organize your report by inserting a header and a footer, than insert page numbers. When you look at the Special characters, a box comes up where you can start to draw what character you are looking for and give suggestions when it finds a match.

A drawing with annotations or a chart are also options to be inserted.

1 Image – You can take your document to the next level and go from boring to quite interesting by just adding a picture. As the saying goes, "A picture is worth a thousand words".

There are six different ways to add an image. Images must be less than 50 MB and be one of the following file types: .gif; .jpg; or .png (3.11).

1. **Upload** – Selecting to upload will take your to your computer's hard drive and select Open.

2. **Take a snapshot** – If your device has a camera, you can take a snapshot and insert it directly into the document.

3. **By URL** – Paste the URL of an image from the web and click Select.

4. **Your albums** – Choose an image from one of your photos albums stored on the web and click Select.

5. **Google Drive** – Choose an image stored in Google Drive and click Select.

6. **Search** – Choose an image from the stock photography archive, or the Google and Life archives, and click Select.

When an image is inserted in a document, you can edit it in various ways.

You must first select the image, the box on the right will appear (3.9) and than you will be able to either, crop it, recolor it. You will also have adjustments such as transparency, brightness, or contrast. You can also replace the image. (3.10)

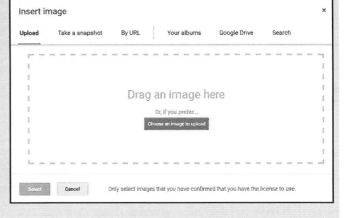

3.9 Edit options

3.10 Edit options

3.11 Adding an image options

Link – Inserting a link into a document will take you to a website or an email.

To insert the line:

1. Select text that you want to have the link.
2. Select Insert > Link.
3. Type the text you want to be linked in the Text field.
4. Enter the URL or email address, or search for a website within the Link field.
5. Click Apply.

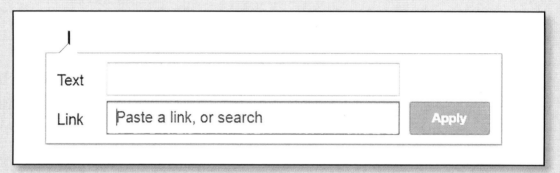

Equation – When you insert an equation, you can insert the symbols you want to add from one of these menus: Greek letters. Miscellaneous operations. Relations. Math operators. Arrows.

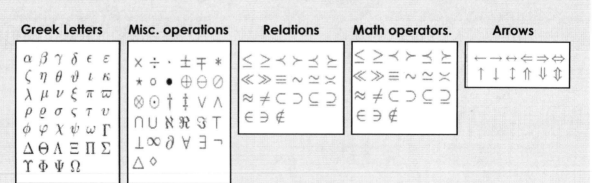

④ **Drawing** – You can not place an image or a text box in a specific location in your Docs. Inserting a drawing gives you the ability to have control where to place them. Selecting Insert > Drawing, a pallet will open (3.12). The background is transparent.

The icon menu in this drawing pallet is similar to the icon menu in Docs

When you select Actions (3.13), you can choose to:

3.12 Drawings Pallet

• Download your drawing as an image format.
• You can also insert Word art.
• The basic editing features are here such as cut, copy, and paste.
• Copy to web clipboard.
• Align your objects.
• Group /ungroup your objects.

You can use the Insert Drawing as a way to annotate an image.

You can not insert a drawing from the Drawings App but you can copy the drawing onto the Web clipboard and paste it into your Drawing that you opened in Docs. You have to watch the size though because the pallet is bigger in Drawings than the Drawings pallet that opens in Docs.

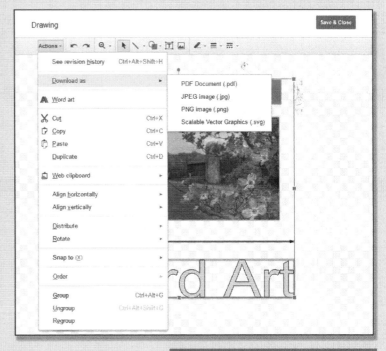

3.13 Actions Menu

5 **Chart** – You have 4 different chart types (3.14) to insert into your Google Doc:

- Bar
- Column
- Line
- Pie
- Plus insert from Sheets

3.14 Chart insertion options

Generic data (3.15) will fill these charts linking to four generic teams. In the upper right corner of these generic charts, are two icons (3.16).

1. The first icon gives you the option to unlink your chart from the Sheets.
2. The second option lets you open up your chart in Sheets and than you can replace the generic data with your own information.

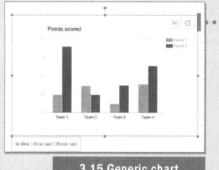

3.15 Generic chart

At the bottom of the CHART insert is the option to insert **From Sheets**. When you choose this option, you will be taken to your existing Sheets (3.17). If there is not a chart currently on that Sheet, you will get the message: *"This spreadsheet has no charts."*

3.15 Generic chart

If the Sheet that your are inserting from your own collection of Sheets has more than one chart within it, you can choose which chart you would like to insert into your Docs (3.18).

3.17 Sheet Chart Options

3.18 Multiple charts

Table – A table is a grid of cells arranged in rows and columns. It can be useful to present data in a table inside a word processing document because it is displayed in an organized and easy to read format. Your table can hold cells from 1x1 up to 20 x 20 and all equations in-between (3.19).

4 x 4

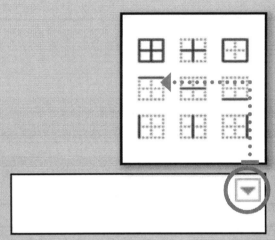

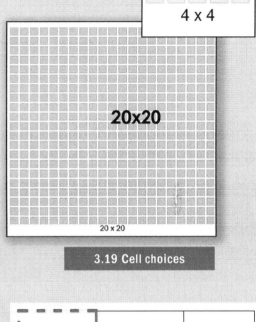

20x20

20 x 20

3.19 Cell choices

When you hover in the upper right corner of every cell, a dropdown carat appears.

Selecting this dropdown (figure above) will bring up a sub-menu giving you the option to customize and colorize individual lines within the cell (3.20).

3.20 Customize

Right-clicking within any cell (3.21) will bring up a sub-menu giving you the option to insert or delete rows or columns, and distribute them.

With table properties you can colorize the background and borders and set specific sizes for cells, cell vertical alignment, table alignment, and padding.

3.21 Right click cell

7 **Comment** – Collaborating is easy when you use a Comment box. A dialog box (3.22) will appear beside your document when you select Insert > Comment. Using this box, you can type in suggestions that you think would improve the file. The Comment box can be used as a running dialog thread with another person who you have shared the document with and have given the rights to either edit or comment.

3.22 Comment box

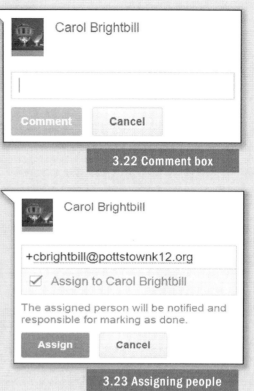

- And right within this dialog box, if you type @ or + in front of it, of the person you want to assign it to (3.23).

- Click the box next to "Assign to [name]."

- Click Assign. The person you assigned the action item to will get an email.

3.23 Assigning people

8 **Footnote** – A footnote provides additional information on the text it refers to. It could include information for how to learn more about the topic, or it could include a citation (a reference to published work) for a quote used in the text. Footnotes are commonly used in research reports and academic writing. They are placed at the bottom of a page.

To use the footnotes:

1. Place the insertion point after the text the footnote will refer to.
2. Click Insert>Footnote.
3. A superscript number will be placed where your cursor was.
4. Place your cursor at the bottom of the page and type the text you want the footnote to reference.

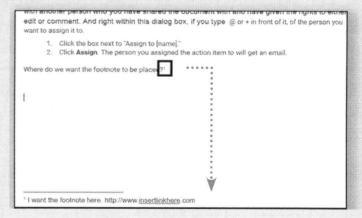

Special Characters

– There are 24 categories (3.24) that spill down when you choose the first button when you select Insert > Special Characters.

There is a sub-menu (3.25) to even filter your selection better.

Google makes it even easier for you if you can't exactly remember what you are looking for but have an idea.

There is a track pad (3.26) and in the middle it states **_Draw a symbol here._** As you start to draw, Google will show you symbols that resemble your drawing. If you insert the same characters frequently, they will show up in your recent characters. Find this list in the first drop-down menu.

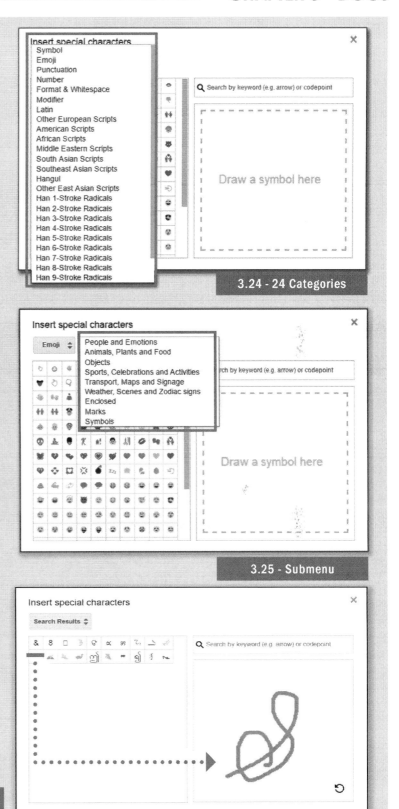

3.24 - 24 Categories

3.25 - Submenu

3.26 Track Pad

10 **Horizontal Line** – A horizontal line is a great way to break your Google Docs into sections and adds order and neatness to your page. If you want to delete the line after you have inserted it, just double clicking on it will highlight it, than it can be deleted.

Simply Google

By Carol Brightbill

My first attempt to write a technical book. I hope that I can give you a greater understanding of the Google Apps interface and how it can be useful to your day-to-day work life.

11 **Page Number** – When you select Insert > Page number, a fly-out menu (3.27) will give you the option to place your page number either on :

1. Page number placed in upper right corner.

2. No page number on first page allowing for Title page, starting on page 2, placing it in the upper right corner.

3. Page number placed in lower right corner.

4. No page number on first page allowing for Title page, starting on page 2, and placing it in the lower right corner.

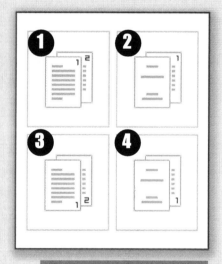

3.27 Page placement options

If you want to display the word Page as part of the page number, you will need to type Page at the desired location in the header.

Page Count – You can automatically display the page count - or how many pages your document has - in the header or footer. Select Insert > Page Count.

Page Break – When you insert a page break, you place your cursor, select Insert > Page break, and the any text where the cursor was will jump to a new page. This would be used to add a lot of white space after such things as a page title.

Column Break – Column break works the same as the page break, it will make the next text start at the top of the next column. So you need to have columns in order to use this function. You can convert your text into columns under the Format tab.

 Header / Footer – Headers and footers add a consistent layout if you have multiple pages. They are comparable to what a template page is because every new page will carry over what is put in that header or footer.

You can format the header or footer by changing fonts, making it bold, colorizing the font. You can also add an image. Great example of a header use is on the business letterhead.

To make the first page header or footer different from the other pages, check Different first page header/footer. You can't add different headers or footers to every page.

 ✓ Different first page header/footer

 Bookmark – A bookmark is what is used in a long document to give you access (a link) to a place further down in that document. A Table of Contents is a great place to use a bookmark.

To add a bookmark:
1. Move cursor to the spot in your Google Doc where you'd to place the bookmark.
2. Select Insert > Bookmark. You'll see a little blue bookmark ribbon added to your document (3.28).
3. Click on the bookmark ribbon and you'll see a Link and a Remove Link option (3.29).
4. Right-click on Link to copy the link to your clipboard or open it in a new tab or window. Now you will have a URL to a specific point in your document.

Today's Session

Bookmark: Link | Remove

3.28 Blue ribbon to add bookmark

One

#bookmark=id.75cezfiohr70 – Change | Remove

3.29 Add / Change link

Table Of Contents – A table of contents is usually found on a page at the beginning of a written document, listing down it's chapters and sections in an organized manner.

Creating a table of contents in Docs is easy to do, and as you add or subtract from it, it will auto-update.

This is really a 2-step process because to initially create the TOC, you must format your text as a Header (3.30). It can be anywhere from Header 1 to Header 4.

Step one:
1. Start each section with what you want to title it:
2. Select, from the Text Menu:
3. Format > Paragraph Styles
4. Choose Header Style.

Step two:
1. After formatting with Header text.
2. Click where you want the table of contents.
3. Click Insert Table of Contents.
4. Choose With page numbers or With blue links (3.31). The table of contents will appear.

3.30 Header text from format

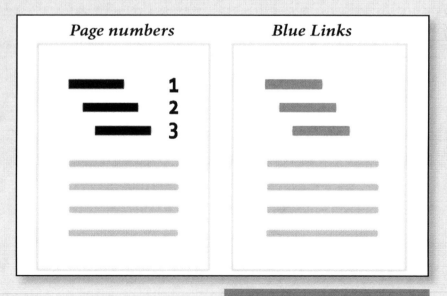

3.31 Page numbers or Blue Links

C-5 Text Menu - FORMAT

Format

1	**B**	Bold	Ctrl+B
	_I_	Italic	Ctrl+I
	U	Underline	Ctrl+U
	S	Strikethrough	Alt+Shift+5
	x²	Superscript	Ctrl+.
	x₂	Subscript	Ctrl+,
2		Font size	►
3		Paragraph styles	►
4		Align	►
5		Line spacing	►
6		Columns	►
7		Lists	►
8		Capitalization	►
	_Tx_	Clear formatting	Ctrl+\
9		Borders & lines	►
10		Crop image	
11		Image options...	
12		Replace image...	
13		Reset image	
14		Alt text...	

1

The beginning part of format is very basic, examples of what you can do are:

Bold

Italic

Underline

~~Strikethrough~~

Super^{script}

Sub$_{script}$

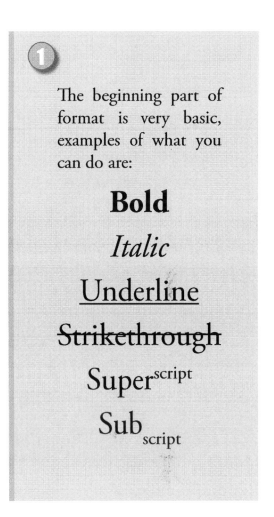

Font size – Starting with **Font size**, you can increase or reduce the size of your fonts.

Increase font size	Ctrl+Shift+.
Decrease font size	Ctrl+Shift+,

Paragraph styles – Paragraph styles opens to a full menu (3.32). The first option is to increase or decrease indent, this is used for creating a block quote. The next options are from Normal Text, Title, Subtitle, Heading 1 to Heading 6. The default text for these styles is ARIAL.

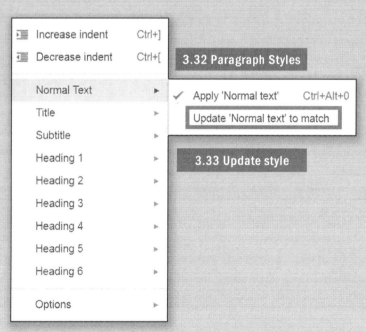

1. Create a text box with text.

2. Change it to the font, size, color and style that you want your new style to be.

3. With the new styled text select, go to any of the options in Paragraph styles, select the right triangle that will have a fly-out menu.

4. Select Update (3.33). Now you have a new paragraph style based on your selected text.

Align – This is the placement of the text within the text box.

Text flushed left

Center text

Right text

When all words are justified their lines are even.

≡	Left	Ctrl+Shift+L
≡	Center	Ctrl+Shift+E
≡	Right	Ctrl+Shift+R
≡	Justified	Ctrl+Shift+J

Line spacing – Line spacing, in desktop publishing terms is called leading. So, as you add space, it can be:

- Single - distance equal to the depth of current line.

- 1.15 - distance equal to depth of current line plus .15% extra.

- 1.5 - distance equal to 1 and 1/2 times size of current line.

- Double - distance equal to two times current line depth.

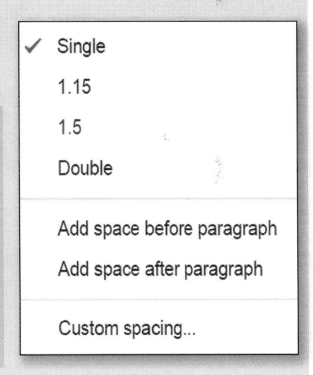

Adding space before and after a paragraph creates a nice break between the paragraphs.

Line spacing (cont'd) –You can add your own custom spacing between lines and between paragraphs or after paragraphs .

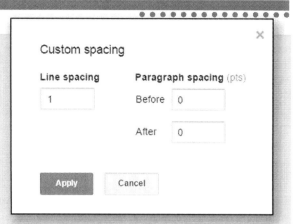

6 Columns – Columns divide your text from one column, to either two or three columns.

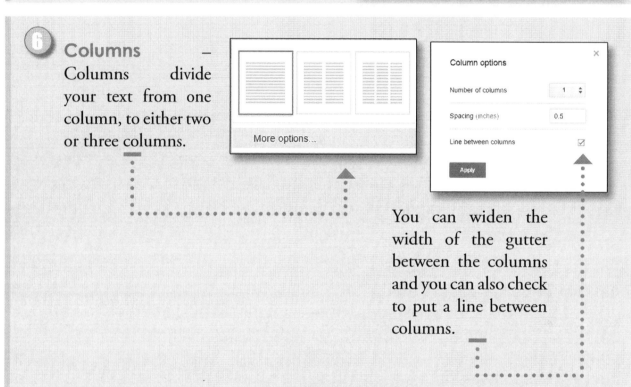

You can widen the width of the gutter between the columns and you can also check to put a line between columns.

Three Column Text with Divider Line

Lorem ipsum dolor sit amet, consectetuer adipiscing elit, sed diam nonummy nibh euismod tincidunt ut laoreet dolore magna aliquam erat volutpat. Duis autem vel eum iriure dolor in hendrerit in

vulputate velit esse molestie consequat, vel illum dolore eu feugiat nulla facilisis at vero eros et accumsan.

Lorem ipsum dolor sit amet, consectetuer adipiscing elit, sed diam nonummy nibh

euismod tincidunt ut laoreet dolore magna aliquam erat volutpat. Duis autem vel eum iriure dolor in hendrerit in vulputate velit esse molestie consequat, vel illum dolore eu feugiat nulla

List – Creating list items in your presentation is a way to help your items stand out or show important steps.

List options ▶

List options gives you the option to restart numbering, edit prefix and suffix.

If you choose More bullets, you will be taken to the number sections of Special Characters, see page 211.

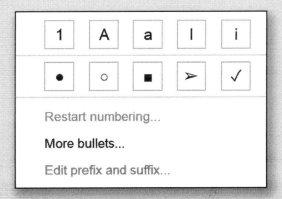

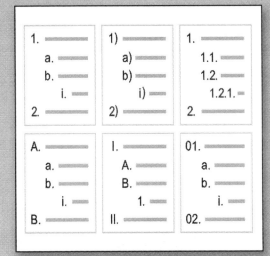

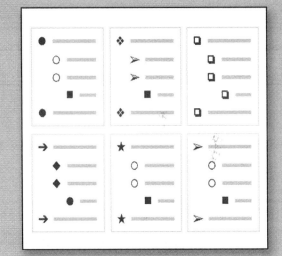

When choosing Numbered list you can list out numerically and indents will be alphabetical, or list out alphabetical and indents will be numbered.

When choosing Bulleted list you can list out with a various shapes, arrows, circles, squares.

8 **Capitalization** – Your text will be converted to what your choose. If your text is all upper case, and you choose lower, all your text will be converted to lower case.

9 **Borders & Lines** – When you insert an object into your Docs, you can change the border weight and the border dash.

Border Weight

Border Dash

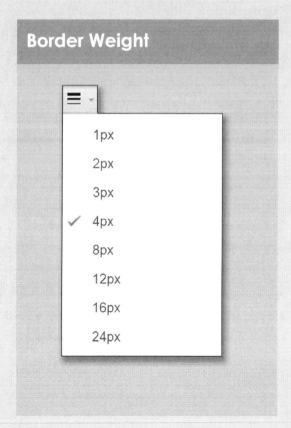

10 **Crop image** – Cropping an image will remove parts of the image without scaling the size of the image.

The darker part of the image is what will show, where it is faded is the cropped part of the image.

11 **Image options** – You can adjust your image's Transparency, Brightness, and Contrast. If you don't like your adjustments, just choose Reset adjustments to put the image back to it's original state.

Image Options ✕

Recolor

Light 1 ▾

Adjustments

Transparency

Brightness

Contrast

Reset adjustments

There are nineteen color options to apply to your image as show on the right.

Image Options ✕

Recolor

Light 7 ▾

No Recolor

Replace image – You have to first have your image selected, than go to Format > Replace image, and the box on the right will appear.

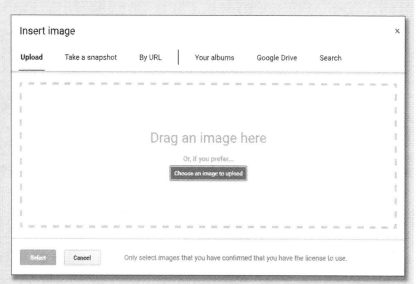

- Once you make your choice, the new image will appear in the box that the old image occupied but any of the formatting will be stripped away.

 Resetting image – Selecting to reset the image will strip away any adjustments you applied such as colorizing, transparency, contrast -- even cropping and line styles will be removed. Your image will be reset to it's original state when your first imported it.

 Alt text – When you add Alt Text to an image, your are giving it a Title and a Description.

This will help your Search Engine Optimization if you post your Slide Deck in a web browser. This was explained in the first chapter of this book.

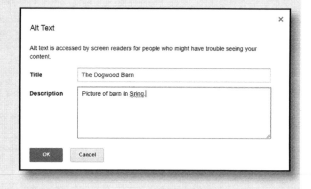

C-6 Text Menu - TOOLS

Tools

(1) Spelling...

(2) ◆ Explore   Ctrl+Alt+Shift+I

(3) Define   Ctrl+Shift+Y

(4) Document outline   Ctrl+Alt+A Ctrl+Alt+H

(5) Word count   Ctrl+Shift+C

(6) 🎤 Voice typing...   Ctrl+Shift+S

(7) 💡 Keep notepad

(8) Translate document...

Script editor...

(9) Preferences...

Personal dictionary...

Tools is a powerhouse feature within Docs.

Take a screwdriver and open the possibilities that Google has to offer. You can Explore the Internet right inside your document and insert it in your Doc. You can dictate using voice typing and you can also translate for various languages and to various languages.

1   It is always good to spell check your file for errors.

When you go to Tools > Spelling, a pop-up box will appear (3.34). It will have suggestions for the correct spelling and you can select Change or Ignore. You can also add a word to the system dictionary.

As you enter text, if Docs thinks it is misspelled, it will have a squiggly line under it (3.35).

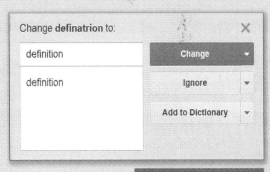

Change **definatrion** to: ✕

definition   Change ▾

definition   Ignore ▾

Add to Dictionary ▾

3.34 Spelling popup

ture within Docs. Just as it is called, imugine getting that Google has to offer feeturing Explore which take nternet opening the world wide web for you right insi

3.35 Spell errors

Explore – When you select **Tools** > Explore, without any words selected, the **artificial intelligence** of **Google** will scan your document and suggestions, from different words in the document, will appear in the Explore panel.

The Explore Panel is broken into three separate sections as listed below:

1. Topics:

Features a number of suggested topics that are related to the content of your document. Click on any topic to access it's information.

2. Images:

The tab provides you with a set of images related to your content which you can add to your document. Added images come with a footnote at the bottom of the document.

3. Related research:

In this section you will be able to view research directly related to the topic of your document.

SEARCH – When you open the Explore panel and type in a search query, the options you will have will be to either search the Web, Images, or your Drive.

The Explore is also in the bottom right of every Doc that is opened. When you select it, the Explore panel will open.

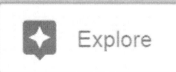

Define – When you select Insert > Define, a Dictionary panel opens. Type in the word that you want a definition of and the breakdown of the word, including it's pronunciation, uses, even synonyms appears.

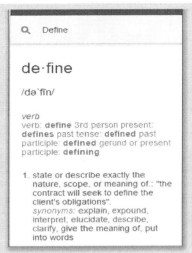

Document Outline – When you select Tools > Document Outline, the outline tool will appear in the left hand panel of your document.

To begin to create your outline:

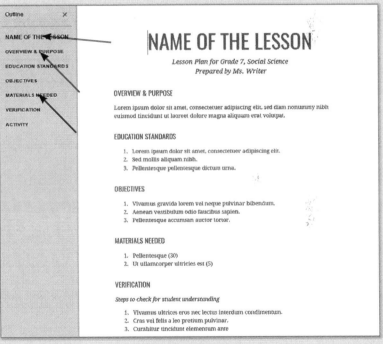

1. Highlight the text you would like in your outline.

2. Either go to Format > Paragraph Styles > Header style or from the Style bar, drop down from Normal text to select a Header style.

3. Your outline will start to build in the left panel. You can nest within your Outline by choosing different Header styles. Title style can be the top level in your outline and Header 1 can follow, than Header 2 to create a sub-header.

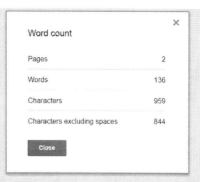

5 **Word Count** – Word count gives you a break down of how many pages, words, characters, and characters excluding spaces are in your Doc.

Word counting may be needed when a text is required to stay within certain numbers of words. Great for legal proceedings, journalism and advertising.

Word count is commonly used by translators to determine the price for the translation job.

6 **Voice Typing** – Dictation made easy! Voice typing is a great time saving tool to use from anything such as dictation of a letter to that next great novel.

Start voice typing in a document

1. Check that your microphone works.
2. Open a document in Google Docs with a Chrome browser.
3. Click Tools and then Voice typing. A microphone box appears.
4. When you're ready to speak, click the microphone.
5. Speak clearly, at a normal volume and pace (see below for more information on using punctuation).
6. When you're done, click the microphone again.

Voice commands are available only in English. The account language and document language must both be English.

If you select the carat drop down at the microphone, you will see the languages and accents it works with.

You can add punctuation with these spoken phrases:
- Period
- Comma
- Exclamation point
- Question mark
- New line
- New paragraph

7 **Keep Notepad** – A mix between personal and work life, Keep tries to bring it all together. As relatively new addition to the Google Docs repertoire of tools, Keep imports those quick notes that you created for yourself in Keep. Some things that Keep can do are:

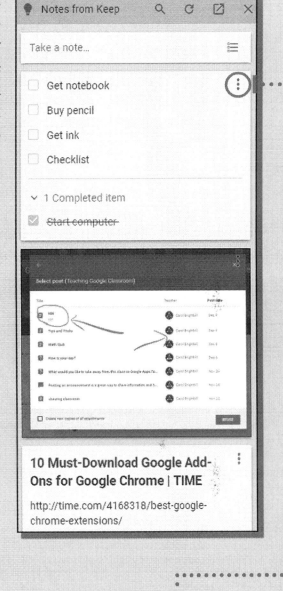

- **Text** – Create a note and all the text within your note will be imported.

- **List** – Adding a list in Keep will keep track of the task to be completed. Once done, the item will have a line through it marking it compete.

- **Images** – You can Grab Image Text from Keep, and than place that text into your Doc. This is called OCR - Optical Character Recognition, is a technology that enables you to convert images captured by a digital camera into editable and search-able data.

- **Audio** – This is an option only available on an Android device.

From within the note, there are three dots, choose what your would like to do with the note such as add it to your Doc, delete, or open in Keep.

Add to document

Delete

Open in Keep

Translate – When you select Tools > Translate, there are **104 different languages** that you can choose from.

This is a good tool for schools with second languages, you can translate to the home language of your student for them to have a better understanding of the topics in your class. It isn't perfect but it is a way to open a door to understanding.

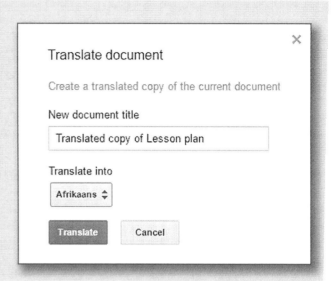

Preferences – Allowing you to customize various aspects within Google Docs, some preference options are:

- Capitalize words.
- Use Smart quotes.
- Detect links.
- Detect list.

Plus, you can type specific words and they will represent a different character.

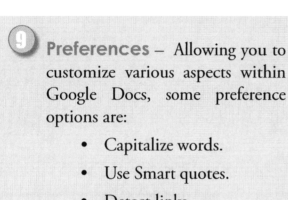

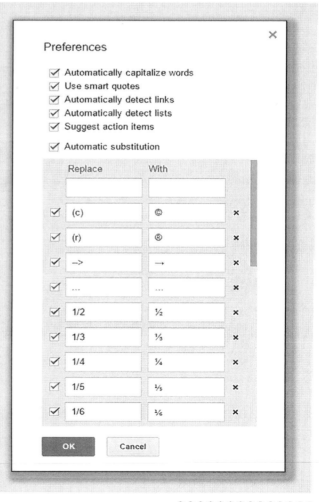

C-7 Text Menu - TABLE

Table – A table is a grid of cells arranged in rows and columns. It can be useful to present data in a table inside a word processing document because it is displayed in an organized and easy to read format.

You can insert a table anywhere from 1x1 up to 20 x 20 and all equations in-between. You can insert and delete rows and columns from within this menu along with merging sells (explained earlier on page 89).

As you travel down the Table Menu, the options are about how to manipulate your table.

1. Insert table - Gives you the option to insert a table anywhere from 1x1 to 20x20 cells.

2. Inserting rows and columns will add additional rows or columns above, below, right or left in your table.

3. Deleting a row or column will remove that row or column.

4. Delete table will remove the table.

5. Distribute rows or columns will give them even spacing.

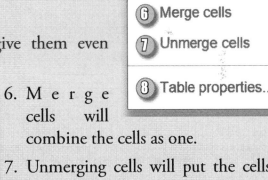

6. Merge cells will combine the cells as one.

7. Unmerging cells will put the cells back in the original order.

8. Table properties - Shown on left. Add border color, background color. Alignment, padding and dimensions.

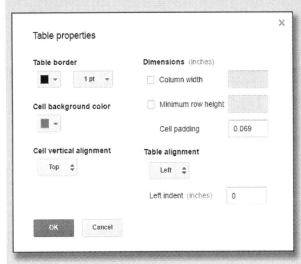

C-8 Text Menu - ADD-ONS

Add-Ons – Add-ons extend the functionality of Google Docs. The are built by third-party developers using Google Apps Script. There are countless add-ons and you can do some research on good ones. If you don't like the add-on, just go to Manage add-ons and delete it.

Add-ons

Get add-ons...

Manage add-ons...

If the documents are shared, other people working on the file will be able to see and use the add-on. The type of add-ons that you can get are anywhere from clip art, Thesaurus, fonts, label makers, highlighters,

All ▼

All

Business Tools

Education

Productivity

Social & Communication

Utilities

and many more. You can filter your search more by selecting All (3.36) and scrolling down.

3.36 Filter your add-ons

C-9 Text Menu - HELP

Help – Any questions you might have, just search the help and a wide variety of answers will be given.

You can also report any issues and report any abuse or copyright issues.

Lastly, the keyboard shortcuts can be found here. A full list of the Doc's shortcuts are on the next page.

Help

Search the menus (Alt+/)

Docs Help

Report a problem

Report abuse/copyright

Keyboard shortcuts   Ctrl+/

C-9 Text Menu - KEYBOARD SHORTCUTS

Text formatting

Bold	Ctrl+B
Italic	Ctrl+I
Underline	Ctrl+U
Strikethrough	Alt+Shift+5
Superscript	Ctrl+.
Subscript	Ctrl+,
Clear formatting	Ctrl+\ or Ctrl+Space

Paragraph formatting

Apply 'Normal text'	Ctrl+Alt+0 or Ctrl+Alt+Num-0
Apply 'Heading 1'	Ctrl+Alt+1 or Ctrl+Alt+Num-1
Apply 'Heading 2'	Ctrl+Alt+2 or Ctrl+Alt+Num-2
Apply 'Heading 3'	Ctrl+Alt+3 or Ctrl+Alt+Num-3
Apply 'Heading 4'	Ctrl+Alt+4 or Ctrl+Alt+Num-4
Apply 'Heading 5'	Ctrl+Alt+5 or Ctrl+Alt+Num-5
Apply 'Heading 6'	Ctrl+Alt+6 or Ctrl+Alt+Num-6
Left align text	Ctrl+Shift+L
Center align text	Ctrl+Shift+E
Right align text	Ctrl+Shift+R
Justify text	Ctrl+Shift+J
Toggle numbered list	Ctrl+Shift+7
Toggle bulleted list	Ctrl+Shift+8

With objects

Resize larger	Ctrl+Alt+K
Resize smaller	Ctrl+Alt+J

Editing

Insert link...	Ctrl+K
Find...	Ctrl+F
Find and replace...	Ctrl+H
Define word	Ctrl+Shift+Y

Copy formatting	Ctrl+Alt+C
Paste formatting	Ctrl+Alt+V
Switch to editing	Ctrl+Alt+Shift+Z
Switch to suggesting	Ctrl+Alt+Shift+X
Switch to viewing	Ctrl+Alt+Shift+C

Navigation

Chat	Shift+Esc
Insert or move to header	Ctrl+Alt+O Ctrl+Alt+H
Insert or move to footer	Ctrl+Alt+O Ctrl+Alt+F
Insert footnote	Ctrl+Alt+F
Move to next heading	Ctrl+Alt+N Ctrl+Alt+H
Move to previous heading	Ctrl+Alt+P Ctrl+Alt+H
Move to next heading 1	Ctrl+Alt+N Ctrl+Alt+1
Move to previous heading 1	Ctrl+Alt+P Ctrl+Alt+1
Move to next heading 2	Ctrl+Alt+N Ctrl+Alt+2
Move to previous heading 2	Ctrl+Alt+P Ctrl+Alt+2
Move to next heading 3	Ctrl+Alt+N Ctrl+Alt+3
Move to previous heading 3	Ctrl+Alt+P Ctrl+Alt+3
Move to next heading 4	Ctrl+Alt+N Ctrl+Alt+4
Move to previous heading 4	Ctrl+Alt+P Ctrl+Alt+4
Move to next heading 5	Ctrl+Alt+N Ctrl+Alt+5
Move to previous heading 5	Ctrl+Alt+P Ctrl+Alt+5
Move to next heading 6	Ctrl+Alt+N Ctrl+Alt+6
Move to previous heading 6	Ctrl+Alt+P Ctrl+Alt+6

Move into current footnote	Ctrl+Alt+E Ctrl+Alt+F
Move to next misspelling	Ctrl+'
Move to previous misspelling	Ctrl+;
Explore	Ctrl+Alt+Shift+I

Menus

File menu	Alt+Shift+F or Alt+F
Edit menu	Alt+Shift+E or Alt+E
View menu	Alt+Shift+V or Alt+V
Insert menu	Alt+Shift+I or Alt+I
Format menu	Alt+Shift+O or Alt+O
Tools menu	Alt+Shift+T or Alt+T
Add-ons menu	Alt+Shift+N or Alt+N
Count words	Ctrl+Shift+C
Table menu	Alt+Shift+B or Alt+B
Help menu	Alt+Shift+H or Alt+H
Context menu	Ctrl+Shift+\ or Ctrl+Shift+X

Comments

Add comment	Ctrl+Alt+M
Open comments thread...	Ctrl+Alt+Shift+A
Enter current comment	Ctrl+Alt+E Ctrl+Alt+C
Move to next comment	Ctrl+Alt+N Ctrl+Alt+C
Move to previous comment	Ctrl+Alt+P Ctrl+Alt+C

④ SHEETS

Create, update and modify spreadsheets

*Create a new file and share collaboratively -
available on or offline.*

This Ajax-based program compares with Microsoft Excel. You can upload your Excel and convert it to the Google Sheets format. Your files can be saved as HTML. All the typical spreadsheet features, such as the ability to add, delete and sort rows and columns, are available in Sheets. As with all the other Google products, the any where, any time collaboration between users on a spreadsheet in real time and chat through a built-in instant messaging program.

A. HOW TO GET TO YOUR SHEETS

1

After your have logged into your Chrome account, type in

https://sheets.google.com

2

Go to the waffle and select the green rectangle icon.

3

From your Drive, select BLUE **NEW** button and go down to Sheets.

Spreadsheet

'spred,SHēt/

noun

- 1. - an electronic document in which data is arranged in the rows and columns of a grid and can be manipulated and used in calculations.
- "we have a color-coded Excel spreadsheet of all of our trip expenses"

verb

- 1. - use or create a spreadsheet.

Templates List:

- **EDUCATION:** Attendance; Grade book.
- **PERSONAL:** To-do list; Annual budget; Monthly budget; 2017 Calendar; Schedule; Travel planner; Wedding planner; Team roster.
- **WORK:** Invoice; Weekly time sheet; Financial statements by Xera; Annual business budget by Intuit Quickbooks; Expense report; Purchase order.

B. TERMINOLOGY

Terminology:

- **Cell:** A single data point or element in a spreadsheet.
- **Column:** A vertical set of cells.
- **Row:** A horizontal set of cells.
- **Range:** A selection of cells extending across a row, column, or both.
- **Function:** A built-in operation from the spreadsheet app, which can be used to calculate cell, row, column, or range values, manipulate data, and more.
- **Formula:** The combination of functions, cells, rows, columns, and ranges used to obtain a specific result.
- **Worksheet (Sheet):** The named sets of rows and columns making up your spreadsheet; one spreadsheet can have multiple sheets.
- **Spreadsheet:** The entire document containing your worksheets.

Facts:

- Spreadsheets: Up to 2 million cells for spreadsheets that are created in or converted to Google Sheets.
- Limit to 200 sheets.
- Good for organizing numbers and text.

C. FEATURES OVERVIEW

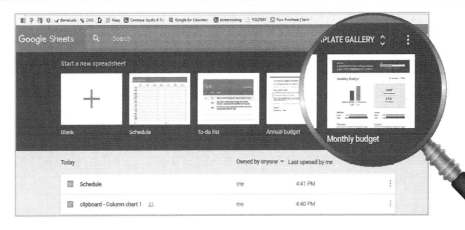

With revision history, multiple versions of spreadsheets to be stored, allowing users to roll them back to previous versions without losing any information.

Sheets also allows the document owner to determine what privileges are given to each user. This means that you can have multiple viewers and editors on a single project. When complete, your file can be downloaded as an Excel file.

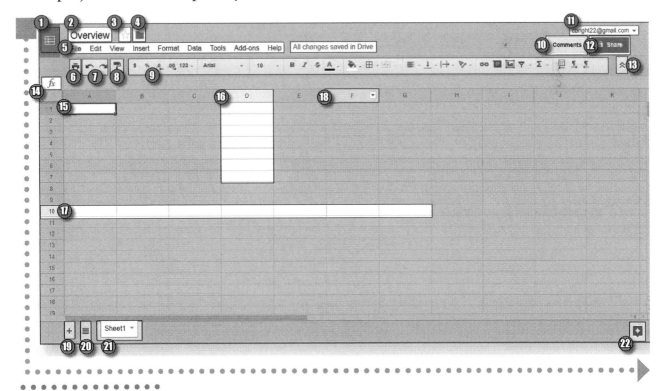

1 Home – Selecting the green rectangle with white lines in the upper corner of your window will return you to your Sheets Repository. It is a quick, easy navigation tool. From here, you can start a new blank spreadsheet, use a template or open a previously created Sheet.

2 Title – After you have created your first blank spreadsheet, it will be an Untitled document. You will want to give your new spreadsheet a title right away because Sheets auto-saves.

3 Star – Starring a document gives it importance and makes your file easier in a search.

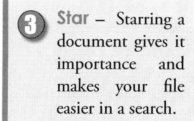

4 Move to – Selecting the folder icon will give you the option to move your document to another location.

5 Text Menu – All about the text menu will follow in a later chapter.

6 Print – Your printer will appear and give you the option to print your document.

7 Undo/Redo – Go back one step in your files and go forward to your last move.

8 **Paint Format** – You can use it to copy a format from one highlighted area of text or cell to another.

1. Open a Google file.
2. Select the text, range of cells, or object you want to copy the format of.
3. In the toolbar, click Paint format .
4. Select what you want to paste the formatting onto.

9 **Icon Menu** – Adding style to your document is how you make your file stand out from the competition. This is called formatting. Various ways to format is to change fonts, font sizes, bold, colorize and adding a bullet list. The Style menu is located below the drop-down menus.

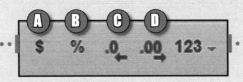

A. **Format as currency** - You can display a number with the default currency symbol by selecting the cell or range of cells with your number and than select the $ symbol. Example placing 1 in cell will be converted to $1.00.

B. **Format as percentage** - Your number will be changed to a percent. Example: 1 is changed to 100.00%

C. **Decrease decimal places** - Decimals are removed from the end of your number. Example: 100.00% is changed to 100.0% with one click.

D. **Increase decimal places** - Decimals are added to the end of your number. Example: 100.00% is changed to 100.000 b % with one click.

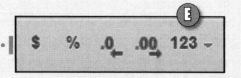

E. More formats - Number format helps to make your spreadsheet easier to use. When you apply a number format, you're telling your spreadsheet exactly what types of values are stored in a cell.

An example is the date format which can tell the spreadsheet that you are entering specific calendar dates allowing the spreadsheet to better understand your information.

If you don't need to use a specific number format, the spreadsheet will usually apply the automatic format by default. However, the automatic format may apply some small formatting changes to your data.

123 ▾	
✓ Automatic	
Plain text	
Number	1,000.12
Percent	10.12%
Scientific	1.01E+03
Accounting	$ (1,000.12)
Financial	(1,000.12)
Currency	$1,000.12
Currency (rounded)	$1,000
Date	9/26/2008
Time	3:59:00 PM
Date time	9/26/2008 15:59:00
Duration	24:01:00
More Formats	▶

More currencies...

More date and time formats...

Custom number format...

F. Font

G. Font Size

H. **Bold**

I. *Italics*

J. ~~Strikethrough~~

K. Font Color

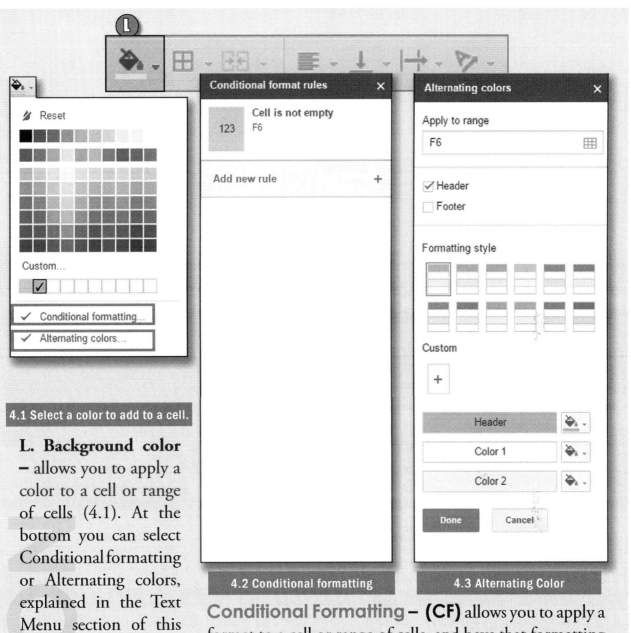

4.1 Select a color to add to a cell.

4.2 Conditional formatting

4.3 Alternating Color

L. Background color – allows you to apply a color to a cell or range of cells (4.1). At the bottom you can select Conditional formatting or Alternating colors, explained in the Text Menu section of this chapter.

Conditional Formatting – (CF) allows you to apply a format to a cell or range of cells, and have that formatting change depending on the value of the cell or the value of a formula (4.2).

Alternating Colors – Choosing alternating colors is a way to add color and an organized style to your spreadsheet by alternating the color every other row (4.3).

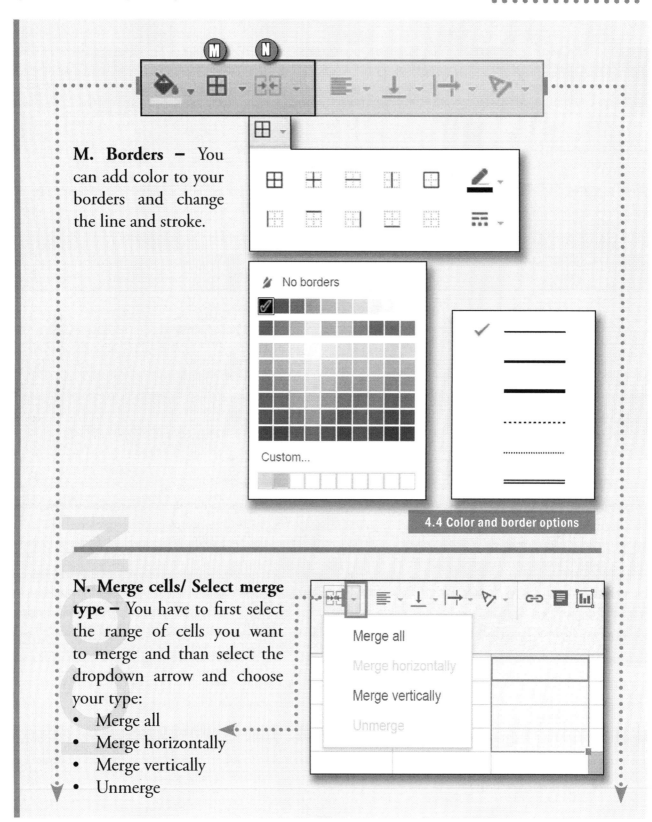

M. Borders – You can add color to your borders and change the line and stroke.

4.4 Color and border options

N. Merge cells/ Select merge type – You have to first select the range of cells you want to merge and than select the dropdown arrow and choose your type:

- Merge all
- Merge horizontally
- Merge vertically
- Unmerge

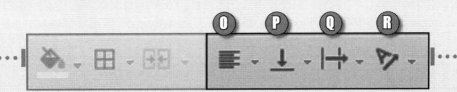

O. Horizontal align - Choose to either flush left, center or flush right.

P. Vertical align - Choose if your data is vertically aligned to either the top of the cell, center of the cell or the bottom of the cell. (4.5)

Top left	Top center	Top right
Middle left	Middle center	Middle Right
Bottom left	Bottom center	Bottom right

4.5 Horizontal and vertical alignment

Q. Text Wrapping - Text wrapping has a fly-out menu giving you three options:

   1. **Overflow** - will go into adjacent cells (left or right depending on text alignment) as long as those cells are empty.

   2. **Wrap** - will change the row's height, making it taller, depending on width, length of text, and font size.

   3. **Clip** - text will only fit into cell, and will be clipped off.

R. Text Rotation – Text rotations angles your text.

H	I	J	K	L	M
Rotation	Rotation	Rotation	Rotation	Rotation	Rotation

S. Insert Link - You first select the cell or cells that you would like to link and the box that popups will have a text area and the link area.

In addition to these two areas, suggested websites will appear beneath the link box based on your selection. This is another area where Google artificial intelligence comes into play by reading your data and searching the web for you. You can also put the link of a shared file here or an email.

T. Insert Comment - When you select this option, a dialog box will appear beside your document. Using this box, you can type in suggestions that you think would improve the file. A comment can be attached to a specific cell and that cell will than have a triangle in the upper right corner to indicate that a comment is there.

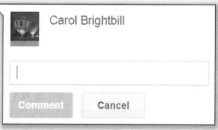

U. Insert Chart - Select your range of data for the chart, and select Insert Chart. A pop-up window will appear with three tab options:
1. **Recommendations** (best options that fit your specific data);
2. **Chart types** (all chart types, see QR Code and url for full list);
3. **Customization** (select font, color, legend, axis).

V. Filter - To see and analyze data in a spreadsheet, use filters. Filters let you hide data that you don't want to see. You'll still be able to see all your data when you turn the filter off. Filters can be useful if you want everyone viewing your spreadsheet to see a specific filter when they open it or you want your data to stay sorted after using the filter.

W. Functions - Choose if your data is vertically aligned to either the top of the cell, center of the cell or the bottom of the cell.

SUM
Returns the sum of a series of numbers and/or cells.

AVERAGE
Returns the numerical average value in a dataset, ignoring text.

COUNT
Returns a count of the number of numeric values in a dataset.

MAX
Returns the maximum value in a numeric dataset.

MIN
Returns the minimum value in a numeric dataset.

SUM
AVERAGE
COUNT
MAX
MIN
More...

10 **Comment** – You must first add a comment to the side of your Google Sheet. Now when you select Comment, at the top, you can see your comment and any additional comments that are added throughout the document, even a multiple page document, well show as a running text stream at the top of the page.

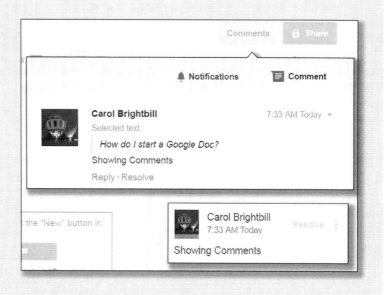

Select the cell where you would like to attach the comment and the comment box will appear for you to insert your comment.

11 **Account** – When you select your email address, a box will open showing you your My Account button to go see an overview of your account settings. You can also add an account, Go to Google +, Privacy settings, and Sign out of your Google account.

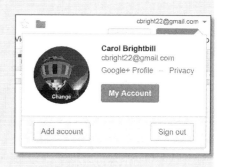

12 **Share** – All about sharing on pages 40-49 of this book.

13 **Show your menu** – Clicking the double arrow will hide the menus and clicking the double arrow again will show the menu.

14 **Formula bar** – By default, the formula bar is hidden, to make it appear, go to View menu and click Show formula bar. To make the formula bar bigger or smaller, click the bottom of it, then drag it up or down. The formula bar is can be used to show a cell that has a lot of text in it, and you can use it to type. You can also type a function within the formula bar.

fx |

15 **Cell** – The information that you usually place within a cell is text, a numeric value, or a formula. The entire spreadsheet is composed of rows and columns of cells. Individual cells are usually identified by a column letter and a row number. For example, D12 specifies the cell in column D and row 12.

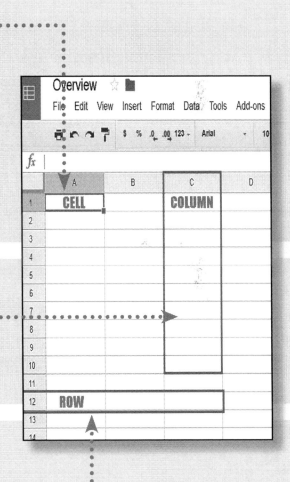

16 **Column** – A column is a vertical series of cells in a chart, table, or spreadsheet. You can add, delete, freeze, move, or hide rows and columns in a spreadsheet in Google Sheets.

17 **Row** – A row is a horizontal series of cells in a chart, table, or spreadsheet. You can add, delete, freeze, move, or hide rows and columns in a spreadsheet in Google Sheets.

18 **Column Options** – When you hover in the upper right corner of any column, a dropdown arrow will appear and a sub-menu will open giving you action items that you perform in the column.

You can cut, copy and paste. Paste special has a sub-menu. (4.6)

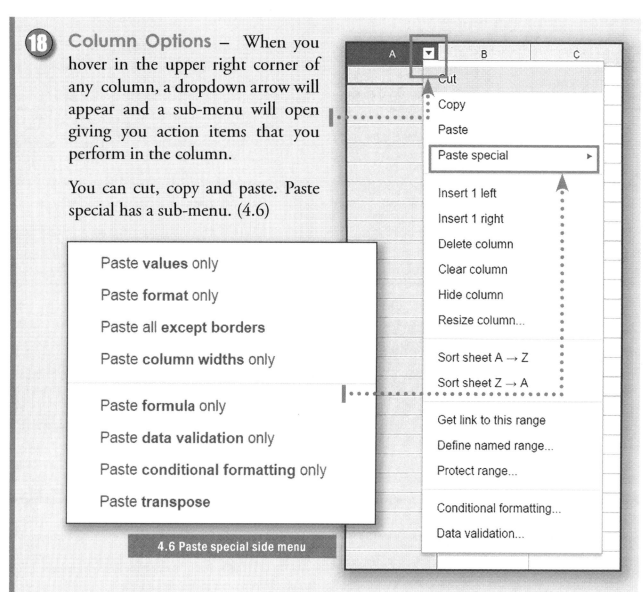

Paste **values** only

Paste **format** only

Paste all **except borders**

Paste **column widths** only

Paste **formula** only

Paste **data validation** only

Paste **conditional formatting** only

Paste **transpose**

4.6 Paste special side menu

You can insert, delete, clear, hide, and resize columns.

You can sort alphabetically, get a link, define and protect a range.

The bottom of the menu is Conditional formatting and Data validation, explained on pages 152-153.

Add sheet – A limit of 200 sheets can be added to a Google Sheets file.

All sheet – Selecting All sheets will open up an index listing your sheets with the first one at the top and listing downward. It is a good idea to name your sheets so you know where to go.

Current sheet – Selecting the current sheet opens a menu giving you actions items such as:

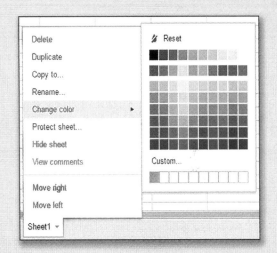

- Delete

- Duplicate

- Copy to - You can copy that sheet to another sheet within your Drive.

- Rename

- Change color - See side flyout menu with standard or custom color options.

- Protect sheet - If you don't want people to change the content in a spreadsheet, you can protect it. People can print, copy, paste, and import and export copies of a protected spreadsheet.

- Hide sheet - You can hide sheets that are old or are placeholders for calculations used by other sheets.

- View Comments

- Move right

- Move left.

22 **Explore** – Select some data, and then hover over the Explore button (4.7), it will slide open (4.8) will then offer you information on functions, formatting, and more based on what you have selected.

This is a quick means to easily format a collection of cells. With your cells highlighted, open up Explore and then click the option you like best under the FORMATTING section. It's that easy. Need a chart? Explore will create an on-the-fly chart based on the data you've highlighted. Click and drag the chart onto your document and you're ready to go

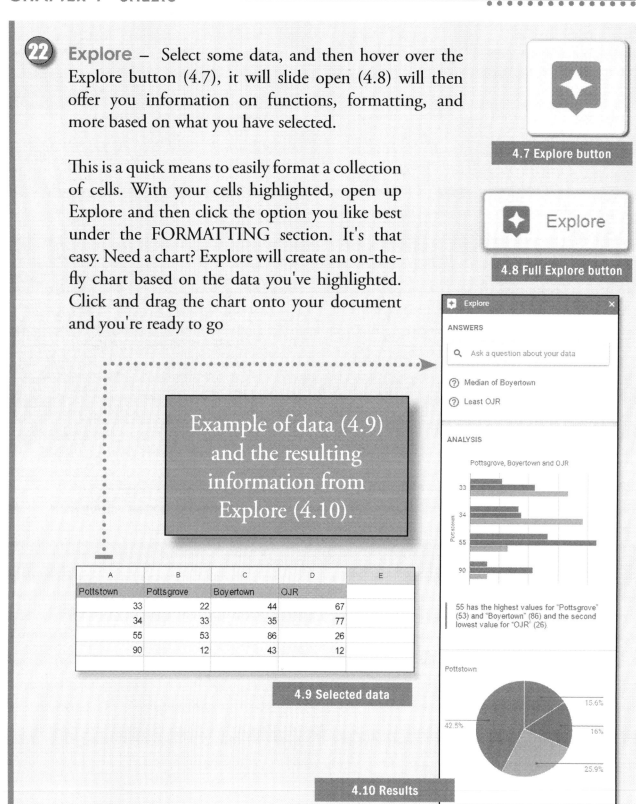

4.7 Explore button

4.8 Full Explore button

Example of data (4.9) and the resulting information from Explore (4.10).

4.9 Selected data

4.10 Results

D. TEXT MENU OVERVIEW

Menus are used for organization... providing a list of action items for the user to select, and a way for users to navigate the program.

Maneuvering through the Text Menu and familiarizing yourself with all the sub-menus helps to increase your productivity.

Sheets Text Menu

File   Edit   View   Insert   Format   Data   Tools   Add-ons   Help

D-1 Text Menu - FILE

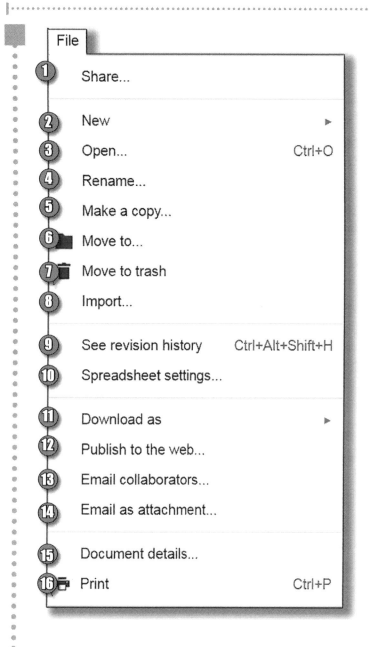

File

1. Share...
2. New ►
3. Open... Ctrl+O
4. Rename...
5. Make a copy...
6. Move to...
7. Move to trash
8. Import...
9. See revision history Ctrl+Alt+Shift+H
10. Spreadsheet settings...
11. Download as ►
12. Publish to the web...
13. Email collaborators...
14. Email as attachment...
15. Document details...
16. Print Ctrl+P

1 **Share** – The first thing under the file menu is one of the most important things about Google Apps, the ability to **Share** your file. I covered this intensively in the Drive section, pages 40-49.

2 **New** – Clicking the New will show how dynamic the Google Apps are. From the New, you can create any one of the Google core apps. Additionally, you can select to create a new Sheet from a template.

- Document
- Spreadsheet
- Presentation
- Form
- Drawing
- From template...

3 **Open** – Selecting **Open** gives you the choices of going to:

- My Drive
- Shared with Me
- Starred
- Recent
- Upload

Selecting dropdown arrow will let you open by file type.

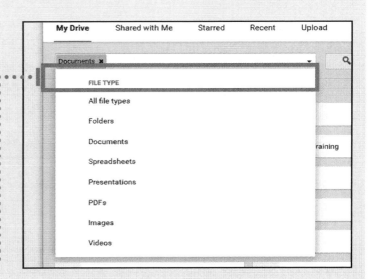

4 **Rename** – When you select Rename, your cursor will instantly pop up to where your file has it's existing name and it will be highlighted. Renaming does not make an additional file, it just gives your existing file a new name.

5 **Make A Copy** – There are two reasons to make a copy of your file:

1. When a file is shared and the rights are **View Only**, you can not edit the file. This is a smart practice to maintain the integrity of your file. If you select **Make a Copy**, you can rename it, now it is yours to go into and edit.

2. You want to update a file with new information but you want to keep the original file. This is another reason to make a copy of your original, so you can have a different version with the new information and keep your old version.

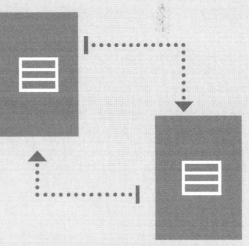

Move to – Selecting the folder icon will give you the option to move your document to another location.

This file is in 1 folder: ×

My Drive

Move this item

Move to trash – This will delete your file from your drive but it is not permanently deleted until you delete it from your trash.

8 **Import** - Selecting File > Import will take you to four options:

- My Drive;
- Shared with me;
- Recent; and
- Upload.

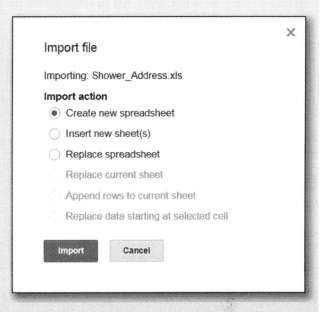

From the above import options, if you select a Microsoft Excel file, you will be given 6 choices (not all file types will have all six options):

Create new spreadsheet: Does just what it states, a new spreadsheet will be created that you will have to name.

Insert new sheets: An additional worksheet tab will be created.

Replace spreadsheet: All data currently in the existing spreadsheet will be replaced.

Replace current sheet: This option replaces the current sheet with the imported data. Formatting and data previously on this sheet is replaced.

Append rows to current sheet: This option adds the imported data to the row after the last row with any data in it on your current sheet. Your existing data will remain intact.

Replace data starting at selected cell: This option pastes the imported data in a range of cells you have selected. It will replace any data that was previously on the sheet where the imported data has been pasted, but preserves existing data everywhere else.

See Revision History – Gone are the days of paper drafts that teachers reviewed to see the thought process of their student. This is where Revision History comes in handy. It is also a great way to keep students, working on teams collaborating honest! You can see who has done what in the file.

When you choose **File > See Revision History**, another window opens showing the document, and a side bar will appear that details all the changes within the document.

You can select various dates or times and see the changes that occurred. You can also restore a previous version from this area.

When you restore a previous version, you do not loose any of the other versions, the restored version just jumps to the top.

Revision history

Yesterday

▶ **May 3, 5:53 PM**
   ■ Carol Brightbill

▼ May 3, 9:12 AM
   ■ Carol Brightbill

   May 3, 8:52 AM
   ■ Carol Brightbill

   May 3, 8:52 AM
   ■ Carol Brightbill

   May 3, 8:51 AM
   ■ Carol Brightbill

Tuesday

▶ May 2, 9:07 PM
   ■ Carol Brightbill

▶ May 2, 7:46 PM
   ■ Carol Brightbill

   May 2, 6:36 PM
   ■ Carol Brightbill

   May 2, 5:19 PM
   ■ Carol Brightbill

   May 2, 5:18 PM
   ■ Carol Brightbill

✓ Show changes

10 **S p r e a d s h e e t Settings** – It is a good idea to customize your Settings tab.

- **GENERAL** – Choosing your location will affect details such as functions, dates and default currency. Choosing United States gives you dollars, Europe would give you Euro. Calculation part will recalculate your formulas depending what setting you choose (4.11).

- **CALCULATION** – Sets how often certain formulas are updated (4.12). Iterative calculation: Sets the number of times a formula with a circular reference can take place.
  - On Change (4.13)
  - On change and every minute
  - On change and every hour

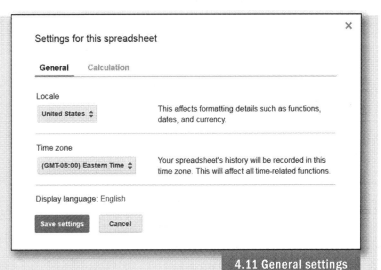

4.11 General settings

4.12 Calculation settings

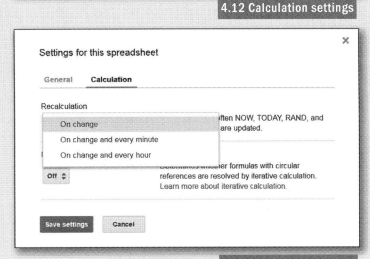

4.13 On Change

Download As- There are six options to download as:

Microsoft Excel (.xlsx)

OpenDocument format (.ods)

PDF document (.pdf)

Web page (.html, zipped)

Comma-separated values (.csv, current sheet)

Tab-separated values (.tsv, current sheet)

- **MICROSOFT EXCEL** – Microsoft Office Excel has a lot more powerful formulas but Excel should retain all the formulas from Google spreadsheet provided they are compatible with Excel. Google spreadsheet formulas that are not compatible with Excel with show up with error, such as #VALUE!

- **OPEN DOCUMENT FORMAT** – ODF is an ISO International Standard format for office documents, created in 2006. The advantage of ODF is that it is not tied to any one office application suite. It is an open standard that any company can implement in their software. OpenOffice uses ODF format as its default document format.[1]

- **PDF DOCUMENT** – Portable document file, created by Adobe as a format that any file type can be transferred without loosing their fonts and file layout.

- **WEB PAGE** – Your file is automatically downloaded in a zipped file that contains an html file and a css file.

- **COMMA-SEPARATED VALUES** – An Excel .csv file is automatically downloaded.

- **TAB-SEPARATED VALUES** – A notepad text file is downloaded.

---

[1]Open Office: https://www.openoffice.org/why/why_odf.html

12 **Publish to the web** – Publishing to the web creates a webpage where anyone with the link can view your document. A URL is created for your Sheet.

When a file is published, a copy of the original file is made. The copy is the file that people see when they visit your website. It doesn't carry over sharing permissions, so anyone will be able to see it.

When you publish, you can do the following:

- Create an embeddable HTML version of a doc. The HTML version can be embedded in blogs, Google Sites, and more.

- Show your doc to large web audiences. Only 50 people can view a shared doc at a time, but a lightweight webpage has much, much higher limits.

- Provide quick access to file downloads.

- Publish a one-time snapshot of a your document. To create such a snapshot, make sure you un-check "Automatically republish" when you publish your doc.

To publish to the web:

- **Link** – Either entire document of a specific sheet, your link can be either one of the 6 options on the right.

- **Embed** – When you publish as embed, you are given an iframe code which specifies an inline frame. An IFrame is an HTML document embedded inside another HTML document on a website. The IFrame HTML element is often used to insert content from another source, such as an advertisement, into a Web page.

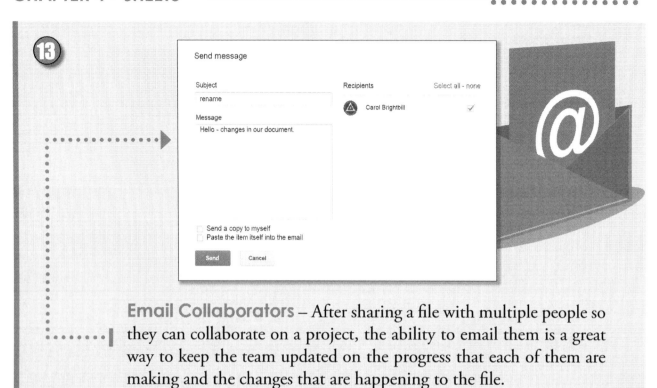

Email Collaborators – After sharing a file with multiple people so they can collaborate on a project, the ability to email them is a great way to keep the team updated on the progress that each of them are making and the changes that are happening to the file.

Email as Attachment – Not everyone has or uses Google Sheets so when you want to send the file to someone, you do have the option to attached it as a different file type. When you attach the file, you have two options: PDF or Microsoft Excel (4.14).

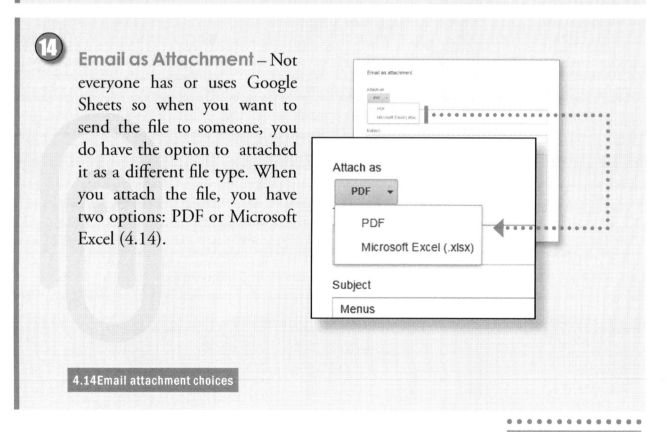

4.14 Email attachment choices

15

Document details – The details of the document provides useful information, especially if you don't know what folder your file is located or who the owner is.

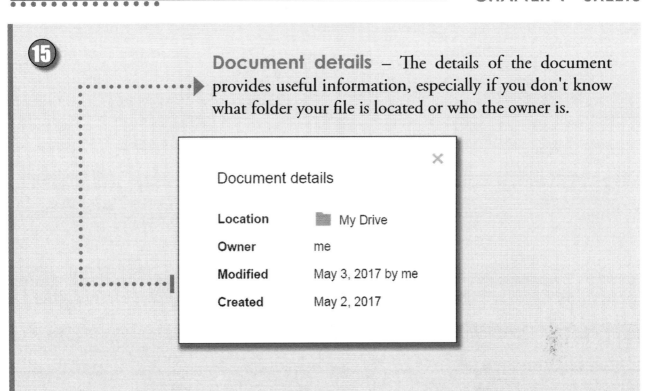

16

Print – Your printer will appear and give you the option to print your document.

D-2 Text Menu - EDIT

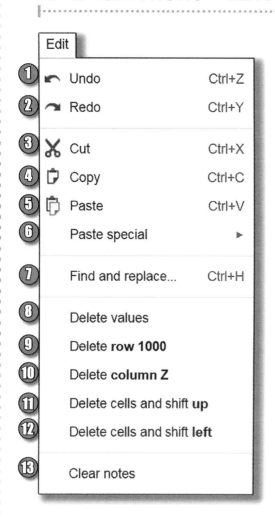

Edit	
① ↶ Undo	Ctrl+Z
② ↷ Redo	Ctrl+Y
③ ✂ Cut	Ctrl+X
④ 📋 Copy	Ctrl+C
⑤ 📋 Paste	Ctrl+V
⑥ Paste special	▶
⑦ Find and replace...	Ctrl+H
⑧ Delete values	
⑨ Delete **row 1000**	
⑩ Delete **column Z**	
⑪ Delete cells and shift **up**	
⑫ Delete cells and shift **left**	
⑬ Clear notes	

Where would word processing be without cut, copy, paste! And Control Z!! The best ever! Let's go down the menu:

1. **Undo** – action that takes you back one step in your editing.

2. **Redo** – action that jumps you back to where your were before your Undo.

3. **Cut** – places what you cut onto the computer clipboard and removes it from your file.

4. **Copy** – places what you copy onto the computer clipboard and leaves it in your file. Your computer clipboard only holds one item, the last thing you either copied or cut.

5. **Paste** – pasting will put whatever you cut or copied, from the computer's clipboard onto your file.

Undo, Redo, Cut, Copy, and Paste are the very basic of editing tools.

But a word from the wise, don't do the Cut command and than Paste, that is a dangerous way of moving content. Imagine that you select the Cut command and plan to paste it immediately, but than your computer froze and you now lose what is Cut. It is much wiser to Copy and Paste and than after you have pasted your content, now you can cut it from your file.

Paste Special – When you read down the list of Paste special, the eight different options are pretty self-explanatory. The options are as follows:

Paste **values** only	Ctrl+Shift+V
Paste **format** only	Ctrl+Alt+V
Paste all **except borders**	
Paste **column widths** only	
Paste **formula** only	
Paste **data validation** only	
Paste **conditional formatting** only	
Paste **transpose**	

- **Paste values only:** Pastes only the text from the original range of cells.
- **Paste format only:** This option is identical to using the paint format tool -- it only copies cell formatting, and won't change existing text or formulas.
- **Paste all except borders:** Pastes everything except cell borders.
- **Paste formula only:** Pastes the formulas contained in a copied range of cells, not the resulting calculations of the formulas.
- **Paste data validation only:** Pastes a data validation rule over a range of cells without changing existing formatting, formulas, or text.
- **Paste conditional formatting only:** Only applies conditional formatting rules to a range of cells.
- **Paste transpose:** Pastes a rotated version of the copied cells. For example, if you copy a column of cells and use paste transpose, it will paste them into a row, and vice versa.

7 **Find and replace** – You can search for a specific word, phrase and select find and replace it with another word or phrase.

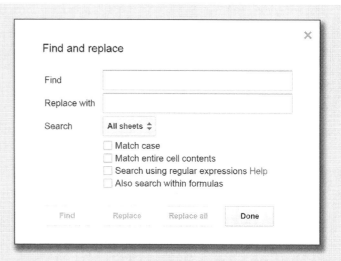

You can search in all sheets, current sheet, or a specific range.

Narrow your search by using an option below.

- **Match case:** Makes your search case-sensitive.
- **Match entire cell contents:** Searches for cells that are an exact match.
- **Search using regular expressions:** Searches for cells that match a pattern.
- **Also search within formulas:** Searches include formulas.

8 **Column or row move or deletion** – The bottom part of the edit menu deals with what column, row, or cell you have selected. When selected, you will be given the choices to move it or delete it.

When you have a full row or a full column selected, you can move it up or down, left or right.

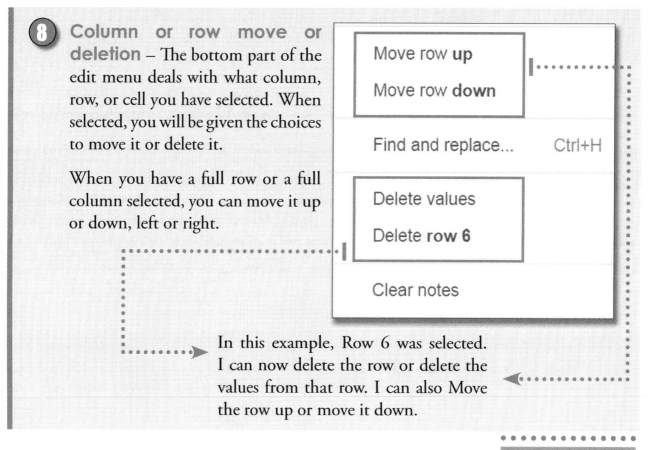

In this example, Row 6 was selected. I can now delete the row or delete the values from that row. I can also Move the row up or move it down.

8   **Delete value** – delete what is in the cell.

9   **Delete row** – delete the entire selected row.

10   **Delete column** – deletes the selected column.

11   **Delete cells and shift up** – deletes selected cells and moves them up.

12   **Delete cells and shift left** – deletes selected cells and moves them left.

Delete values

Delete **row 1**

Delete **column A**

Delete cells and shift **up**

Delete cells and shift **left**

Delete values

Delete **rows 9 - 18**

Delete **columns C - E**

Delete cells and shift **up**

Delete cells and shift **left**

You can see the entire range of cells selected.

Just the top cell was selected.

  Clear notes – This will remove any notes you have placed on your spreadsheet.

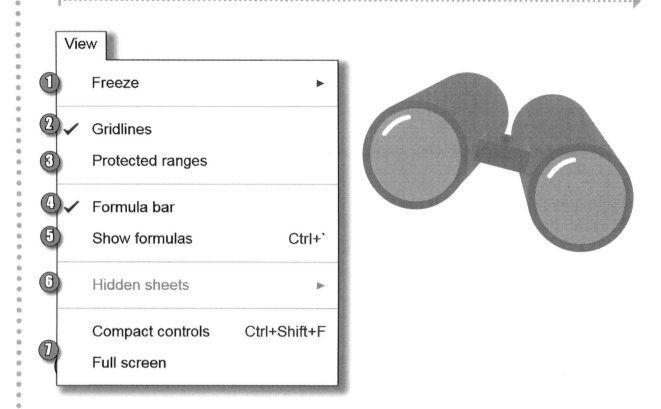

View

① Freeze ▶

② ✓ Gridlines

③ Protected ranges

④ ✓ Formula bar

⑤ Show formulas   Ctrl+`

⑥ Hidden sheets ▶

Compact controls   Ctrl+Shift+F

⑦ Full screen

①

No rows

1 row

2 rows

Up to current row (1)

No columns

1 column

2 columns

Up to current column (A)

Freeze – Freezing rows and columns allows you to keep some of your cells in the same place as the rest of your spreadsheet scrolls. You can freeze up to ten rows or five columns in any single sheet.

Before you choose to freeze rows or columns in a worksheet, it's important to consider the following:

- You can freeze only rows at the top and columns on the left side of the worksheet.

- You cannot freeze rows and columns in the middle of the worksheet.

2 **Gridlines** – Gridlines are the borders within your cells.

- You can turn the lines on and off within your Sheets file.
- Gridlines cannot be customized in the same manner that borders can.
- You can still see background colors if you turn gridlines off.

3 **Protected Ranges** – If you don't want people to change the content in a spreadsheet, you can protect it. This shouldn't be used as a security measure. People can print, copy, paste, and import and export copies of a protected spreadsheet. Only share spreadsheets with people you trust.

4 **Formula Bar** – By default, the formula bar is hidden, to make it appear, go to View menu and click Show formula bar. To make the formula bar bigger or smaller, click the bottom of it, then drag it up or down. The formula bar is can be used to show a cell that has a lot of text in it, and you can use it to type. You can also type a function within the formula bar.

5 **Show Formulas** - Switch between displaying formulas and formula results on a worksheet This method is a toggle between two different display modes. It does not change the state of the cells.

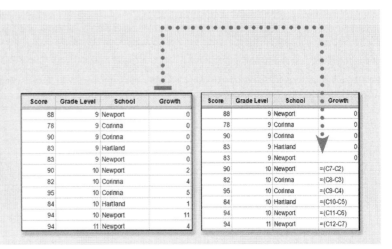

Hidden sheets – You can hide sheets that are old or are placeholders for calculations used by other sheets.

- Hiding a sheet is not the same as protecting a sheet.
- All spreadsheet editors can unhide and view these sheets.
- Spreadsheet viewers can't see hidden sheets. If someone makes a copy of the spreadsheet, the sheets will stay hidden, but they'll be able to unhide the sheets.

To hide a sheet:

1. Open a spreadsheet in Google Sheets.

2. Click the sheet you want to hide.

3. On the sheet tab, click the Down arrow Down Arrow.

4. Click Hide sheet. This option won't show if your spreadsheet doesn't contain two or more sheets.

To unhide a sheet:

1. Click View and then Hidden sheets. If your spreadsheet doesn't have any hidden sheets, this option will be grayed out.

2. Click the sheet that you no longer want hidden.

3. The spreadsheet will reappear.

 Compact controls / Full screen – These controls will hide the menus and clicking them again will show the menu. Also clicking the double arrows will show and hide the menus.

D-4 Text Menu - INSERT

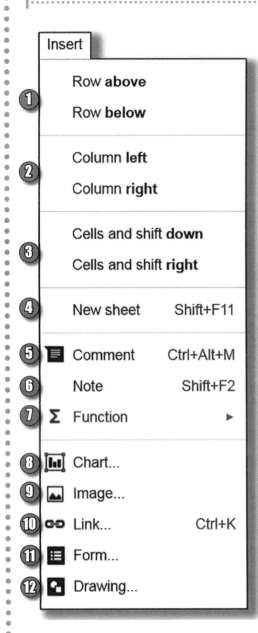

1 **Row above / Row below** - Selecting this will insert a row above or below but if you have a specific number of rows selected, it will insert that many rows above or below. Example, if you have 3 rows selected, it will state it is inserting 3 rows.

2 **Column left / Column right** - Inserting a column right or left works the same as inserting a row where if you select specific number of columns, it will insert that many columns right or left.

3 **Cells and shift down / right** - This will insert your cells and either shift you existing content down or shift it to the right.

4 **New sheet** - A new worksheet will be inserted, it can be viewed at the bottom of your spreadsheet. You will want to name your worksheets.

⑤ Comment – Select the cell where you would like to attach the comment and the comment box will appear for you to insert your comment. That cell will than have a triangle in the upper right corner to indicate that a comment is there.

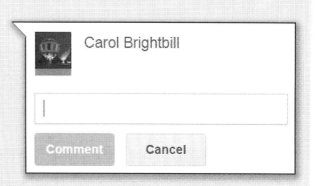

Using this box, you can type in suggestions that you think would improve the file.

⑥ Note – You place your cursor within a cell, and select Insert > Note and a white, scalable box will appear that you can place the information that you want to share or just remember at a later date.

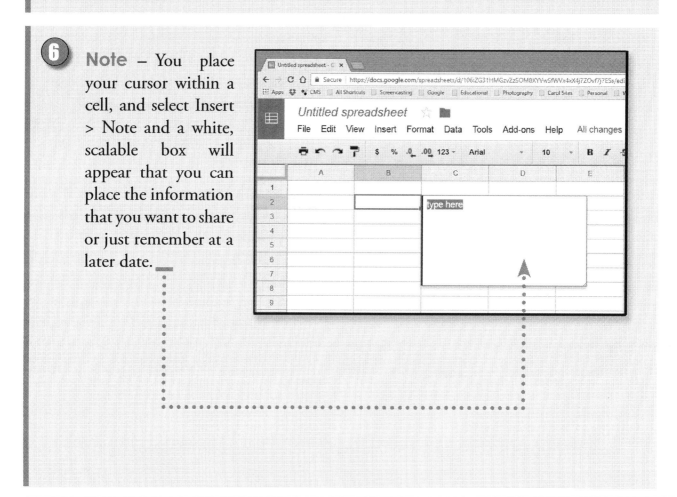

7 **Function** – When you select Function, a fly out menu appears listing five options and More at the bottom.

SUM
Returns the sum of a series of numbers and/or cells.

AVERAGE
Returns the numerical average value in a dataset, ignoring text.

COUNT
Returns a count of the number of numeric values in a dataset.

MAX
Returns the maximum value in a numeric dataset.

MIN
Returns the minimum value in a numeric dataset.

SUM
AVERAGE
COUNT
MAX
MIN
More...

4.14 Function Flyout menu

https://goo.gl/u3jMwD

MORE – Google Spreadsheets supports cell formulas typically found in most desktop spreadsheet packages. These formulas can be used to create functions that manipulate data and calculate strings and numbers.

Either scan the QR Code or type in the URL on the left and you will be taken to a list of all the functions available in each category.

When using them, don't forget to add quotation marks around all function components made of alphabetic characters that aren't referring to cells or columns.

8 **Chart** – The Chart function is an automated task that Sheets performs. The chart allows for data visualization which creates a graphical view of your information. The chart create a clearer picture of the information that you would like to relay to your team or in a presentation.

To create your chart:
- Select the cells that you want the chart to be created from.
- If you want headers in your chart, add a header or column row.
- Select Insert > Chart.
- A pop-up window will appear with three tab options:
    1. **Recommendations** (best options that fit your specific data)(4.15);
    2. **Chart types** (all chart types, see QR Code and URL for full list)(4.16);
    3. **Customization** (select font, color, legend, axis) (4.17).

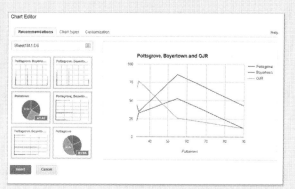

4.15 Recommendations

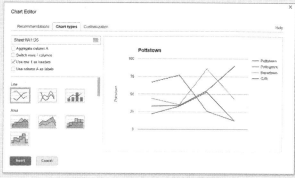

4.16 Chart types

4.17 Customization

- **Chart title:** Change the font style, size, or color.
- **Horizontal or vertical axis labels:** Change the font style, size, or color.
- **Legend:** Change the font style, size, data series color, or position.
- **Data series:** Change the color, line thickness, dot size, or axis it belongs to. For example, click on a line you want to edit in a line chart or click on a bar in a bar chart.
- **Chart background:** Resize your chart, move it within the chart area, change the font or background color, or adjust the number of grid lines shown.

Image – Inserting an image will give you six options:

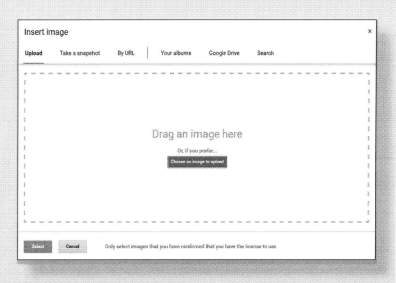

Upload - Upload from your computer.

Take a snapshop - If your device has a camera, it will take a picture.

By URL - You can put a url from a website's image.

Your Albums - This will be your Google Photos album.

Google Drive - Insert from your Drive.

Search - Search results take you to results that are labeled for commercial use with modification for the Google images and LIFE search but the third search is only for personal use because they are copyrighted.

Link – Inserting a link in Sheets is very intuitive. You first select the cell or cells that you would like to link and the box that popups will have a text area and the link area. In addition to these two areas, suggested websites will appear beneath the link box based on your selection. This is another area where Google artificial intelligence comes into play by reading your data and searching the web for you.

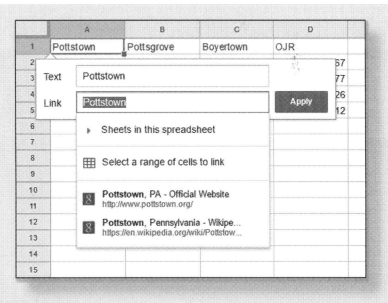

11 **Form** – To poll, survey, quiz, or otherwise collect information using a form from a spreadsheet in Google Sheets:

1. While working with a spreadsheet, click Insert and then Form.
2. A message will display at the top of the page notifying you that a new form has been created.
3. To begin editing your form, click Add questions here in the message.
4. To get rid of this message and continue editing your spreadsheet, click Dismiss.
5. If you dismiss this message, you can edit your form at any time. Click Form and then Edit form.
6. A new form will automatically be created. A new tab will appear at the bottom of your spreadsheet labeled "Form responses," where all responses to your form will be added.

12 **Drawing** – Inserting a drawing in a sheet creates a transparent annotation on top of your sheet. The drawing can include:

- text boxes, inserting color in the background;
- importing images from your drive or the web;
- multiple shapes that you can add color.

And this drawing can be easily moved and placed anywhere within your sheets. It is really fun to play with and see the full capabilities that this feature offers.

D-5 Text Menu - FORMAT

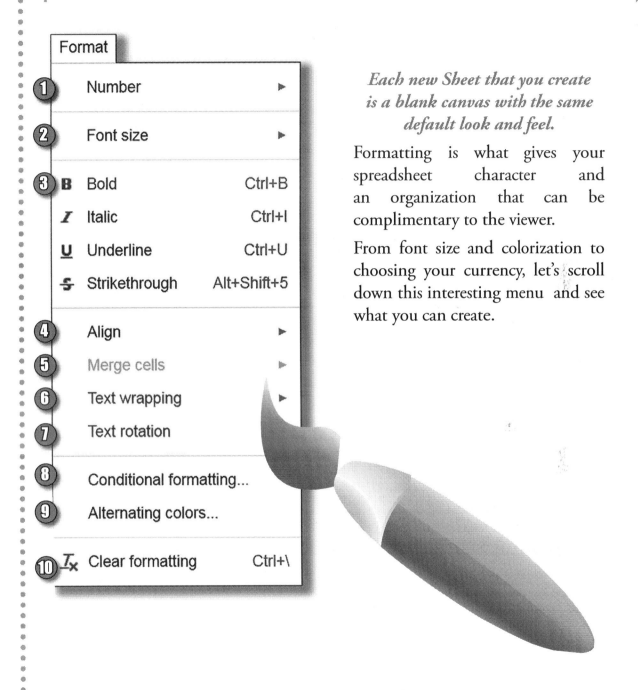

Format

1. Number ▶
2. Font size ▶
3. **B** Bold   Ctrl+B
   I Italic   Ctrl+I
   <u>U</u> Underline   Ctrl+U
   S̶ Strikethrough   Alt+Shift+5
4. Align ▶
5. Merge cells ▶
6. Text wrapping ▶
7. Text rotation
8. Conditional formatting...
9. Alternating colors...
10. *T*x Clear formatting   Ctrl+\

Each new Sheet that you create is a blank canvas with the same default look and feel.

Formatting is what gives your spreadsheet character and an organization that can be complimentary to the viewer.

From font size and colorization to choosing your currency, let's scroll down this interesting menu and see what you can create.

Number – The first option in the Format Menu is Number that has a fly-out menu (4.18), allowing you to format or change the format of numbers, dates or currencies in a spreadsheet.

If you want to add more detailed time or date values to your formatting, for example the hour or minute, click the down arrow in the right corner of the menu text box and select an additional value. You can adjust the specific formatting for these values by clicking on the arrows in the value and choosing an option. To delete a value from your formatting, click the value and select Delete.

You can also change a few properties about the currency (for example, how many decimal places to show) by clicking the drop-down menu in the right corner of the input box and choosing a desired option. [1]

✓ Automatic	
Plain text	
Number	1,000.12
Percent	10.12%
Scientific	1.01E+03
Accounting	$ (1,000.12)
Financial	(1,000.12)
Currency	$1,000.12
Currency (rounded)	$1,000
Date	9/26/2008
Time	3:59:00 PM
Date time	9/26/2008 15:59:00
Duration	24:01:00
More Formats	▶

4.18 Flyout Menu

---

1 https://support.google.com/docs/answer/56470?hl=en&co=GENIE.Platform=Desktop

②

Font Size – Listed on this image are all the font sizes available.

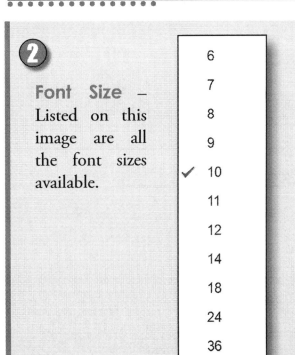

③

Always the basic formatting examples of what you can do are:

Bold

Italic

<u>Underline</u>

~~Strikethrough~~

④

Align – Selecting Align, a flyout menu (4.19) presents your options. Yes you can align your text left, center, and right, but you can also align the top of the cell, middle and bottom of the cell.

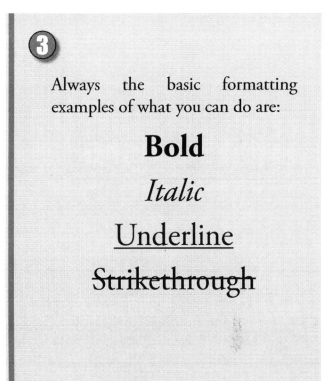

4.19 Flyout Menu

Top left	Top center	Top right
Middle left	Middle center	Middle Right
Bottom left	Bottom center	Bottom right

⑤ Merge Cells – Merging cells is a way of combining the cells either:

1. Merge Horizontally;

2. Merge Vertically;

3. Merge All.

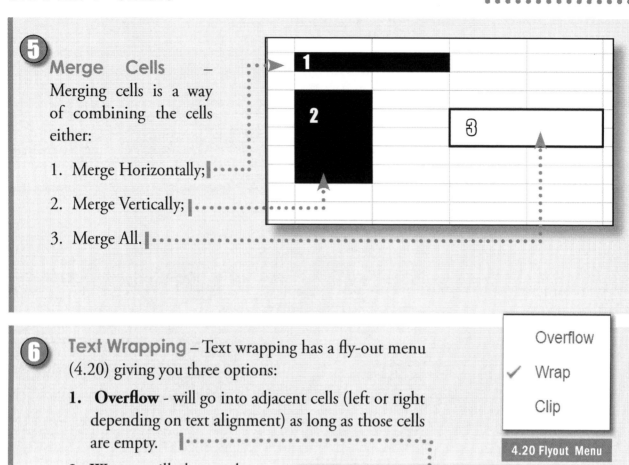

⑥ Text Wrapping – Text wrapping has a fly-out menu (4.20) giving you three options:

1. **Overflow** - will go into adjacent cells (left or right depending on text alignment) as long as those cells are empty.

2. **Wrap** - will change the row's height, making it taller, depending on width, length of text, and font size.

3. **Clip** - text will only fit into cell, and will be clipped off.

Overflow	
✓	Wrap
	Clip

4.20 Flyout Menu

① The brown cow jumped over the moon.	
② The brown cow jumped over the moon.	
③ The brown cow ju	

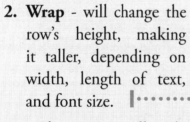

Style Menu - The style menu (icon menu under the text list of menus) has icons for text wrap shown at the right picture starting with overflow icon first, wrap icon, than the clip icon.

Text Rotation – Text rotations fly-out menu (4.21) is shown on the left and the bottom image shows the examples of each option.

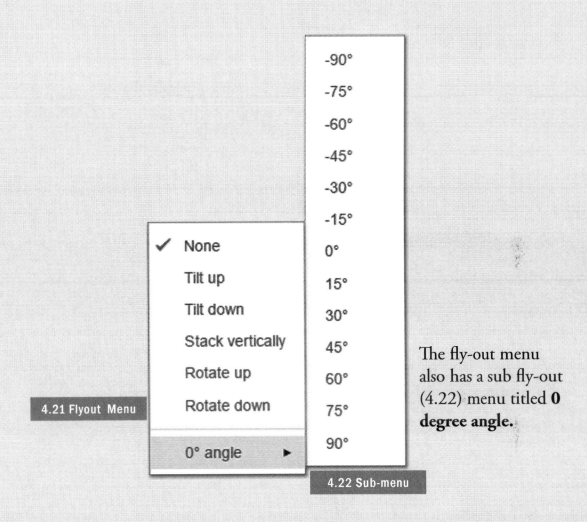

4.21 Flyout Menu

4.22 Sub-menu

The fly-out menu also has a sub fly-out (4.22) menu titled **0 degree angle.**

Conditional Formatting – (CF) allows you to apply a format to a cell or range of cells, and have that formatting change depending on the value of the cell or the value of a formula.

SINGLE COLOR

COLOR SCALE

How to create a Conditional Formatting:

- Select Format > Conditional Formatting, the two windows on the left appear with the choices of **Single color** or **Color scale.**

- Next, select your range of cells that you would like the CF to be applied to. That range will be seen where it says **Apply to range.**

- Now choose the **Format cells if. . .** and the various conditions you can select are listed in the image at the right.

- Now you have a choice of formatting to choose from adding bold, italics, strike-through, or you can change the fort or cell color.

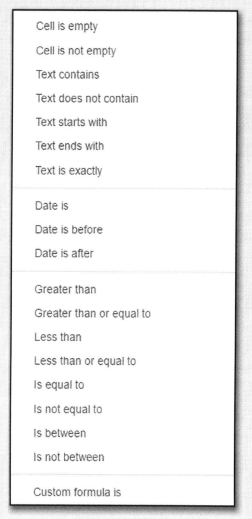

Cell is empty

Cell is not empty

Text contains

Text does not contain

Text starts with

Text ends with

Text is exactly

Date is

Date is before

Date is after

Greater than

Greater than or equal to

Less than

Less than or equal to

Is equal to

Is not equal to

Is between

Is not between

Custom formula is

⑨ Alternating Colors – Choosing alternating colors (4.23) is a way to add color and an organized style to your spreadsheet by alternating the color every other row.

- There are twelve styles offered under Formatting style.

- You can also customize your alternating colors by choosing the paint bucket under Custom. Than you can pick from 80 different color choices.

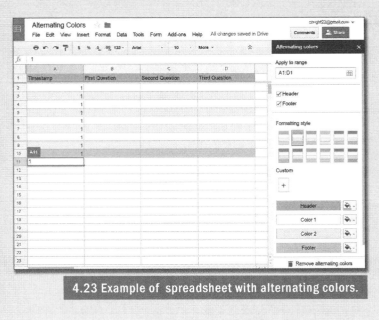

4.23 Example of spreadsheet with alternating colors.

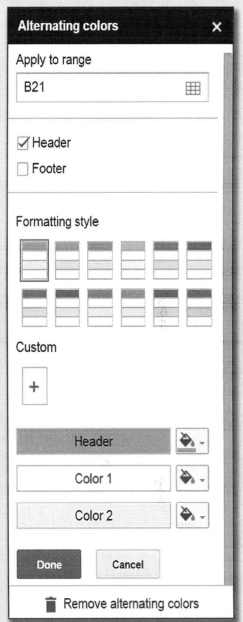

⑩ Clear Formatting – You have to first select the range of cells that you would like the formatting removed, after selected, select Clear Formatting and all formatting will be removed.

D-6 Text Menu - DATA

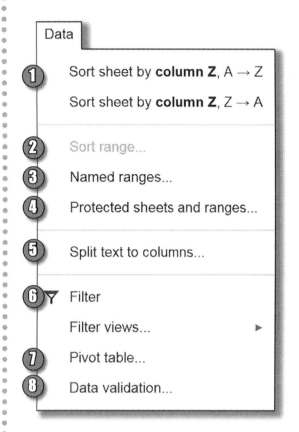

1 **Data Sort** – To sort data is to arrange it in a meaningful order so you can review it effectively.

Sort by A to Z or Z to A, great way to stay organized, listing names in alphabetical order. When you sort this way, you are given a better visual view to better understand your information. This is also used to find duplicates and remove extra spaces.

Sort by numerical order, high to low or low to high.

2 **Sort range** – When you select a range of cells, rows, and columns, you can sort just that specific range of cells.

If you look at the image on the right, cells from B17 to C28 were selected and this data can be sorted A to Z or Z to A and you can also sort by either Column B or Column C.

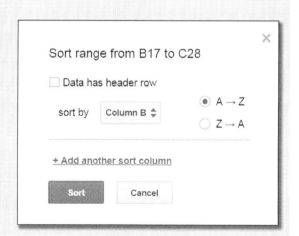

Named ranges - You can name ranges in Google Sheets to keep better track of them and create cleaner formulas.

For example, instead of using "A1:B2" to describe a range of cells, you could name the range "budget_total." This way, a formula like "=SUM(A1:B2, D4:E6)" could be written as "=SUM(budget_total, quarter2)."

Name a range
1. Open a spreadsheet in Google Sheets.
2. Select the cells you want to name.
3. Click Data and then Named ranges. A menu will open on the right.
4. Type the range name you want.
5. To change the range, click Spreadsheet Grid.
6. Select a range in the spreadsheet or type the new range into the text box, then click Ok.
7. Click Done.

Range names:
- Can contain only letters, numbers, and underscores.
- Can't start with a number, or the words "true" or "false."
- Can't contain any spaces or punctuation.
- Must be 1–250 characters.
- Can't be in either A1 or R1C1 syntax. For example, you might get an error if you give your range a name like "A1:B2" or "R1C1:R2C2."

Edit or delete a named range
1. Open a spreadsheet in Google Sheets.
2. Click Data and then Named ranges.
3. On the named range you want to edit or delete, click Edit.
4. To edit the range, enter a new name or range, then click Done.
5. To delete the named range, next to the name, click Delete Trash.
6. On the menu that opens, click Remove.

Note: When you delete a named range, any formulas that reference it will no longer work. Protected ranges that reference a named range will use the cell values and continue to work.

Protected sheets and ranges — If you don't want people to change the content in a spreadsheet, you can protect it. This shouldn't be used as a security measure. People can print, copy, paste, and import and export copies of a protected spreadsheet. Only share spreadsheets with people you trust.

Protect a range or sheet

1. Open a spreadsheet in Google Sheets.
2. Click Data and then Protected sheets and ranges. A box will open on the right.
3. Click Add a sheet or range or click an existing protection to edit it.
4. To protect a range, click Range. To protect a sheet, click Sheet.
   - Range: To change or enter the range you're protecting, click the spreadsheet icon and highlight the range in the spreadsheet.
   - Sheet: Choose a sheet to protect. If you want a set of cells to be unprotected in a sheet, check the box next to "Except certain cells."
5. Click Set permissions or Change permissions.
6. Choose how you want to limit editing:
   - To show a warning when anyone makes an edit: Select "Show a warning when editing this range." It doesn't block people from editing, but they'll see a message asking them to confirm if they really want to make an edit.
   - To choose who can edit the range or sheet: select "Restrict who can edit this range." Choose:
     - Only you: Only you (and the owner if you're not the owner) can edit the range or sheet.
     - Only domain: If you use Google Sheets for work or school, only people in your domain can edit the range or sheet. This option is only available when everyone in your domain can edit the spreadsheet.
     - Custom: Only the people you choose can edit the range or sheet.
     - Copy permissions from another range: Reuse the same permissions you set up on a different set of cells or sheet.
7. Click Save or Done.

To see protected cells, click View and then Protected ranges. A striped background will appear over the cells.

Split text to columns – You can split delimited data, such as text separated by a comma, into several columns with Google Sheets. For example, a column with "Last name, First name" can be split into 2 columns: "Last name" and "First name."

Split data into columns

1. Data isn't in a spreadsheet yet.
2. Open a spreadsheet in Google Sheets.
3. Paste the data you want to split into columns.
4. In the bottom right corner of your data, click Paste.
5. Click Split text to columns. Your data will split into different columns.
6. To change the delimiter, in the separator box, click Comma.

Filter / Filter views – You can sort and filter data in Google Sheets to organize and analyze it. To see and analyze data in a spreadsheet, use filters. Filters let you hide data that you don't want to see. You'll still be able to see all your data when you turn the filter off.

Filter views can be useful if:

- You want to save multiple views.
- You want to name your view.
- You want others to be able to view the data differently. Since filter views need to be turned on by each person viewing a spreadsheet, each person can view a different filter view at the same time.
- You want to share different filters with people. You can send different filter view links to different people so everyone will see the most relevant information for them.
- You want to make a copy or create another view with similar rules.
- You don't have edit access to a spreadsheet and still want to filter or sort. In this case, a temporary filter view will be created.

Note: You can import and export filters, but not filter views.

Pivot table – You can use pivot tables to narrow down a large data set or analyze relationships between data points.

Add and edit pivot tables

1. On your computer, open Google Sheets.

2. Open the spreadsheet with the data you want to put in a table.

3. Select the cells with data you want to use.

4. Put the data you want to use into columns. Each column is one data set.

5. Each column needs a header.

6. In the menu, click Data and then Pivot table. Click the pivot table sheet, if it's not already open.

7. Next to each category in the "Report editor" window, click Add field, then click a column to use.

8. Your table has one row or column for each number in the column you use, even if the number is in more than one cell.

9. Data from the columns you use for "Values" is sorted into the matching rows and columns.

10. If you want to add a field to the "Values" category that calculates values based on a formula, click Calculated field and enter the formula.

11. "Filters" hide data that you don't want to show in the table.

12. You can change how your data is listed, sorted, summarized or filtered. Next to what you want to change, click the Down Arrow Down Arrow.

13. To format the pivot tables, use the buttons in the toolbar.

14. Change or remove data

15. To move a data set from one category to another, drag it to the category you want.

16. To remove a data set from a category, click Remove.

17. To expand the range of data used for your pivot table, click Edit range.

18. The pivot table refreshes any time you change the cells it's drawn from.

Data validation – Create drop-down lists in a cell with Google Sheets.

Create a drop-down list

1. Open a spreadsheet in Google Sheets.

2. Select the cell or cells where you want to create a drop-down list.

3. Click Data and then Validation.

4. Next to "Criteria," choose an option:

5. List from a range: Choose the cells that will be included in the list.

6. List of items: Enter items, separated by commas and no spaces.

7. The cells will have a Down Arrow. To remove the arrow, uncheck "Display in-cell button to show list."

8. If you enter data in a cell that doesn't match an item on the list, you'll see a warning. If you want people to only enter items from the list, choose "Reject input" next to "On invalid data."

9. Click Save. The cells will show a drop-down list.

D-7 Text Menu - TOOLS

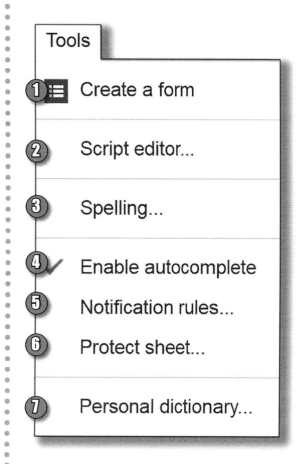

Tools

① Create a form

② Script editor...

③ Spelling...

④ ✓ Enable autocomplete

⑤ Notification rules...

⑥ Protect sheet...

⑦ Personal dictionary...

 Create a form –

1. Click the Tools drop-down menu, scroll to Form, and select Create a form. A new tab will be created at the bottom for form responses to be collected.

2. In the form template that opens, you can add any questions and options you'd like.

To edit this form, go to the Form tab, see page 172.

② Script editor – To learn all about Script editing and how to create your first script, go here:

https://developers.google.com/apps-script/articles

③ Spelling – Your sheets will be scanned for spelling errors and suggested replacements for the errors will appear.

4 **Enable autocomplete** – Autocomplete feature helps users by automatically filling the content of cell when users starting entering the first couple of letters in the Cell. The automatic entry is picked from the previously entered values for the same column.

5 **Notification rules** – Set notifications to find out when other people have changed your spreadsheets, and see what they've modified.

1. Open a spreadsheet in Google Sheets.
2. At the top, click Tools Notification rules.
3. In the window that appears, select "when" you want to receive
notifications. Notify you when: ...
4. In the window that appears, select "how often" you want to receive notifications. Notify you with: ...
5. Click Save

6 **Protect sheet** – If you don't want people to change the content in a spreadsheet, you can protect it. Select a range on your spreadsheet than choose Protected range and a box will open, choose Set permissions. In the next box choose who you would give permission to.

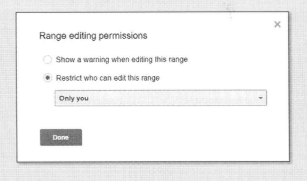

7 **Personal dictionary** – Add the words to your personal dictionary that the spell check keeps finding but you are allowing.

D-8 Text Menu - FORM

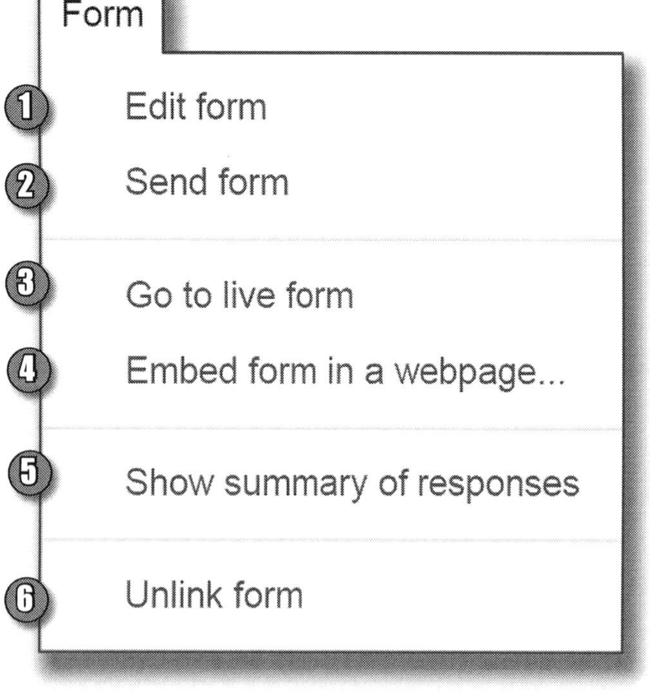

Form

① Edit form

② Send form

③ Go to live form

④ Embed form in a webpage...

⑤ Show summary of responses

⑥ Unlink form

① **Edit form –** Selecting to edit your form will take you to your form so you can add your questions. As you build the form, on the form side, the new questions will appear in a new column in Sheets.

② **Send form –** Selecting to send your form will take you to your form's send section. To learn more about sending a form, go to page 262.

③ **Go to live form –** Choosing to go to live form will take you to what the recipients will see. There is a pencil icon in the upper right corner if you want to edit the form.

Embed form in a webpage – You embed the form in a webpage via an iFrame code. You are also given the option to change the width and height for you code.

 Show summary of responses – The whole reason your are creating a form, survey, or quiz is to obtain the responses. Google Forms breaks down the responses by offering charts and graphs so you can analyze the data, or grade the test.

You can view your responses two ways:

1. **Summary** - The Summary section will display your answers in bar graphs or list, even pie charts.

2. **Individual** - You can scroll through the individual answers to your form in the Individual tab. Clicking on the forward arrows will take you to each individual answer. You can also print and trash each response separately.

 Unlink form – Unlinking the form will remove your access to the existing form and you will not be able to perform any of the action items in this menu.

D-9 Text Menu - ADD ONS

Add-ons

① Get add-ons...

Manage add-ons...

① **Add-ons** – Spreadsheets are amazing, powerful tools. They can do anything—almost anything, at least.

And to enhance your sheets, go to the add-ons section and scroll through them and see what is available.

Try one, if you don't like it, you can always uninstall it through the Manage add-ons section.

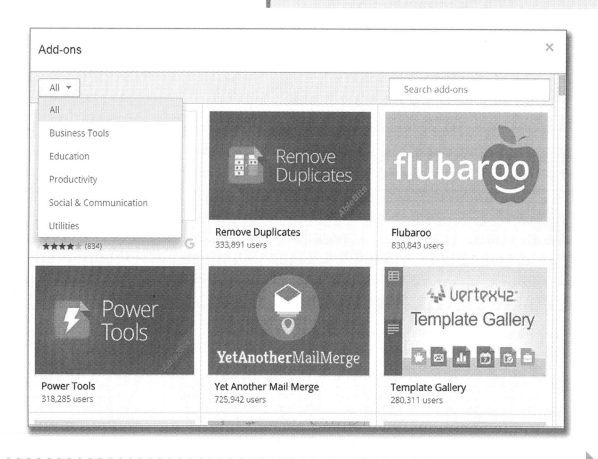

D-10 Text Menu - HELP

Sheets Help – Go to the Sheets Help for answers to any questions you might have regarding Sheets.

Report a problem – Reporting a problem goes right to Google. They take their customers very seriously and it is important to them that they are informed of any issues.

Report abuse/copyright – Copyright is something that should be taken seriously. People put a lot of time and effort into their projects and it is important to respect that.

Editing	
Absolute/relative references (when entering a formula)	F4
Fill down	Ctrl+D
Fill range	Ctrl+Enter
Fill right	Ctrl+R
Input tools on/off	Ctrl+Shift+K
Insert array formula	Ctrl+Shift+Enter
Insert comment	Ctrl+Alt+M
Insert current date	Ctrl+;
Insert current date and time	Ctrl+Alt+Shift+;
Insert current time	Ctrl+Shift+;
Insert link	Ctrl+K
Insert new sheet	Shift+F11
Insert/edit note	Shift+F2
Open delete cells menu	Ctrl+Alt+-
Open insert cells menu	Ctrl+Alt+Shift+= or Ctrl+Alt+=
Override browser shortcuts	Ctrl+Alt+K
Paste values only	Ctrl+Shift+V
Redo	Ctrl+Y or Ctrl+Shift+Z or F4
Select input tools	Ctrl+Alt+Shift+K
Undo	Ctrl+Z

Movement	
Find...	Ctrl+F
Move to next sheet	Ctrl+Shift+Pg-Down
Move to previous sheet	Ctrl+Shift+Pg-Up

Menus	
Accessibility menu	Alt+Shift+A or Alt+A
Add-ons menu	Alt+Shift+N or Alt+N
Data menu	Alt+Shift+D or Alt+D
Display sheet menu	Alt+Shift+S
Edit menu	Alt+Shift+E or Alt+E
File menu	Alt+Shift+F or Alt+F
Form menu	Alt+Shift+M or Alt+M
Format menu	Alt+Shift+O or Alt+O

Help menu	Alt+Shift+H or Alt+H
Insert menu	Alt+Shift+I or Alt+I
Show context menu	Ctrl+Shift+\
Show sheet list	Shift+Alt+K
Tools menu	Alt+Shift+T or Alt+T
View menu	Alt+Shift+V or Alt+V

Formatting	
Align center	Ctrl+Shift+E
Align left	Ctrl+Shift+L
Align right	Ctrl+Shift+R
Apply bottom border	Alt+Shift+3
Apply left border	Alt+Shift+4
Apply outer border	Alt+Shift+7
Apply right border	Alt+Shift+2
Apply top border	Alt+Shift+1
Bold	Ctrl+B
Clear formatting	Ctrl+\
Italic	Ctrl+I
Number format: currency	Ctrl+Shift+4
Number format: date	Ctrl+Shift+3
Number format: number	Ctrl+Shift+1
Number format: percent	Ctrl+Shift+5
Number format: scientific	Ctrl+Shift+6
Number format: time	Ctrl+Shift+2
Remove borders	Alt+Shift+6
Strikethrough	Alt+Shift+5
Underline	Ctrl+U

Selection	
Select all	Ctrl+A or Ctrl+Shift+Space
Select column	Ctrl+Space
Select row	Shift+Space

Screen reader support	
Read column	Ctrl+Alt+Shift+C
Read row	Ctrl+Alt+Shift+R
Summarize chart content	Ctrl+Alt+V
Toggle screen reader support	Ctrl+Alt+Z

File commands	
Open...	Ctrl+O
Print	Ctrl+P

View	
Compact controls	Ctrl+Shift+F
Hide columns	Ctrl+Alt+0
Hide rows	Ctrl+Alt+9
Show all formulas	Ctrl+`
Unhide columns	Ctrl+Shift+0
Unhide rows	Ctrl+Shift+9

Navigation	
Chat	Shift+Esc
Enter current comment	Ctrl+Alt+E Ctrl+Alt+C
Focus pop up	Ctrl+Alt+E Ctrl+Alt+P
Focus quicksum	Alt+Shift+Q
Move focus out of editing area	Ctrl+Alt+Shift+M
Move to beginning of sheet	Ctrl+Home
Move to end of row	End
Move to end of sheet	Ctrl+End
Move to next comment	Ctrl+Alt+N Ctrl+Alt+C
Move to next edit	Ctrl+Alt+K or Ctrl+Alt+N Ctrl+Alt+R
Move to previous comment	Ctrl+Alt+P Ctrl+Alt+C
Move to previous edit	Ctrl+Alt+J or Ctrl+Alt+P Ctrl+Alt+R
Move to start of row	Home
Open comments thread...	Ctrl+Alt+Shift+A
Open Explore	Alt+Shift+X
Open filter dropdown menu	Ctrl+Alt+R
Open hyperlink	Alt+Enter
Scroll to active cell	Ctrl+BackSpace
See revision history	Ctrl+Alt+Shift+H

Help	
Help Center	Shift+F1
See keyboard shortcuts	Ctrl+/

Google spreadsheets function list

Google Spreadsheets supports cell formulas typically found in most desktop spreadsheet packages. These formulas can be used to create functions that manipulate data and calculate strings and numbers. Here's a list of all the functions available in each category. When using them, don't forget to add quotation marks around all function components made of alphabetic characters that aren't referring to cells or columns.

Type	Name		Description
Array	ARRAY_CONSTRAIN	ARRAY_CONSTRAIN(input_range, num_rows, num_cols)	Constrains an array result to a specified size. Learn more
Array	TREND	TREND(known_data_y, known_data_x, [new_data_x], [b])	Given partial data about a linear trend, fits an ideal linear trend using the least squares method and/or predicts further values. Learn more
Array	SUMXMY2	SUMXMY2(array_x, array_y)	Calculates the sum of the squares of differences of values in two arrays. Learn more
Array	SUMX2PY2	SUMX2PY2(array_x, array_y)	Calculates the sum of the sums of the squares of values in two arrays. Learn more
Array	SUMX2MY2	SUMX2MY2(array_x, array_y)	Calculates the sum of the differences of the squares of values in two arrays. Learn more
Array	SUMPRODUCT	SUMPRODUCT(array1, array2)	Calculates the sum of the products of corresponding entries in two equal-sized arrays or ranges. Learn more
Array	MMULT	MMULT(matrix1, matrix2)	Calculates the matrix product of two matrices specified as arrays or ranges. Learn more
Array	MINVERSE	MINVERSE(square_matrix)	Returns the multiplicative inverse of a square matrix specified as an array or range. Learn more
Array	MDETERM	MDETERM(square_matrix)	Returns the matrix determinant of a square matrix specified as an array or range. Learn more
Array	LOGEST	LOGEST(known_data_y, [known_data_x], [b], [verbose])	Given partial data about an exponential growth curve, calculates various parameters about the best fit ideal exponential growth curve. Learn more
Array	LINEST	LINEST(known_data_y, [known_data_x], [b], [verbose])	Given partial data about a linear trend, calculates various parameters about the ideal linear trend using the least-squares method. Learn more
Array	GROWTH	GROWTH(known_data_y, [known_data_x], [new_data_x], [b])	Given partial data about an exponential growth trend, fits an ideal exponential growth trend and/or predicts further values. Learn more
Array	FREQUENCY	FREQUENCY(data, classes)	Calculates the frequency distribution of a one-column array into specified classes. Learn more
Array	TRANSPOSE	TRANSPOSE(array_or_range)	Transposes the rows and columns of an array or range of cells. Learn more
Database	DMIN	DMIN(database, field, criteria)	Returns the minimum value selected from a database table-like array or range using a SQL-like query. Learn more
Database	DVARP	DVARP(database, field, criteria)	Returns the variance of an entire population selected from a database table-like array or range using a SQL-like query. Learn more
Database	DSUM	DSUM(database, field, criteria)	Returns the sum of values selected from a database table-like array or range using a SQL-like query. Learn more

Type	Name		Description
Database	DSTDEVP	DSTDEVP(database, field, criteria)	Returns the standard deviation of an entire population selected from a database table-like array or range using a SQL-like query. Learn more
Database	DSTDEV	DSTDEV(database, field, criteria)	Returns the standard deviation of a population sample selected from a database table-like array or range using a SQL-like query. Learn more
Database	DPRODUCT	DPRODUCT(database, field, criteria)	Returns the product of values selected from a database table-like array or range using a SQL-like query. Learn more
Database	DVAR	DVAR(database, field, criteria)	Returns the variance of a population sample selected from a database table-like array or range using a SQL-like query. Learn more
Database	DMAX	DMAX(database, field, criteria)	Returns the maximum value selected from a database table-like array or range using a SQL-like query. Learn more
Database	DGET	DGET(database, field, criteria)	Returns a single value from a database table-like array or range using a SQL-like query. Learn more
Database	DCOUNTA	DCOUNTA(database, field, criteria)	Counts values, including text, selected from a database table-like array or range using a SQL-like query. Learn more
Database	DCOUNT	DCOUNT(database, field, criteria)	Counts numeric values selected from a database table-like array or range using a SQL-like query. Learn more
Database	DAVERAGE	DAVERAGE(database, field, criteria)	Returns the average of a set of values selected from a database table-like array or range using a SQL-like query. Learn more
Date	DAYS360	DAYS360(start_date, end_date, [method])	Returns the difference between two days based on the 360 day year used in some financial interest calculations. Learn more
Date	EDATE	EDATE(start_date)	Returns a date a specified number of months before or after another date. Learn more
Date	EOMONTH	EOMONTH(start_date, months)	Returns a date representing the last day of a month which falls a specified number of months before or after another date. Learn more
Date	HOUR	HOUR(time)	Returns the hour component of a specific time, in numeric format. Learn more
Date	MINUTE	MINUTE(time)	Returns the minute component of a specific time, in numeric format. Learn more
Date	MONTH	MONTH(date)	Returns the month of the year a specific date falls in, in numeric format. Learn more
Date	NETWORKDAYS	NETWORKDAYS(start_date, end_date, [holidays])	Returns the number of net working days between two provided days. Learn more
Date	NETWORKDAYS. INTL	NETWORKDAYS.INTL(start_date, end_date, [weekend], [holidays])	Returns the number of net working days between two provided days excluding specified weekend days and holidays. Learn more
Date	NOW	NOW()	Returns the current date and time as a date value. Learn more
Date	SECOND	SECOND(time)	Returns the second component of a specific time, in numeric format. Learn more
Date	TIME	TIME(hour, minute, second)	Converts a provided hour, minute, and second into a time. Learn more
Date	TIMEVALUE	TIMEVALUE(time_string)	Returns the fraction of a 24-hour day the time represents. Learn more
Date	TODAY	TODAY()	Returns the current date as a date value. Learn more
Date	WEEKDAY	WEEKDAY(date, type)	Returns a number representing the day of the week of the date provided. Learn more

Type	Name		Description
Date	WEEKNUM	WEEKNUM(date, [type])	Returns a number representing the week of the year where the provided date falls. Learn more
Date	WORKDAY	WORKDAY(start_date, num_days, [holidays])	Calculates the end date after a specified number of working days. Learn more
Date	WORKDAY.INTL	WORKDAY.INTL(start_date, num_days, [weekend], [holidays])	Calculates the date after a specified number of workdays excluding specified weekend days and holidays. Learn more
Date	YEAR	YEAR(date)	Returns the year specified by a given date. Learn more
Date	YEARFRAC	YEARFRAC(start_date, end_date, [day_count_convention])	Returns the number of years, including fractional years, between two dates using a specified day count convention. Learn more
Date	DATE	DATE(year, month, day)	Converts a provided year, month, and day into a date. Learn more
Date	DATEVALUE	DATEVALUE(date_string)	Converts a provided date string in a known format to a date value. Learn more
Date	DAY	DAY(date)	Returns the day of the month that a specific date falls on, in numeric format. Learn more
Date	DATEDIF	DATEDIF(start_date, end_date, unit)	Calculates the number of days, months, or years between two dates. Learn more
Engineering	HEX2DEC	HEX2DEC(signed_hexadecimal_number)	Converts a signed hexadecimal number to decimal format. Learn more
Engineering	BIN2DEC	BIN2DEC(signed_binary_number)	Converts a signed binary number to decimal format. Learn more
Engineering	BIN2HEX	BIN2HEX(signed_binary_number, [significant_digits])	Converts a signed binary number to signed hexadecimal format. Learn more
Engineering	BIN2OCT	BIN2OCT(signed_binary_number, [significant_digits])	Converts a signed binary number to signed octal format. Learn more
Engineering	OCT2HEX	OCT2HEX(signed_octal_number, [significant_digits])	Converts a signed octal number to signed hexadecimal format. Learn more
Engineering	OCT2DEC	OCT2DEC(signed_octal_number)	Converts a signed octal number to decimal format. Learn more
Engineering	OCT2BIN	OCT2BIN(signed_octal_number, [significant_digits])	Converts a signed octal number to signed binary format. Learn more
Engineering	HEX2OCT	HEX2OCT(signed_hexadecimal_number, significant_digits)	Converts a signed hexadecimal number to signed octal format. Learn more
Engineering	DEC2BIN	DEC2BIN(decimal_number, [significant_digits])	Converts a decimal number to signed binary format. Learn more
Engineering	HEX2BIN	HEX2BIN(signed_hexadecimal_number, [significant_digits])	Converts a signed hexadecimal number to signed binary format. Learn more
Engineering	DELTA	DELTA(number1, [number2])	Compare two numeric values, returning 1 if they're equal. Learn more
Engineering	DEC2OCT	DEC2OCT(decimal_number, [significant_digits])	Converts a decimal number to signed octal format. Learn more
Engineering	DEC2HEX	DEC2HEX(decimal_number, [significant_digits])	Converts a decimal number to signed hexadecimal format. Learn more
Filter	UNIQUE	UNIQUE(range)	Returns unique rows in the provided source range, discarding duplicates. Rows are returned in the order in which they first appear in the source range. Learn more
Filter	FILTER	FILTER(range, condition1, [condition2])	Returns a filtered version of the source range, returning only rows or columns which meet the specified conditions. Learn more
Filter	SORT	SORT(range, sort_column, is_ascending, [sort_column2], [is_ascending2])	Sorts the rows of a given array or range by the values in one or more columns. Learn more

Type	Name		Description
Financial	DB	DB(cost, salvage, life, period, [month])	Calculates the depreciation of an asset for a specified period using the arithmetic declining balance method. Learn more
Financial	PPMT	PPMT(rate, period, number_of_periods, present_value, future_value, end_or_beginning)	Calculates the payment on the principal of an investment based on constant-amount periodic payments and a constant interest rate. Learn more
Financial	PRICE	PRICE(settlement, maturity, rate, yield, redemption, frequency, [day_count_convention])	Calculates the price of a security paying periodic interest, such as a US Treasury Bond, based on expected yield. Learn more
Financial	PRICEDISC	PRICEDISC(settlement, maturity, discount, redemption, [day_count_convention])	Calculates the price of a discount (non-interest-bearing) security, based on expected yield. Learn more
Financial	PRICEMAT	PRICEMAT(settlement, maturity, issue, rate, yield, [day_count_convention])	Calculates the price of a security paying interest at maturity, based on expected yield. Learn more
Financial	PV	PV(rate, number_of_periods, payment_amount, [future_value], [end_or_beginning])	Calculates the present value of an annuity investment based on constant-amount periodic payments and a constant interest rate. Learn more
Financial	RATE	RATE(number_of_periods, payment_per_period, present_value, [future_value], [end_or_beginning], [rate_guess])	Calculates the interest rate of an annuity investment based on constant-amount periodic payments and the assumption of a constant interest rate. Learn more
Financial	RECEIVED	RECEIVED(settlement, maturity, investment, discount, [day_count_convention])	Calculates the amount received at maturity for an investment in fixed-income securities purchased on a given date. Learn more
Financial	SLN	SLN(cost, salvage, life)	Calculates the depreciation of an asset for one period using the straight-line method. Learn more
Financial	SYD	SYD(cost, salvage, life, period)	Calculates the depreciation of an asset for a specified period using the sum of years digits method. Learn more
Financial	TBILLEQ	TBILLEQ(settlement, maturity, discount)	Calculates the equivalent annualized rate of return of a US Treasury Bill based on discount rate. Learn more
Financial	TBILLPRICE	TBILLPRICE(settlement, maturity, discount)	Calculates the price of a US Treasury Bill based on discount rate. Learn more
Financial	TBILLYIELD	TBILLYIELD(settlement, maturity, price)	Calculates the yield of a US Treasury Bill based on price. Learn more
Financial	XIRR	XIRR(cashflow_amounts, cashflow_dates, [rate_guess])	Calculates the internal rate of return of an investment based on a specified series of potentially irregularly spaced cash flows. Learn more
Financial	XNPV	XNPV(discount, cashflow_amounts, cashflow_dates)	Calculates the net present value of an investment based on a specified series of potentially irregularly spaced cash flows and a discount rate. Learn more
Financial	YIELD	YIELD(settlement, maturity, rate, price, redemption, frequency, [day_count_convention])	Calculates the annual yield of a security paying periodic interest, such as a US Treasury Bond, based on price. Learn more
Financial	YIELDDISC	YIELDDISC(settlement, maturity, price, redemption, [day_count_convention])	Calculates the annual yield of a discount (non-interest-bearing) security, based on price. Learn more
Financial	COUPPCD	COUPPCD(settlement, maturity, frequency, [day_count_convention])	Calculates last coupon, or interest payment, date before the settlement date. Learn more
Financial	COUPNUM	COUPNUM(settlement, maturity, frequency, [day_count_convention])	Calculates the number of coupons, or interest payments, between the settlement date and the maturity date of the investment. Learn more
Financial	COUPNCD	COUPNCD(settlement, maturity, frequency, [day_count_convention])	Calculates next coupon, or interest payment, date after the settlement date. Learn more

Type	Name		Description
Financial	COUPDAYSNC	COUPDAYSNC(settlement, maturity, frequency, [day_count_convention])	Calculates the number of days from the settlement date until the next coupon, or interest payment. Learn more
Financial	COUPDAYS	COUPDAYS(settlement, maturity, frequency, [day_count_convention])	Calculates the number of days in the coupon, or interest payment, period that contains the specified settlement date. Learn more
Financial	COUPDAYBS	COUPDAYBS(settlement, maturity, frequency, [day_count_convention])	Calculates the number of days from the first coupon, or interest payment, until settlement. Learn more
Financial	ACCRINTM	ACCRINTM(issue, maturity, rate, [redemption], [day_count_convention])	Calculates the accrued interest of a security that pays interest at maturity. Learn more
Financial	ACCRINT	ACCRINT(issue, first_payment, settlement, rate, redemption, frequency, [day_count_convention])	Calculates the accrued interest of a security that has periodic payments. Learn more
Financial	CUMIPMT	CUMIPMT(rate, number_of_periods, present_value, first_period, last_period, end_or_beginning)	Calculates the cumulative interest over a range of payment periods for an investment based on constant-amount periodic payments and a constant interest rate. Learn more
Financial	DOLLARDE	DOLLARDE(fractional_price, unit)	Converts a price quotation given as a decimal fraction into a decimal value. Learn more
Financial	DOLLARFR	DOLLARFR(decimal_price, unit)	Converts a price quotation given as a decimal value into a decimal fraction. Learn more
Financial	DURATION	DURATION(settlement, maturity, rate, yield, frequency, [day_count_convention]) .	Calculates the number of compounding periods required for an investment of a specified present value appreciating at a given rate to reach a target value. Learn more
Financial	EFFECT	EFFECT(nominal_rate, periods_per_year)	Calculates the annual effective interest rate given the nominal rate and number of compounding periods per year. Learn more
Financial	FV	FV(rate, number_of_periods, payment_amount, present_value, [end_or_beginning])	Calculates the future value of an annuity investment based on constant-amount periodic payments and a constant interest rate. Learn more
Financial	FVSCHEDULE	FVSCHEDULE(principal, rate_schedule)	Calculates the future value of some principal based on a specified series of potentially varying interest rates. Learn more
Financial	INTRATE	INTRATE(buy_date, sell_date, buy_price, sell_price, [day_count_convention])	Calculates the effective interest rate generated when an investment is purchased at one price and sold at another with no interest or dividends generated by the investment itself. Learn more
Financial	IPMT	IPMT(rate, period, number_of_periods, present_value, [future_value], [end_or_beginning])	Calculates the payment on interest for an investment based on constant-amount periodic payments and a constant interest rate. Learn more
Financial	IRR	IRR(cashflow_amounts, [rate_guess])	Calculates the internal rate of return on an investment based on a series of periodic cash flows. Learn more
Financial	MDURATION	MDURATION(settlement, maturity, rate, yield, frequency, [day_count_convention])	Calculates the modified Macaulay duration of a security paying periodic interest, such as a US Treasury Bond, based on expected yield. Learn more
Financial	MIRR	MIRR(cashflow_amounts, financing_rate, reinvestment_return_rate)	Calculates the modified internal rate of return on an investment based on a series of periodic cash flows and the difference between the interest rate paid on financing versus the return received on reinvested income. Learn more
Financial	NOMINAL	NOMINAL(effective_rate, periods_per_year)	Calculates the annual nominal interest rate given the effective rate and number of compounding periods per year. Learn more
Financial	DDB	DDB(cost, salvage, life, period, [factor])	Calculates the depreciation of an asset for a specified period using the double-declining balance method. Learn more

Type	Name		Description
Financial	DISC	DISC(settlement, maturity, price, redemption, [day_count_convention])	Calculates the discount rate of a security based on price. Learn more
Financial	NPER	NPER(rate, payment_amount, present_value, [future_value], [end_or_beginning])	Calculates the number of payment periods for an investment based on constant-amount periodic payments and a constant interest rate. Learn more
Financial	NPV	NPV(discount, cashflow1, [cashflow2])	Calculates the net present value of an investment based on a series of periodic cash flows and a discount rate. Learn more
Financial	PMT	PMT(rate, number_of_periods, present_value, [future_value], [end_or_beginning])	Calculates the periodic payment for an annuity investment based on constant-amount periodic payments and a constant interest rate. Learn more
Financial	CUMPRINC	CUMPRINC(rate, number_of_periods, present_value, first_period, last_period, end_or_beginning)	Calculates the cumulative principal paid over a range of payment periods for an investment based on constant-amount periodic payments and a constant interest rate. Learn more
Google	IMPORTDATA	IMPORTDATA(url)	Imports data at a given URL in .csv (comma-separated value) or .tsv (tab-separated value) format. Learn more
Google	SPARKLINE	SPARKLINE(data, options)	Creates a miniature chart contained within a single cell. Learn more
Google	DETECT LANGUAGE	DETECTLANGUAGE(text_or_range)	Identifies the language used in text within the specified range. Learn more
Google	GOOGLE FINANCE	GOOGLEFINANCE(ticker, attribute, start_date, end_date|num_days, interval)	Fetches current or historical securities information from Google Finance. Learn more
Google	GOOGLE TRANSLATE	GOOGLETRANSLATE(text, [source_language], [target_language])	Translates text from one language into another Learn more
Google	IMAGE	IMAGE(url, mode)	Inserts an image into a cell. Learn more
Google	ARRAY FORMULA	ARRAYFORMULA(array_formula)	Enables the display of values returned from an array formula into multiple rows and/or columns and the use of non-array functions with arrays. Learn more
Google	IMPORTFEED	IMPORTFEED(url, [query], [headers], [num_items])	Imports a RSS or ATOM feed. Learn more
Google	IMPORTHTML	IMPORTHTML(url, query, index)	Imports data from a table or list within an HTML page. Learn more
Google	IMPORTRANGE	IMPORTRANGE(spreadsheet_key, range_string)	Imports a range of cells from a specified spreadsheet. Learn more
Google	IMPORTXML	IMPORTXML(url, xpath_query)	Imports data from any of various structured data types including XML, HTML, CSV, TSV, and RSS and ATOM XML feeds. Learn more
Google	QUERY	QUERY(data, query, headers)	Runs a Google Visualization API Query Language query across data. Learn more
Info	N	N(value)	Returns the argument provided as a number. Learn more
Info	TYPE	TYPE(value)	Returns a number associated with the type of data passed into the function. Learn more
Info	ERROR.TYPE	ERROR.TYPE(reference)	Returns a number corresponding to the error value in a different cell. Learn more
Info	ISBLANK	ISBLANK(value)	Checks whether the referenced cell is empty. Learn more
Info	ISEMAIL	ISEMAIL(value)	Checks whether a value is a valid email address. Learn more
Info	ISERR	ISERR(value)	Checks whether a value is an error other than `#N/A`. Learn more
Info	ISERROR	ISERROR(value)	Checks whether a value is an error. Learn more
Info	ISFORMULA	ISFORMULA(cell)	Checks whether a formula is in the referenced cell. Learn more

Type	Name		Description
Info	ISLOGICAL	ISLOGICAL(value)	Checks whether a value is `TRUE` or `FALSE`. Learn more
Info	ISNA	ISNA(value)	Checks whether a value is the error `#N/A`. Learn more
Info	ISNONTEXT	ISNONTEXT(value)	Checks whether a value is non-textual. Learn more
Info	ISNUMBER	ISNUMBER(value)	Checks whether a value is a number. Learn more
Info	NA	NA()	Returns the "value not available" error, `#N/A`. Learn more
Info	CELL	CELL(info_type, reference)	Returns the requested information about the specified cell. Learn more
Info	ISURL	ISURL(value)	Checks whether a value is a valid URL. Learn more
Info	ISTEXT	ISTEXT(value)	Checks whether a value is text. Learn more
Info	ISREF	ISREF(value)	Checks whether a value is a valid cell reference. Learn more
Logical	TRUE	TRUE()	Returns the logical value `TRUE`. Learn more
Logical	OR	OR(logical_expression1, [logical_expression2])	Returns true if any of the provided arguments are logically true, and false if all of the provided arguments are logically false. Learn more
Logical	NOT	NOT(logical_expression)	Returns the opposite of a logical value - `NOT(TRUE)` returns `FALSE`; `NOT(FALSE)` returns `TRUE`. Learn more
Logical	IFERROR	IFERROR(value, value_if_error)	Returns the first argument if it is not an error value, otherwise returns the second argument if present, or a blank if the second argument is absent. Learn more
Logical	IF	IF(logical_expression, value_if_true, value_if_false)	Returns one value if a logical expression is `TRUE` and another if it is `FALSE`. Learn more
Logical	FALSE	FALSE()	Returns the logical value `FALSE`. Learn more
Logical	AND	AND(logical_expression1, logical_expression2)	Returns true if all of the provided arguments are logically true, and false if any of the provided arguments are logically false. Learn more
Lookup	HYPERLINK	HYPERLINK(url, link_label)	Creates a hyperlink inside a cell. Learn more
Lookup	HLOOKUP	HLOOKUP(search_key, range, index, is_sorted)	Horizontal lookup. Searches across the first row of a range for a key and returns the value of a specified cell in the column found. Learn more
Lookup	GETPIVOTDATA	GETPIVOTDATA(value_name, any_pivot_table_cell, [original_column_1, pivot_item_1], [original_column_2, pivot_item_2, ...])	Extracts an aggregated value from a pivot table that corresponds to the specified row and column headings. Learn more
Lookup	ROWS	ROWS(range)	Returns the number of rows in a specified array or range. Learn more
Lookup	COLUMN	COLUMN([cell_reference])	Returns the column number of a specified cell, with `A=1`. Learn more
Lookup	CHOOSE	CHOOSE(index, choice1, choice2)	Returns an element from a list of choices based on index. Learn more
Lookup	ADDRESS	ADDRESS(row, column, absolute_relative_mode, use_a1_notation, sheet)	Returns a cell reference as a string. Learn more
Lookup	VLOOKUP	VLOOKUP(search_key, range, index, is_sorted)	Vertical lookup. Searches down the first column of a range for a key and returns the value of a specified cell in the row found. Learn more
Lookup	ROW	ROW(cell_reference)	Returns the row number of a specified cell. Learn more
Lookup	OFFSET	OFFSET(cell_reference, offset_rows, offset_columns, height, width)	Returns a range reference shifted a specified number of rows and columns from a starting cell reference. Learn more

Type	Name		Description
Lookup	MATCH	MATCH(search_key, range, search_type)	Returns the relative position of an item in a range that matches a specified value. Learn more
Lookup	LOOKUP	LOOKUP(search_key, search_range|search_result_array, [result_range])	Looks through a row or column for a key and returns the value of the cell in a result range located in the same position as the search row or column. Learn more
Lookup	INDIRECT	INDIRECT(cell_reference_as_string)	Returns a cell reference specified by a string. Learn more
Lookup	INDEX	INDEX(reference, row, column)	Returns the content of a cell, specified by row and column offset. Learn more
Lookup	COLUMNS	COLUMNS(range)	Returns the number of columns in a specified array or range. Learn more
Math	ISEVEN	ISEVEN(value)	Checks whether the provided value is even. Learn more
Math	ISODD	ISODD(value)	Checks whether the provided value is odd. Learn more
Math	LCM	LCM(value1, value2)	Returns the least common multiple of one or more integers. Learn more
Math	LN	LN(value)	Returns the the logarithm of a number, base e (Euler's number). Learn more
Math	LOG	LOG(value, base)	Returns the the logarithm of a number given a base. Learn more
Math	LOG10	LOG10(value)	Returns the the logarithm of a number, base 10. Learn more
Math	MOD	MOD(dividend, divisor)	Returns the result of the modulo operator, the remainder after a division operation. Learn more
Math	MROUND	MROUND(value, factor)	Rounds one number to the nearest integer multiple of another. Learn more
Math	MULTINOMIAL	MULTINOMIAL(value1, value2)	Returns the factorial of the sum of values divided by the product of the values' factorials. Learn more
Math	ODD	ODD(value)	Rounds a number up to the nearest odd integer. Learn more
Math	PI	PI()	Returns the value of Pi to 14 decimal places. Learn more
Math	POWER	POWER(base, exponent)	Returns a number raised to a power. Learn more
Math	PRODUCT	PRODUCT(factor1, factor2)	Returns the result of multiplying a series of numbers together. Learn more
Math	QUOTIENT	QUOTIENT(dividend, divisor)	Returns one number divided by another. Learn more
Math	RADIANS	RADIANS(angle)	Converts an angle value in degrees to radians. Learn more
Math	RAND	RAND()	Returns a random number between 0 inclusive and 1 exclusive. Learn more
Math	RANDBETWEEN	RANDBETWEEN(low, high)	Returns a uniformly random integer between two values, inclusive. Learn more
Math	ROUND	ROUND(value, places)	Rounds a number to a certain number of decimal places according to standard rules. Learn more
Math	ROUNDDOWN	ROUNDDOWN(value, [places])	Rounds a number to a certain number of decimal places, always rounding down to the next valid increment. Learn more
Math	ROUNDUP	ROUNDUP(value, places)	Rounds a number to a certain number of decimal places, always rounding up to the next valid increment. Learn more
Math	SERIESSUM	SERIESSUM(x, n, m, a)	Given parameters x, n, m, and a, returns the power series sum a1xn + a2x(n+m) + ... + aix(n+(i-1)m), where i is the number of entries in range `a`. Learn more
Math	SIGN	SIGN(value)	Given an input number, returns `-1` if it is negative, `1` if positive, and `0` if it is zero. Learn more

Type	Name		Description
Math	SIN	SIN(angle)	Returns the sine of an angle provided in radians. Learn more
Math	SINH	SINH(value)	Returns the hyperbolic sine of any real number. Learn more
Math	SQRT	SQRT(value)	Returns the positive square root of a positive number. Learn more
Math	SQRTPI	SQRTPI(value)	Returns the positive square root of the product of Pi and the given positive number. Learn more
Math	SUBTOTAL	SUBTOTAL(function_code, range1, range2)	Returns a subtotal for a vertical range of cells using a specified aggregation function. Learn more
Math	SUM	SUM(value1, value2)	Returns the sum of a series of numbers and/or cells. Learn more
Math	SUMIF	SUMIF(range, criterion, sum_range)	Returns a conditional sum across a range. Learn more
Math	SUMIFS	SUMIFS(sum_range, criteria_range1, criterion1, [criteria_range2, criterion2, ...])	Returns the sum of a range depending on multiple criteria. Learn more
Math	SUMSQ	SUMSQ(value1, [value2])	Returns the sum of the squares of a series of numbers and/or cells. Learn more
Math	TAN	TAN(angle)	Returns the tangent of an angle provided in radians. Learn more
Math	TANH	TANH(value)	Returns the hyperbolic tangent of any real number. Learn more
Math	TRUNC	TRUNC(value, [places])	Truncates a number to a certain number of significant digits by omitting less significant digits. Learn more
Math	ABS	ABS(value)	Returns the absolute value of a number. Learn more
Math	ACOS	ACOS(value)	Returns the inverse cosine of a value, in radians. Learn more
Math	ACOSH	ACOSH(value)	Returns the inverse hyperbolic cosine of a number. Learn more
Math	ASIN	ASIN(value)	Returns the inverse sine of a value, in radians. Learn more
Math	ASINH	ASINH(value)	Returns the inverse hyperbolic sine of a number. Learn more
Math	ATAN	ATAN(value)	Returns the inverse tangent of a value, in radians. Learn more
Math	ATAN2	ATAN2(x, y)	Returns the angle between the x-axis and a line segment from the origin (0,0) to specified coordinate pair (`x`,`y`), in radians. Learn more
Math	ATANH	ATANH(value)	Returns the inverse hyperbolic tangent of a number. Learn more
Math	CEILING	CEILING(value, [factor])	Rounds a number up to the nearest integer multiple of specified significance. Learn more
Math	COMBIN	COMBIN(n, k)	Returns the number of ways to choose some number of objects from a pool of a given size of objects. Learn more
Math	COS	COS(angle)	Returns the cosine of an angle provided in radians. Learn more
Math	COSH	COSH(value)	Returns the hyperbolic cosine of any real number. Learn more
Math	COUNTBLANK	COUNTBLANK(range)	Returns the number of empty cells in a given range. Learn more
Math	COUNTIF	COUNTIF(range, criterion)	Returns a conditional count across a range. Learn more
Math	COUNTIFS	COUNTIFS(criteria_range1, criterion1, [criteria_range2, criterion2, ...])	Returns the count of a range depending on multiple criteria. Learn more
Math	COUNTUNIQUE	COUNTUNIQUE(value1, value2)	Counts the number of unique values in a list of specified values and ranges. Learn more
Math	DEGREES	DEGREES(angle)	Converts an angle value in radians to degrees. Learn more
Math	ERFC	ERFC(z)	Returns the complementary Gauss error function of a value. Learn more
Math	EVEN	EVEN(value)	Rounds a number up to the nearest even integer. Learn more
Math	EXP	EXP(exponent)	Returns Euler's number, e (~2.718) raised to a power. Learn more
Math	FACT	FACT(value)	Returns the factorial of a number. Learn more

Type	Name		Description
Math	FACTDOUBLE	FACTDOUBLE(value)	Returns the "double factorial" of a number. Learn more
Math	FLOOR	FLOOR(value, [factor])	Rounds a number down to the nearest integer multiple of specified significance. Learn more
Math	GAMMALN	GAMMALN(value)	Returns the the logarithm of a specified Gamma function, base e (Euler's number). Learn more
Math	GCD	GCD(value1, value2)	Returns the greatest common divisor of one or more integers. Learn more
Math	INT	INT(value)	Rounds a number down to the nearest integer that is less than or equal to it. Learn more
Operator	NE	NE(value1, value2)	Returns `TRUE` if two specified values are not equal and `FALSE` otherwise. Equivalent to the `<>` operator. Learn more
Operator	EQ	EQ(value1, value2)	Returns `TRUE` if two specified values are equal and `FALSE` otherwise. Equivalent to the `=` operator. Learn more
Operator	CONCAT	CONCAT(value1, value2)	Returns the concatenation of two values. Equivalent to the `&` operator. Learn more
Operator	DIVIDE	DIVIDE(dividend, divisor)	Returns one number divided by another. Equivalent to the `/` operator. Learn more
Operator	GT	GT(value1, value2)	Returns `TRUE` if the first argument is strictly greater than the second, and `FALSE` otherwise. Equivalent to the `>` operator. Learn more
Operator	GTE	GTE(value1, value2)	Returns `TRUE` if the first argument is greater than or equal to the second, and `FALSE` otherwise. Equivalent to the `>=` operator. Learn more
Operator	LT	LT(value1, value2)	Returns `TRUE` if the first argument is strictly less than the second, and `FALSE` otherwise. Equivalent to the `<` operator. Learn more
Operator	LTE	LTE(value1, value2)	Returns `TRUE` if the first argument is less than or equal to the second, and `FALSE` otherwise. Equivalent to the `<=` operator. Learn more
Operator	MINUS	MINUS(value1, value2)	Returns the difference of two numbers. Equivalent to the `-` operator. Learn more
Operator	MULTIPLY	MULTIPLY(factor1, factor2)	Returns the product of two numbers. Equivalent to the `*` operator. Learn more
Operator	ADD	ADD(value1, value2)	Returns the sum of two numbers. Equivalent to the `+` operator. Learn more
Operator	POW	POW(base, exponent)	Returns a number raised to a power. Learn more
Operator	UMINUS	UMINUS(value)	Returns a number with the sign reversed. Learn more
Operator	UNARY_PERCENT	UNARY_PERCENT(percentage)	Returns a value interpreted as a percentage; that is, `UNARY_PERCENT(100)` equals `1`. Learn more
Operator	UPLUS	UPLUS(value)	Returns a specified number, unchanged. Learn more
Parser	TO_TEXT	TO_TEXT(value)	Converts a provided numeric value to a text value. Learn more
Parser	TO_PURE_NUMBER	TO_PURE_NUMBER(value)	Converts a provided date/time, percentage, currency or other formatted numeric value to a pure number without formatting. Learn more
Parser	TO_PERCENT	TO_PERCENT(value)	Converts a provided number to a percentage. Learn more
Parser	TO_DOLLARS	TO_DOLLARS(value)	Converts a provided number to a dollar value. Learn more
Parser	TO_DATE	TO_DATE(value)	Converts a provided number to a date. Learn more

Type	Name		Description
Parser	CONVERT	CONVERT(value, start_unit, end_unit)	Converts a numeric value to a different unit of measure. Learn more
Statistical	MINA	MINA(value1, value2)	Returns the minimum numeric value in a dataset. Learn more
Statistical	MODE	MODE(value1, [value2])	Returns the most commonly occurring value in a dataset. Learn more
Statistical	NEGBINOMDIST	NEGBINOMDIST(num_failures, num_successes, prob_success)	Calculates the probability of drawing a certain number of failures before a certain number of successes given a probability of success in independent trials. Learn more
Statistical	NORMDIST	NORMDIST(x, mean, standard_deviation, cumulative)	Returns the value of the normal distribution function (or normal cumulative distribution function) for a specified value, mean, and standard deviation. Learn more
Statistical	NORMINV	NORMINV(x, mean, standard_deviation)	Returns the value of the inverse normal distribution function for a specified value, mean, and standard deviation. Learn more
Statistical	NORMSDIST	NORMSDIST(x)	Returns the value of the standard normal cumulative distribution function for a specified value. Learn more
Statistical	NORMSINV	NORMSINV(x)	Returns the value of the inverse standard normal distribution function for a specified value. Learn more
Statistical	PEARSON	PEARSON(data_y, data_x)	Calculates r, the Pearson product-moment correlation coefficient of a dataset. Learn more
Statistical	PERCENTILE	PERCENTILE(data, percentile)	Returns the value at a given percentile of a dataset. Learn more
Statistical	PERCENTRANK	PERCENTRANK(data, value, [significant_digits])	Returns the percentage rank (percentile) of a specified value in a dataset. Learn more
Statistical	PERCENTRANK. EXC	PERCENTRANK.EXC(data, value, [significant_digits])	Returns the percentage rank (percentile) from 0 to 1 exclusive of a specified value in a dataset. Learn more
Statistical	PERCENTRANK. INC	PERCENTRANK.INC(data, value, [significant_digits])	Returns the percentage rank (percentile) from 0 to 1 inclusive of a specified value in a dataset. Learn more
Statistical	PERMUT	PERMUT(n, k)	Returns the number of ways to choose some number of objects from a pool of a given size of objects, considering order. Learn more
Statistical	POISSON	POISSON(x, mean, cumulative)	Returns the value of the Poisson distribution function (or Poisson cumulative distribution function) for a specified value and mean. Learn more
Statistical	PROB	PROB(data, probabilities, low_limit, [high_limit])	Given a set of values and corresponding probabilities, calculates the probability that a value chosen at random falls between two limits. Learn more
Statistical	QUARTILE	QUARTILE(data, quartile_number)	Returns a value nearest to a specified quartile of a dataset. Learn more
Statistical	RANK	RANK(value, data, [is_ascending])	Returns the rank of a specified value in a dataset. Learn more
Statistical	RANK.AVG	RANK.AVG(value, data, [is_ascending])	Returns the rank of a specified value in a dataset. If there is more than one entry of the same value in the dataset, the average rank of the entries will be returned. Learn more
Statistical	RANK.EQ	RANK.EQ(value, data, [is_ascending])	Returns the rank of a specified value in a dataset. If there is more than one entry of the same value in the dataset, the top rank of the entries will be returned. Learn more
Statistical	RSQ	RSQ(data_y, data_x)	Calculates the square of r, the Pearson product-moment correlation coefficient of a dataset. Learn more
Statistical	SKEW	SKEW(value1, value2)	Calculates the skewness of a dataset, which describes the symmetry of that dataset about the mean. Learn more

Type	Name		Description
Statistical	SLOPE	SLOPE(data_y, data_x)	Calculates the slope of the line resulting from linear regression of a dataset. Learn more
Statistical	SMALL	SMALL(data, n)	Returns the nth smallest element from a data set, where n is user-defined. Learn more
Statistical	STANDARDIZE	STANDARDIZE(value, mean, standard_deviation)	Calculates the normalized equivalent of a random variable given mean and standard deviation of the distribution. Learn more
Statistical	STDEV	STDEV(value1, value2)	Calculates the standard deviation based on a sample. Learn more
Statistical	STDEVA	STDEVA(value1, value2)	Calculates the standard deviation based on a sample, setting text to the value `0`. Learn more
Statistical	STDEVP	STDEVP(value1, value2)	Calculates the standard deviation based on an entire population. Learn more
Statistical	STDEVPA	STDEVPA(value1, value2)	Calculates the standard deviation based on an entire population, setting text to the value `0`. Learn more
Statistical	STEYX	STEYX(data_y, data_x)	Calculates the standard error of the predicted y-value for each x in the regression of a dataset. Learn more
Statistical	T.INV	T.INV(probability, degrees_freedom)	Calculates the negative inverse of the one-tailed TDIST function. Learn more
Statistical	T.INV.2T	T.INV.2T(probability, degrees_freedom)	Calculates the inverse of the two-tailed TDIST function. Learn more
Statistical	TDIST	TDIST(x, degrees_freedom, tails)	Calculates the probability for Student's t-distribution with a given input (x). Learn more
Statistical	TINV	TINV(probability, degrees_freedom)	Calculates the inverse of the two-tailed TDIST function. Learn more
Statistical	TRIMMEAN	TRIMMEAN(data, exclude_proportion)	Calculates the mean of a dataset excluding some proportion of data from the high and low ends of the dataset. Learn more
Statistical	TTEST	TTEST(range1, range2, tails, type)	Returns the probability associated with t-test. Determines whether two samples are likely to have come from the same two underlying populations that have the same mean. Learn more
Statistical	VAR	VAR(value1, [value2])	Calculates the variance based on a sample. Learn more
Statistical	VARA	VARA(value1, value2)	Calculates an estimate of variance based on a sample, setting text to the value `0`. Learn more
Statistical	VARP	VARP(value1, value2)	Calculates the variance based on an entire population. Learn more
Statistical	VARPA	VARPA(value1, value2)	Calculates the variance based on an entire population, setting text to the value `0`. Learn more
Statistical	WEIBULL	WEIBULL(x, shape, scale, cumulative)	Returns the value of the Weibull distribution function (or Weibull cumulative distribution function) for a specified shape and scale. Learn more
Statistical	ZTEST	ZTEST(data, value, [standard_deviation])	Returns the two-tailed P-value of a Z-test with standard distribution. Learn more
Statistical	CRITBINOM	CRITBINOM(num_trials, prob_success, target_prob)	Calculates the smallest value for which the cumulative binomial distribution is greater than or equal to a specified criteria. Learn more
Statistical	DEVSQ	DEVSQ(value1, value2)	Calculates the sum of squares of deviations based on a sample. Learn more
Statistical	EXPONDIST	EXPONDIST(x, lambda, cumulative)	Returns the value of the exponential distribution function with a specified lambda at a specified value. Learn more
Statistical	F.DIST	F.DIST(x, degrees_freedom1, degrees_freedom2, cumulative)	Calculates the left-tailed F probability distribution (degree of diversity) for two data sets with given input x. Alternately called Fisher-Snedecor distribution or Snedecor's F distribution. Learn more

Type	Name		Description
Statistical	F.DIST.RT	F.DIST.RT(x, degrees_freedom1, degrees_freedom2)	Calculates the right-tailed F probability distribution (degree of diversity) for two data sets with given input x. Alternately called Fisher-Snedecor distribution or Snedecor's F distribution. Learn more
Statistical	FDIST	FDIST(x, degrees_freedom1, degrees_freedom2)	Calculates the right-tailed F probability distribution (degree of diversity) for two data sets with given input x. Alternately called Fisher-Snedecor distribution or Snedecor's F distribution. Learn more
Statistical	FISHER	FISHER(value)	Returns the Fisher transformation of a specified value. Learn more
Statistical	FISHERINV	FISHERINV(value)	Returns the inverse Fisher transformation of a specified value. Learn more
Statistical	FORECAST	FORECAST(x, data_y, data_x)	Calculates the expected y-value for a specified x based on a linear regression of a dataset. Learn more
Statistical	GEOMEAN	GEOMEAN(value1, value2)	Calculates the geometric mean of a dataset. Learn more
Statistical	HARMEAN	HARMEAN(value1, value2)	Calculates the harmonic mean of a dataset. Learn more
Statistical	HYPGEOMDIST	HYPGEOMDIST(num_successes, num_draws, successes_in_pop, pop_size)	Calculates the probability of drawing a certain number of successes in a certain number of tries given a population of a certain size containing a certain number of successes, without replacement of draws. Learn more
Statistical	INTERCEPT	INTERCEPT(data_y, data_x)	Calculates the y-value at which the line resulting from linear regression of a dataset will intersect the y-axis (x=0). Learn more
Statistical	KURT	KURT(value1, value2)	Calculates the kurtosis of a dataset, which describes the shape, and in particular the "peakedness" of that dataset. Learn more
Statistical	LARGE	LARGE(data, n)	Returns the nth largest element from a data set, where n is user-defined. Learn more
Statistical	LOGINV	LOGINV(x, mean, standard_deviation)	Returns the value of the inverse log-normal cumulative distribution with given mean and standard deviation at a specified value. Learn more
Statistical	LOGNORMDIST	LOGNORMDIST(x, mean, standard_deviation)	Returns the value of the log-normal cumulative distribution with given mean and standard deviation at a specified value. Learn more
Statistical	MAX	MAX(value1, [value2])	Returns the maximum value in a numeric dataset. Learn more
Statistical	MAXA	MAXA(value1, value2)	Returns the maximum numeric value in a dataset. Learn more
Statistical	MEDIAN	MEDIAN(value1, value2)	Returns the median value in a numeric dataset. Learn more
Statistical	MIN	MIN(value1, [value2])	Returns the minimum value in a numeric dataset. Learn more
Statistical	AVEDEV	AVEDEV(value1, [value2])	Calculates the average of the magnitudes of deviations of data from a dataset's mean. Learn more
Statistical	AVERAGE	AVERAGE(value1, value2)	Returns the numerical average value in a dataset, ignoring text. Learn more
Statistical	AVERAGEA	AVERAGEA(value1, [value2])	Returns the numerical average value in a dataset. Learn more
Statistical	AVERAGEIF	AVERAGEIF(criteria_range, criterion, [average_range])	Returns the average of a range depending on criteria. Learn more
Statistical	AVERAGEIFS	AVERAGEIFS(average_range, criteria_range1, criterion1, [criteria_range2, criterion2, ...])	Returns the average of a range depending on multiple criteria. Learn more

Type	Name		Description
Statistical	BINOMDIST	BINOMDIST(num_successes, num_trials, prob_success, cumulative)	Calculates the probability of drawing a certain number of successes (or a maximum number of successes) in a certain number of tries given a population of a certain size containing a certain number of successes, with replacement of draws. Learn more
Statistical	CONFIDENCE	CONFIDENCE(alpha, standard_deviation, pop_size)	Calculates the width of half the confidence interval for a normal distribution. Learn more
Statistical	CORREL	CORREL(data_y, data_x)	Calculates r, the Pearson product-moment correlation coefficient of a dataset. Learn more
Statistical	COUNT	COUNT(value1, value2)	Returns the a count of the number of numeric values in a dataset. Learn more
Statistical	COUNTA	COUNTA(value1, value2)	Returns the a count of the number of values in a dataset. Learn more
Statistical	COVAR	COVAR(data_y, data_x)	Calculates the covariance of a dataset. Learn more
Text	PROPER	PROPER(text_to_capitalize)	Capitalizes each word in a specified string. Learn more
Text	VALUE	VALUE(text)	Converts a string in any of the date, time or number formats that Google Sheets understands into a number. Learn more
Text	TRIM	TRIM(text)	Removes leading and trailing spaces in a specified string. Learn more
Text	TEXT	TEXT(number, format)	Converts a number into text according to a specified format. Learn more
Text	T	T(value)	Returns string arguments as text. Learn more
Text	SUBSTITUTE	SUBSTITUTE(text_to_search, search_for, replace_with, occurrence_number)	Replaces existing text with new text in a string. Learn more
Text	SPLIT	SPLIT(text, delimiter, split_by_each)	Divides text around a specified character or string, and puts each fragment into a separate cell in the row. Learn more
Text	SEARCHB	SEARCHB(search_for, text_to_search, [starting_at])	Returns the position at which a string is first found within text counting each double-character as 2. Learn more
Text	SEARCH	SEARCH(search_for, text_to_search, [starting_at])	Returns the position at which a string is first found within text. Learn more
Text	ROMAN	ROMAN(number, [rule_relaxation])	Formats a number in Roman numerals. Learn more
Text	RIGHT	RIGHT(string, [number_of_characters])	Returns a substring from the end of a specified string. Learn more
Text	REPT	REPT(text_to_repeat, number_of_repetitions)	Returns specified text repeated a number of times. Learn more
Text	REPLACE	REPLACE(text, position, length, new_text)	Replaces part of a text string with a different text string. Learn more
Text	REGEXREPLACE	REGEXREPLACE(text, regular_expression, replacement)	Replaces part of a text string with a different text string using regular expressions. Learn more
Text	REGEXMATCH	REGEXMATCH(text, regular_expression)	Whether a piece of text matches a regular expression. Learn more
Text	REGEXEXTRACT	REGEXEXTRACT(text, regular_expression)	Extracts matching substrings according to a regular expression. Learn more
Text	UPPER	UPPER(text)	Converts a specified string to uppercase. Learn more
Text	MID	MID(string, starting_at, extract_length)	Returns a segment of a string. Learn more
Text	LOWER	LOWER(text)	Converts a specified string to lowercase. Learn more
Text	LEN	LEN(text)	Returns the length of a string. Learn more
Text	LEFT	LEFT(string, [number_of_characters])	Returns a substring from the beginning of a specified string. Learn more

Type	Name		Description
Text	JOIN	JOIN(delimiter, value_or_array1, [value_or_array2])	Concatenates the elements of one or more one-dimensional arrays using a specified delimiter. Learn more
Text	FIXED	FIXED(number, number_of_places, [suppress_separator])	Formats a number with a fixed number of decimal places. Learn more
Text	FINDB	FINDB(search_for, text_to_search, [starting_at])	Returns the position at which a string is first found within text counting each double-character as 2. Learn more
Text	FIND	FIND(search_for, text_to_search, starting_at)	Returns the position at which a string is first found within text. Learn more
Text	EXACT	EXACT(string1, string2)	Tests whether two strings are identical. Learn more
Text	DOLLAR	DOLLAR(number, number_of_places)	Formats a number into the locale-specific currency format. Learn more
Text	CONCATENATE	CONCATENATE(string1, string2)	Appends strings to one another. Learn more
Text	CODE	CODE(string)	Returns the numeric Unicode map value of the first character in the string provided. Learn more
Text	CLEAN	CLEAN(text)	Returns the text with the non-printable ASCII characters removed. Learn more
Text	ARABIC	ARABIC(roman_numeral)	Computes the value of a Roman numeral. Learn more
Text	CHAR	CHAR(table_number)	Convert a number into a character according to the current Unicode table. Learn more

5 SLIDES

Created, Edited And Stored Online

*More than a presentation tool,
it is also a layout tool.*

Everything from presentations to posters. . . can be created with Slides. I have been in the design business for a long time, using a lot of professional products, from Quark Express to In-Design and I find that Slides ranks up there as a really great layout program. Of course it is also an excellent presentation platform, but as you use this robust program, you will understand how I have come to this conclusion.

A. HOW TO GET TO YOUR SLIDES

1

After your have logged into your Chrome account, type in

https://slides.google.com

2

Go to the waffle and select the yellow rectangle icon.

3

From your Drive, select **BLUE NEW** button and go down to Slides.

Let me list some of the best Slides features:

Layering capabilities - This means that you can bring an item to the front and send an item back. The first item you place on your background will be the bottom layer, and as you add items, they start to stack on top. Layering gives you the capability to bring that back layer and place it on top of any layer.

Grouping - To group items, either text boxes, shapes, or images, connects them so that they become one item and can move around together. You can than select ungroup to break them apart.

Transparency - You can change the opacity of a shape with fill or an image to be 0% to 100% transparent.

Crop - You can crop an image. To crop means to remove a portion of the image so it does not show in your layout but it is there if you want to bring it back by uncropping it.

Mask - There are different shapes and you can mask your image in one of the various shapes that are there for you to choose from.

Text boxes - A text box can be inserted and moved to any location that you choose on your page.

Selecting the Waffle Icon or typing into the omnibox slides.google.com, will take you to the repository of all your slides.

Templates .. similar to Docs and Sheets, Slides has ready made templates for your usage to help save your time.

B. FEATURES OVERVIEW

With revision history, multiple versions of documents to be stored, allowing users to roll them back to previous versions without losing any information.

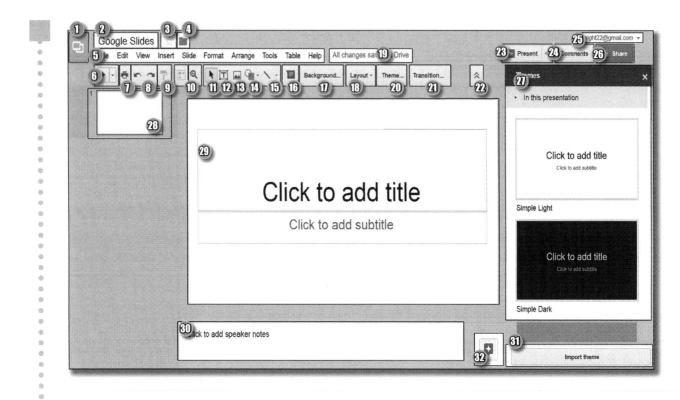

1 **Home** – Selecting the gold rectangle with white rectangle in the upper corner of your window will return you to your Slides Repository. It is a quick, easy navigation tool. From here, you can start a new blank Slide, use a template or open a previously created Slide.

2 **Title** – After you have created your first blank doc, it will be an Untitled presentation. You will want to give it a title right away because, one of Slide's powerful features is that it auto-saves.

3 **Star** – Starring a slide gives it importance and makes your file easier to search for.

4 **Move to** – Selecting the folder icon will give you the option to move your presentation to another location.

5 **Text Menu** – Part C of this Chapter gives an in-depth overview of the Menu.

6 **New Slide (ctr M)** – Selecting the + will automatically add a new page based on the last page inserted.

Selecting the carat drop down (5.1) will open the choices of different sides that you can insert, color and layout is based on the theme that is selected but each choice of specific page i.e. Title slide; Section header - stays consistent in each theme.

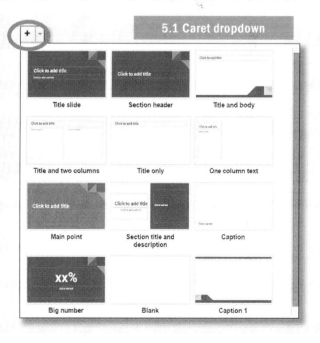

5.1 Caret dropdown

7 **Print** – Brings up your print menu and if your have drivers installed and a printer, you can print. If not, print to PDF and save your file.

8 **Undo/Redo** – Go back one step in your files and go forward to your last move.

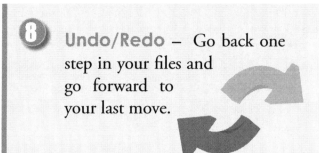

9 **Paint Format** – This tool will copy the formatting of text, cells, or an object with the paint format tool and instantly put it on the object / text that you select.

1. Open a Google file.
2. Select the text, range of cells, or object you want to copy the format of.
3. In the toolbar, click Paint format .
4. Select what you want to paste the formatting onto.

10 **Zoom** – You first select the magnifying glass icon (5.2) and touch the slide canvas and it will increase size each time you touch it.

You select the Fit to view (5.3) icon to fit the screen back to normal size.

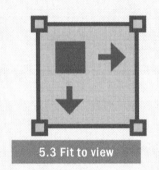

5.3 Fit to view

5.2 Magnifying glass

11 **Select** – The arrow is the select tool. When you choose this action item, you can move any object on your page, from text box, shapes, or images, to a different position.

12. **Text Box** – The text box is an entry field where the user can enter the information that they want to present.

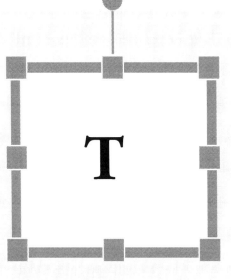

A text box is what makes Slides stand out from Docs, it turns your presentation tool into a layout program. A layout programs gives you control over where you can place your items on your page creating a design.

The things you can do with a text box are:

- Resize it to whatever size you want.
- Enter verbiage.
- Rotate it.

- Add a stroke.
- Add a background fill.
- Change the text color.

13. **Image**– You can take your slides to the next level and go from boring to quite interesting by just adding a picture. As the saying goes, "A picture is worth a thousand words". There are six different ways to add an image. Images must be less than 50 MB and be one of the following file types: .gif; .jpg; or.png.

1. **Upload** – Selecting to upload will take your to your computer's hard drive and select Open.
2. **Take a snapshot** – If your device has a camera, you can take a snapshot and insert it directly into the document.
3. **By URL** – Paste the URL of an image from the web and click Select.
4. **Your albums** – Choose an image from one of your photos albums stored on the web and click Select.
5. **Google Drive** – Choose an image stored in Google Drive and click Select.
6. **Search** – Choose an image from the stock photography archive, or the Google and Life archives, and click Select.

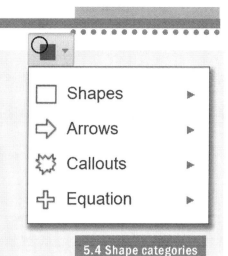

14 Shape – There are four category of shapes (5.4). The shapes use mathematic equations and geometric primitives (points, lines, and shapes) to create art that is clean and can be scaled infinitely, without any loss of quality.

The things you can do with a text box are:

5.4 Shape categories

Some of the shapes have a yellow diamond joint (5.5) and when you grab this circle, you can adjust and change the shape.

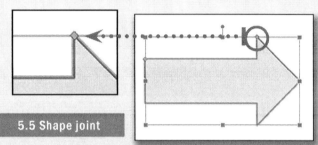

5.5 Shape joint

Shapes

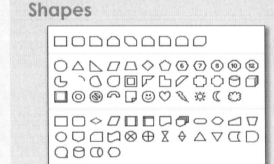

Arrows

Callouts

Equation

15 **Line** – There are seven line options (5.6). The lines and the shapes are good to combine together to make flowcharts and diagrams.

To create a flowchart, you can select the line tool and pick an arrow or connector to connect two shapes. You can place the shapes anywhere on the screen and the connectors would follow (5.7).

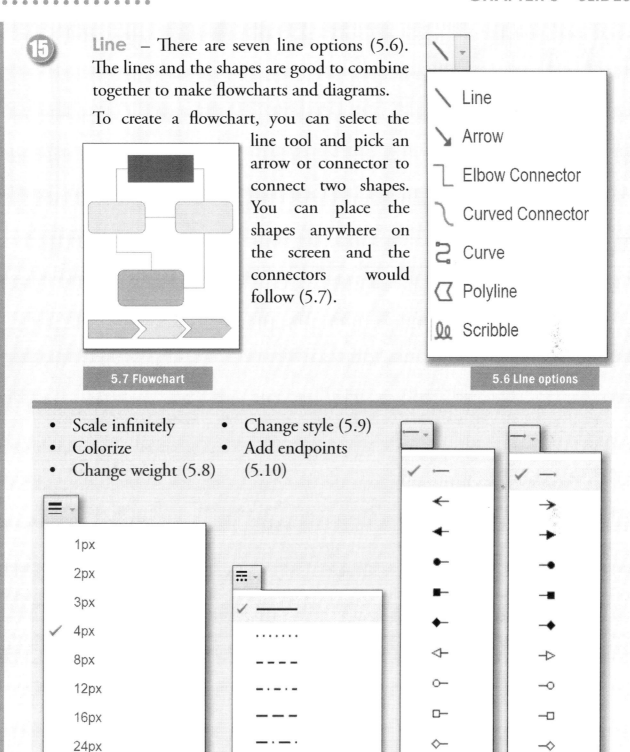

5.7 Flowchart

5.6 Line options

- Scale infinitely
- Colorize
- Change weight (5.8)
- Change style (5.9)
- Add endpoints (5.10)

5.8 Line weight

5.9 Line style

5.10 Line endpoints

16 **Comment** – Select this icon and a comment box will appear for you to insert your comment.

Using this box, you can type in suggestions that you think would improve the file.

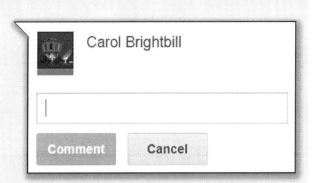

17 **Background** – The following options are available when you choose background:

A. **Color** - You can change the color of the background to a solid color or a gradient color (5.11). Once you choose the color, you can select Add to theme. Now the entire theme is based on your selected color.

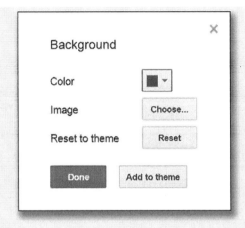

B. **Image** - Selecting Choose... takes you to the six options (5.12): Upload; Take a snapshot; By URL; Your albums; Google Drive; and Search. Once you choose your image, it will fill the entire background of your slide and become part of your theme.

C. **Reset** - To reset the theme, you must choose a new color or background, and than select Reset.

5.11 Background color

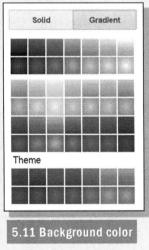

| Upload | Take a snapshot | By URL | Your albums | Google Drive | Search |

5.12 Background image

18 **Layout** – If your slide is a Title slide and you want it to be a different slide in the Theme, just choose Layout and you can choose one of the eleven different slide layouts available. All choices are represented in the image on the right.

19 **All changes saved in Drive** – This text line will tell you your file is saved in the drive and if you click on this line, you will be taken to your Revision History.

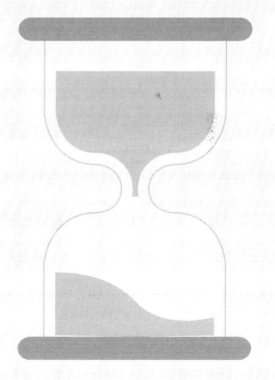

20 Theme – Slides has eighteen different installed themes available. You can import themes from your Drive or upload a theme. Selecting Theme will open all themes that are available for you to use. Your current theme will be the top theme, and all the rest will be underneath it.

You can not mix and match themes, but your can edit the theme by going to View > Master. Within the Master slide area, you can change the background color or add an image as shown in the previous page of this chapter. You can also select an

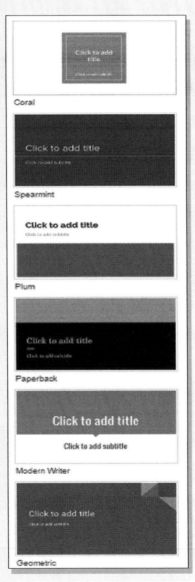

21 Transition – Webster's definition of transition is a passage from one state, stage, subject, or place to another. There are two separate types of transition you can do in Slides, first is the transition of the slide and the second is the transition of an object.

A. **Slide Transition** – The transition of a slide is how it appears in your presentation.

You can have no transition and let it appear normally or choose one of the six options (5.13) listed in the image on the left.

Once you choose the transition, you can change the speed from Slow, Medium, to Fast (5.14).

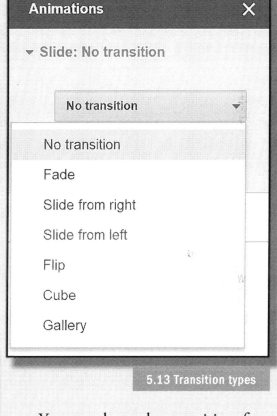

5.13 Transition types

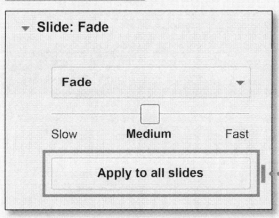

5.14 Choose Speed

You can have the transition for only the slide you are on or you can Apply to all slides.

B. **Object Animation** – The transition of an object is how it appears and moves in the presentation, it is called animation. There are fifteen animations to choose from(5.15).

Once you choose the animation, the choices on it's appearance are (5.16):

- **On click** - you have to touch it for interaction;
- **After previous** - appears after the last animation;
- **With previous** - appears with another animation.

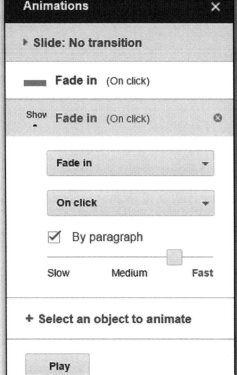

5.16 Additional choices

Fade in	▼

Appear

Disappear

Fade in

Fade out

Fly in from left

Fly in from right

Fly in from bottom

Fly in from top

Fly out to left

Fly out to right

Fly out to bottom

Fly out to top

Zoom in

Zoom out

Spin

5.15 Animation choices

You can also change the speed from Slow, Medium, to Fast. If you select By paragraph, than bullet points or paragraphs will appear, by your selected animation, speed, appearance as separate items.

22 Show your menu – Clicking the double arrow will hide the menus and clicking them again will show the menu.

23 Present – You have put a lot of time into creating your presentation and now it's showtime! To give a flawless presentation, it is important to really familiarizer yourself with the tools within Slides. When you click the Select button, your presentation will go to full screen. A navigation tool-bar till appear at the bottom left of your presentation (5.17).

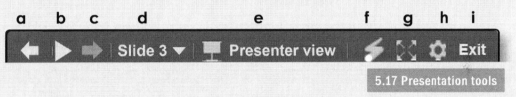

5.17 Presentation tools

a. Previous slide arrow.

b. Play button, plays presentation and you can pause your presentation here also.

c. Next slide arrow.

d. All slides will list out when you select the downward arrow.

e. Presenter view will open so you can take audience Q&A and view speaker notes.

f. Laser pointer enable.

g. Full screen mode on and off.

h. Settings gear, takes you list to either open speaker notes, report copyright infringement, print, download as pdf, or download as pptx.

i. Exit your presentation.

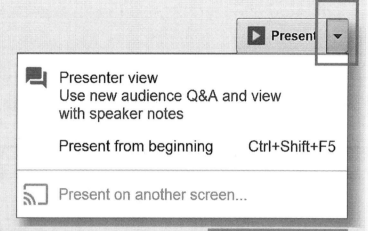

Selecting the dropdown arrow (5.18) in Present gives three options:

- Presenter view
- Present from beginning
- Present on another screen...

Presenter view
Use new audience Q&A and view with speaker notes

Present from beginning   Ctrl+Shift+F5

Present on another screen...

5.18 Dropdown arrow

5.19 Audience tools

With **Presenter view,** you can turn Audience Tools (5.19) on and off. When it is turned on, you can give your audience a provided hyperlink (5.20) that will take them to a Q&A area.

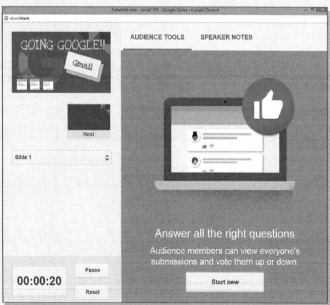

5.20 Presenter View

24 Comment – Select the cell where you would like to attach the comment and the comment box will appear for you to insert your comment. That cell will than have a triangle in the upper right corner to indicate that a comment is there.

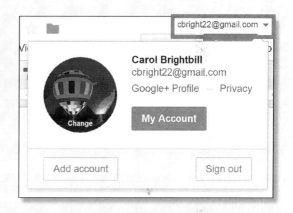

Using this box, you can type in suggestions that you think would improve the file.

25 Account – When you select your email address, a box will open showing you your My Account button to go see an overview of your account settings. You can also add an account, Go to Google +, Privacy settings, and Sign out of your Google account.

26 Share – The first thing under the file menu is one of the most important things about Google Apps, the ability to **Share** your file. I covered this intensively in the Drive section, pages 40-49.

27 Theme – Slides has eighteen different installed themes available. You can import themes from your Drive or upload a theme. Selecting Theme will open all themes that are available for you to use. Your current theme will be the top theme, and all the rest will be underneath it.

You can not mix and match themes, but your can edit the theme by going to View > Master. Within the Master slide area, you can change the background color or add an image as shown in the previous page of this chapter.

28 Page 1 – Pages in your presentation will list down starting with one. The action items you can do when you right click on the page icon are shown on the right (5.21).

5.21 Page action items

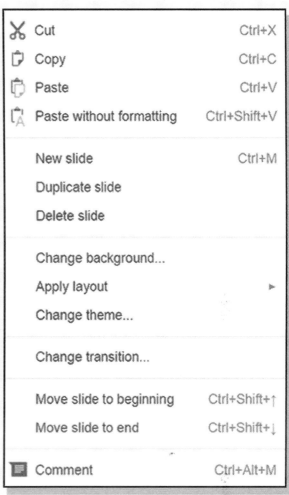

29 Canvas – Each page on the canvas will be based on which page from the theme you have chosen.

30 **Speaker Notes** – Use speaker notes to keep track of your talking points for each slide. In the presentation editor, they are displayed in the text area beneath the current slide.

Public Speaking can be a very nervous experience, and when you get in front of your audience, your worst fear is that your mind will go blank! Having Speaker Notes can be your safety net.

No - you do not want to read them word for word, but having them can ease your mind. Make the font large and easy to read. Set them in bullet points, they can really make your presentation easier. And as time goes by, you will become the speaker who always know what you are talking about!

31 **Import Theme** – Selecting this option will take you to either Presentations, which are your themes in your Drive, ot to Upload a theme your computer.

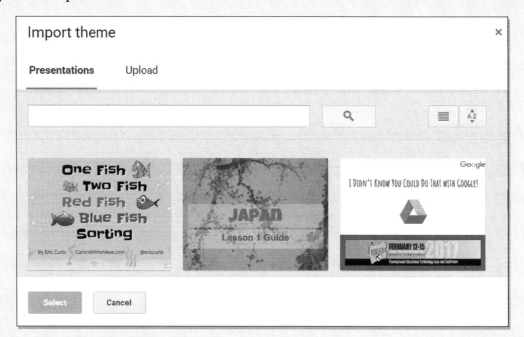

32 **Explore** – Explore in Slides is really a fun tool to use. It is also called Suggested Layouts.

1. Open a presentation in Google Slides.
2. At the bottom right, click Explore.
3. You might see images or information you can use to help finish your work.

- **Layouts:** To choose a new layout for your slide, click the one you want.
- **Web search:** Search the web for information related to your presentation.
- **Images:** To preview an image, click Preview Zoom in. To use an image, click it. This will also add the link to the bottom of the image.
- ***Google Drive:*** You can search Google Drive for content to use with your presentation.

If you don't see suggestions:

You may not always see suggested layouts in Explore. To help suggested layouts appear, you can:

- Use a default Slides theme or default Slides layout.
- Reduce the amount of text on your slides.
- Remove any shapes on your slide.
- Make sure all images are at least 100 x 100 pixels in size.

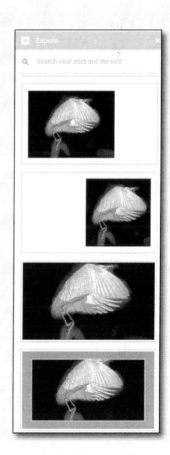

C. TEXT MENU

*Under each item in the Text Menu list action item
that help you create the perfect presentation.*

Text Menu ☆ 📁

File   Edit   View   Insert   Slide   Format   Arrange   Tools   Table   Help

---

File

1. Share...

2. New ►

3. Open... Ctrl+O

4. Rename...

5. Make a copy...

6. 📁 Move to...

7. 🗑 Move to trash

8. Import slides...

9. See revision history Ctrl+Alt+Shift+H

10. Language ►

11. Download as ►

12. Publish to the web...

13. Email collaborators...

14. Email as attachment...

15. Document details...

16. Page setup...

    Print settings and preview

17. 🖶 Print Ctrl+P

TEXT
MENU

C-1 Text Menu - FILE

1 Share – The first thing under the file menu is one of the most important things about Google Apps, the ability to **Share** your file. I covered this intensively in the Drive section, pages 40-49.

2 New – Clicking the New will show how dynamic the Google Apps are. From the New, you can create any one of the Google core apps. Additionally, you can select to create a new Doc from a template.

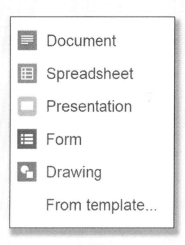

3 Open – Selecting **Open** gives you the choices of going to:
- My Drive
- Shared with Me
- Starred
- Recent
- Upload

Selecting dropdown arrow will let you open by file type.

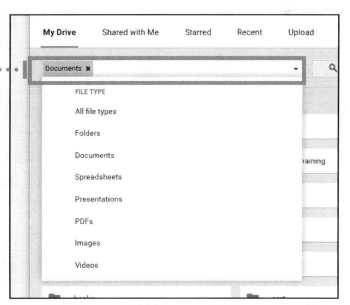

Rename – When you select Rename, your cursor will instantly pop up to where your file has it's existing name and it will be highlighted. Renaming does not make an additional file, it just gives your existing file a new name.

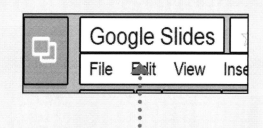

Make A Copy – There are two reasons to make a copy of your file:

1. When a file is shared and the rights are **View Only**, you can not edit the file. This is a smart practice to maintain the integrity of your file. If you select **Make a Copy**, you can rename it, now it is yours to go into and edit.

2. You want to update a file with new information but you want to keep the original file. This is another reason to make a copy of your original, so you can have a different version with the new information and keep your old version.

Move to – Selecting the folder icon will give you the option to move your document to another location. Especially if you created your file in the drive, it is better than just hanging loose with in your Drive folder.

7 Move to trash – This will delete your file from your drive but it is not permanently deleted until you delete it from your trash.

8 Import Slides – Choosing Import Slides, will present two options (5.22):

1. **Presentation** - An existing presentation housed in your Drive.

2. **Upload** - Upload from your computer.

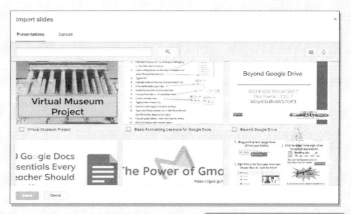

5.22 Import options

Once you have choose your option, click select. Now the second import window will open (5.23).

You can import the entire presentation that you are importing but you can also select certain slides that you want to place into your presentation.

5.23 Import options

See Revision History – Gone are the days of paper drafts that teachers reviewed to see the thought process of their student. This is where Revision History comes in handy. It is also a great way to keep students, working on teams collaborating honest! You can see who has done what in the file.

When you choose **File > See Revision History,** another window opens showing the document, and a side bar will appear that details all the changes within the document.

You can select various dates or times and see the changes that occurred. You can also restore a previous version from this area.

When you restore a previous version, you do not loose any of the other versions, the restored version just jumps to the top.

Revision history

Today

May 6, 7:48 PM
■ Carol Brightbill

May 6, 7:09 AM
■ Carol Brightbill

Yesterday

▶ May 5, 9:54 PM
■ Carol Brightbill

May 5, 9:48 PM
■ Carol Brightbill

☑ Show changes

Language – To change your typing language.

Step 1:

1. Open a document in Google Slides
2. Go to the top menu
3. Click File
4. Then Language and then the language you need.

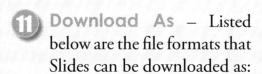 **Download As** – Listed below are the file formats that Slides can be downloaded as:

- **Microsoft Powerpoint** files can be uploaded as a Slides file and re-downloaded as a Powerpoint.

- **ODP** is a file extension for a presentation file format used by OpenOffice.org

Microsoft PowerPoint (.pptx)

ODP Document (.odp)

PDF Document (.pdf)

Plain Text (.txt)

JPEG image (.jpg, current slide)

PNG image (.png, current slide)

Scalable Vector Graphics (.svg, current slide)

- **PDF** stands for portable document format, the universal format that embeds fonts and images.

- **Plain Text** uses no formating or images and can be opened in Notepad.

- **JPEG Image** (current slide) is a file format that is good to use to upload to a website, good for images.

- **PNG Image** (current slide) is a file format used to upload to the web and is good for line items, charts, text and is a small size.

- **Scalable Vector Graphics** (current slide) is good for an interactive web side and is a clean scalable format that keeps the lines smooth.

12 **Publish To The Web** – Choosing to publish to the web opens your file for public viewing. An embeddable HTML version of your Slide deck is created and what gets embedded is not your original file but a copy. This copy does not carry over any sharing privileges that you have granted.

Some of the useful reasons why you would want to publish your presentation:

- File can be embedded in a blog, your Google Sites, your own website.
- Opens your file up to a very large audience.
- Your published Slide deck will automatically update when you make a change to the original.

Selecting Publish to the web opens a pop up box with two options:

Link - Choosing the link option will create a hyperlink that can be placed in an email, Facebook, Twitter, and even a web page. Some of the options are to start slide-show as soon as the player loads and restart the slide-show after the last slide. Selecting to get the link starts publishing the slide deck and any changes will automatically be updated until you select Stop publishing.

Publish to the web

This document is published to the web.
Make your content visible to anyone by publishing it to the web. You can link to or embed your document. Learn more

Link   Embed

Auto-advance slides:

every 3 seconds (default) ⇕

☐ Start slideshow as soon as the player loads
☐ Restart the slideshow after the last slide

https://docs.google.com/presentation/d/17JzF5KoY_hMxnAc6uySjW2a9_NwAGxjR5

Or share this link using: G+ M f 🐦

Published

▼ Published content & settings

Stop publishing

☐ Require viewers to sign in with their Pottstown School District account

Embed - When choosing to embed, you can choose the size of the file your would like to embed and you can also choose the speed of the slide advance. Embedding gives you an iFrame code which can than be placed in your web page.

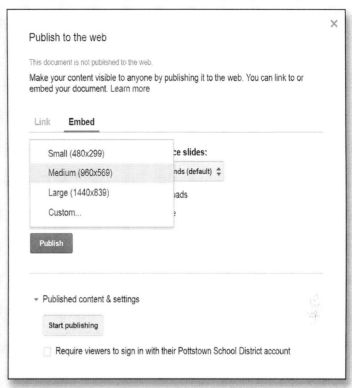

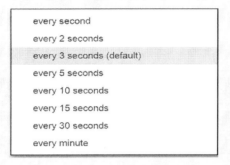

every second
every 2 seconds
every 3 seconds (default)
every 5 seconds
every 10 seconds
every 15 seconds
every 30 seconds
every minute

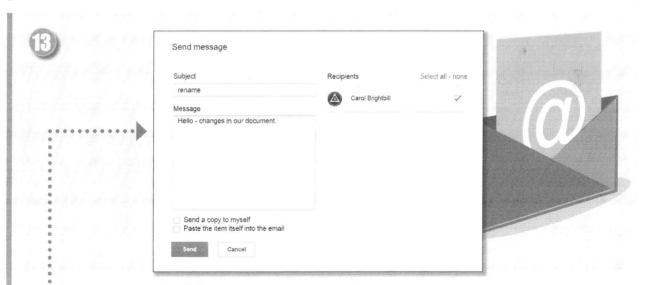

Email Collaborators – After sharing a file with multiple people so they can collaborate on a project, the ability to email them is a great way to keep the team updated on the progress that each of them are making and the changes that are happening to the file.

14 **Email as Attachment–** Not everyone has or uses Google Slides so when you want to send the file to someone, you do have the option to attached it as a different file type. When you attach the file, you have three options:

- PDF
- PowerPoint
- Plain Text

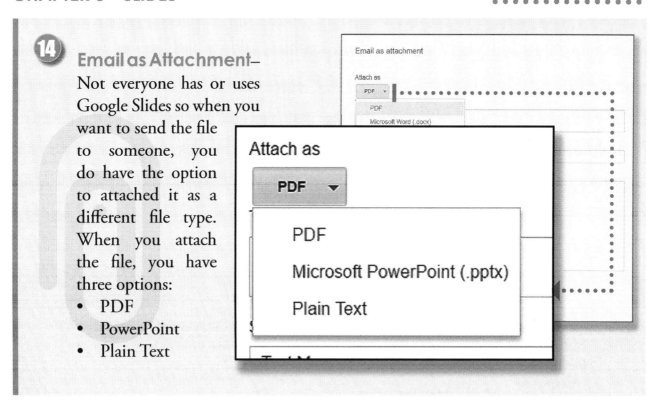

15 Document details – The details of the document provides useful information, especially if you don't know what folder your file is located or who the owner is.

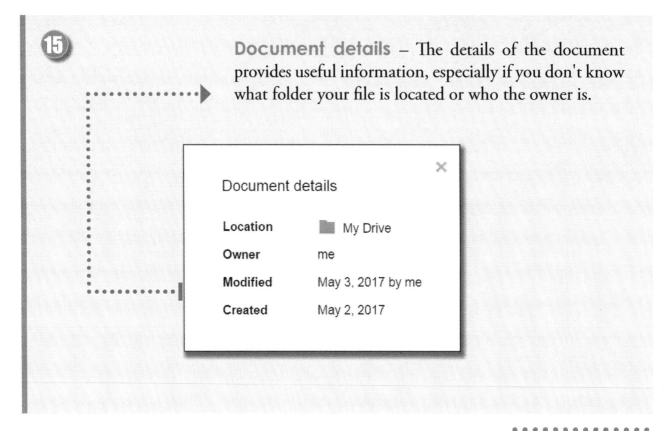

Page Setup – In page setup you can change the size of your page layout to be any size you want it to be.

This is why I think that Slides is a great layout program that can be used similarly to the professional programs. You get there by choosing File > Page setup. In the middle of the box that appears will display Widescreen 16:9, and when you select this, you have 4 options:

- Standard 4:3
- Widescreen 16:10
- Widescreen 16:9
- Custom

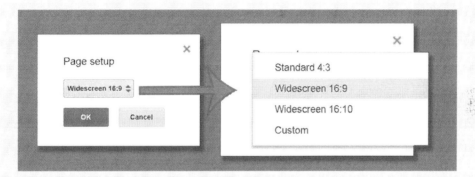

When you select Custom, you can choose 8.5 x 11" for letter size, 8.5 x 14" for legal, 11 x 17" for tabloid size. You can even choose 3.5 x 2" for business cards size and 24" x 36 poster size.

 Print Settings and Preview– Open the presentation you want to print.

1. Click File and then Print settings and preview. A new window with a preview of your presentation and print options will open.

2. Click the 1 slide with notes dropdown menu in the toolbar to print your slides with speaker notes or choose how many slides are printed on each page. To change the orientation of the slides when printed, click Landscape.

3. Click Print in the toolbar.

C-2 Text Menu - EDIT

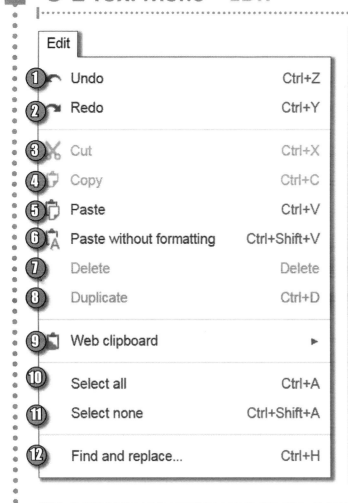

Where would word processing be without cut, copy, paste! And Control Z!! The best ever! Let's go down the menu:

1. **Undo** – action that takes you back one step in your editing.

2. **Redo** – action that jumps you back to where your were before your Undo.

3. **Cut** – places what you cut onto the computer clipboard and removes it from your file.

4. **Copy** – places what you copy onto the computer clipboard and leaves it in your file. Your computer clipboard only holds one item, the last thing you either copied or cut.

5. **Paste** – pasting will put whatever you cut or copied, from the computer's clipboard onto your file.

6. **Paste without formatting** – existing formatting from what your cut or copied will be stripped away when you paste and your content will take on the existing format where it is being pasted into.

7. **Delete** – whatever is selected will be removed from the page when you select delete.

8. **Duplicate** – an exact copy will be created from anything you have selected and you select duplicate.

9 Web clipboard – Copying to the Web clipboard is different than just copying to your computer's clipboard.

This clipboard can hold multiple items at once, across different apps. And since your are signed into your Google account, it is also syncs. Items will clear after 30 days.

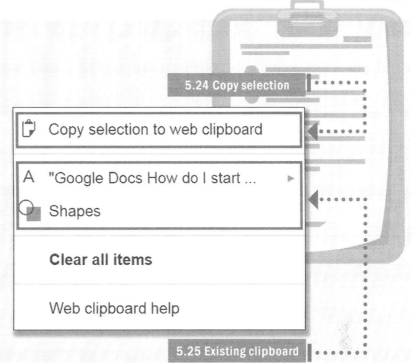

5.24 Copy selection

Copy selection to web clipboard

A "Google Docs How do I start ...

Shapes

Clear all items

Web clipboard help

5.25 Existing clipboard

1. Select what you want to copy.
2. Choose Edit > scroll down to Web clipboard.
3. Choose Copy selection to web clipboard. (5.24)

Under where you select Copy selection to web clipboard, you items that are existing on the clipboard will list down (5.25). The next list item is Clear all items.

10

Select all – Depending on if you are in a text box, all your type will be selected, or if you are just on the page, all the items on the page will be selected.

11

Select none – This will deselect what your have selected.

12

Find and replace – Great time saving way to find specific words to replace.

C-3 Text Menu - VIEW

View	
① Present	Ctrl+F5
② Animations	Ctrl+Alt+Shift+B
③ Master	
④ Fit (78%)	Ctrl+Alt+[
50%	
100%	
200%	
Zoom in	Ctrl+Alt++
Zoom out	Ctrl+Alt+-
⑤ Snap to	►
⑥ HTML view	Ctrl+Alt+Shift+P
⑦ ✓ Show spelling suggestions	
⑧ ✓ Show speaker notes	
⑨ Compact controls	Ctrl+Shift+F
⑩ Full screen	

Present – You have put a lot of time into creating your presentation and now it's showtime! To give a flawless presentation, it is important to really familiarizer yourself with the tools within Slides. When you click the Select button, your presentation will go to full screen. A navigation tool-bar till appear at the bottom left of your presentation (5.26).

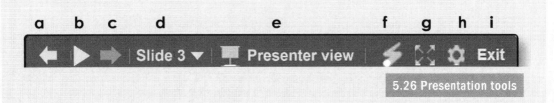

5.26 Presentation tools

a. Previous slide arrow.

b. Play button, plays presentation and you can pause your presentation here also.

c. Next slide arrow.

d. All slides will list out when you select the downward arrow.

e. Presenter view will open so you can take audience Q&A and view speaker notes.

f. Laser pointer enable.

g. Full screen mode on and off.

h. Settings gear, takes you list to either open speaker notes, report copyright infringement, print, download as pdf, or download as pptx.

i. Exit your presentation.

2 **Transition** – Webster's definition of transition is a passage from one state, stage, subject, or place to another. There are two separate types of transition you can do in Slides, first is the transition of the slide and the second is the transition of an object.

A. **Slide Transition** – The transition of a slide is how it appears in your presentation.

You can have no transition and let it appear normally or choose one of the six options (5.27) listed in the image on the left.

Once you choose the transition, you can change the speed from Slow, Medium, to Fast (5.28).

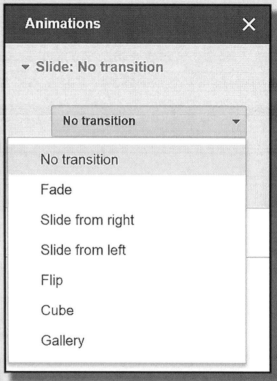

5.27 Transition types

5.28 Choose Speed

You can have the transition for only the slide you are on or you can Apply to all slides.

B. **Object Animation** – The transition of an object is how it appears and moves in the presentation, it is called animation. There are fifteen animations to choose from(5.29).

Once you choose the animation, the choices on it's appearance are (5.30):

- **On click** - you have to touch it for interaction;

- **After previous** - appears after the last animation;

- **With previous** - appears with another animation.

5.30 Additional choices

Fade in

Appear

Disappear

Fade in

Fade out

Fly in from left

Fly in from right

Fly in from bottom

Fly in from top

Fly out to left

Fly out to right

Fly out to bottom

Fly out to top

Zoom in

Zoom out

Spin

Animations ✕

▸ **Slide: No transition**

▬▬ **Fade in** (On click)

Show **Fade in** (On click) ⊗

Fade in ▾

On click ▾

☑ By paragraph

Slow   Medium   Fast

＋ **Select an object to animate**

Play

5.29 Animation choices

You can also change the speed from Slow, Medium, to Fast. If you select By paragraph, than bullet points or paragraphs will appear, by your selected animation, speed, appearance as separate items.

3 **Master** – Master pages gives you control over your presentation. You can change colors, fonts, images, positioning, and backgrounds universally when you use a master. Using a slide master gives you the ability to modify existing pages by changing the master. Even if you are halfway through creating your presentation and you decide that you don't like the master that you are using, you to have the option to change masters and it will cascade on all the pages.

The Master is the theme of your presentation. It carries a consistent look and feel throughout it. This is called branding. Branding is an effective way to get your message across to your audience. Also, branding is a way to create recognition. Use the same color scheme, logo placement, look and feel throughout. You don't need to be fancy, just consistent.

If you want two different Masters in your presentation, you will have to import the second master as a set of slides because you can not change the master without it affecting all slides.

A pecking order is created in the Master list, a type of hierarchy, as listed below:
- Title slide
- Section header
- Title and body
- Title and two columns
- Title only
- One column text
- Main point
- Section title and description
- Caption
- Big number
- Blank

④ Fit / Zoom – You first select the magnifying glass icon (5.32) and touch the screen slide will increase size each time you touch it.

You select the Fit to view (5.31) icon to fit the screen back to normal size.

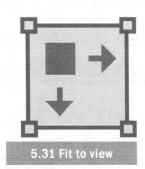

5.31 Fit to view

5.32 Magnifying glass

⑤ Snap to Grids and Guides - Used to align objects more precisely on a slide so you can easily arrange objects in relation to other objects on the slide. Snap to Guides is enabled by default. You can enable or disable the Snap to Grid and Snap to Guides options under the "View" menu. However Google Slides doesn't offer the features of ruler guides or a grid.

6. **HTML view** – HTML view opens your presentation in the browser.

7. **SHOW SPELLING SUGGESTIONS** – A red squiggle line will appear under misspelled words when this is checked.

8. **SHOW SPEAKER NOTES** – Hiding speaker notes gives you more viewing room to work on your presentation. When Speaker Notes are showing there will be a checkmark beside this menu item.

9. **COMPACT CONTROLS** – Takes away the text menu and you must select the double downward arrows in the right corner to bring the full menu system back.

10. **FULL SCREEN** – Your controls are hidden and you have to select the ESC. button to exit full screen.

C-4 Text Menu - INSERT

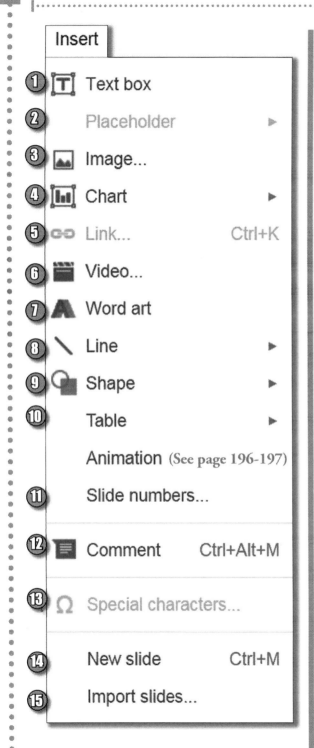

Insert

① ⊤ Text box

② Placeholder ▶

③ 🖼 Image...

④ 📊 Chart ▶

⑤ 🔗 Link... Ctrl+K

⑥ 🎬 Video...

⑦ 🅰 Word art

⑧ ╲ Line ▶

⑨ 🔲 Shape ▶

⑩ Table ▶

Animation (See page 196-197)

⑪ Slide numbers...

⑫ 📋 Comment Ctrl+Alt+M

⑬ Ω Special characters...

⑭ New slide Ctrl+M

⑮ Import slides...

① **ext Box** – The text box is an entry field where the user can enter the information that they want to present.

A text box is what makes Slides stand out from Docs, it turns your presentation tool into a layout program. A layout programs gives you control over where you can place your items on your page creating a design.

This actually turns your program into a desktop publishing program.

The things you can do with a text box are:

- Resize it to whatever size you want.
- Enter verbiage.
- Rotate it 360.
- Change opacity from 0 to 100.
- Add a stroke from 1, 2, 3, 4, 8, 12, 16, and 24 pixels.
- Add a background fill.
- Change the text color.

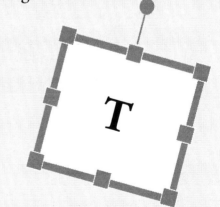

② Placeholder – Placeholder text can only be inserted into a master slide. It will stay inactive until you open the Master and than it becomes active and usable. You would use placeholder text is just how it sounds, it places text boxes when you want them to be in the master. Once placed in the master, you can stylize it how you want it to look by either changing font size, color, font, background.

The three types of placeholder you can insert are:

- Title placeholder
- Subtitle placeholder
- Body text placeholder

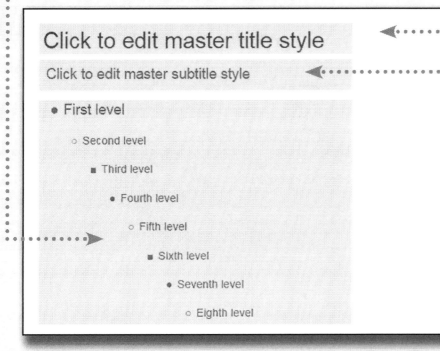

③ Image– You can take your slides to the next level and go from boring to quite interesting by just adding a picture. As the saying goes, "A picture is worth a thousand words". There are six different ways to add an image. Images must be less than 50 MB and be one of the following file types: .gif; .jpg; or.png.

1. **Upload** – Selecting to upload will take your to your computer's hard drive and select Open.

2. **Take a snapshot** – If your device has a camera, you can take a snapshot and insert it directly into the document.

3. **By URL** – Paste the URL of an image from the web and click Select.

4. **Your albums** – Choose an image from one of your photos albums stored on the web and click Select.

5. **Google Drive** – Choose an image stored in Google Drive and click Select.

6. **Search** – Choose an image from the stock photography archive, or the Google and Life archives, and click Select.

When an image is inserted in a document, you can edit it in various ways. You must first select the image and than you will be able to either, crop it, recolor it. You will also have adjustments such as transparency, brightness, or contrast. You can also replace the image.

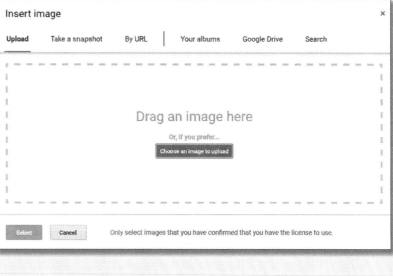

④ Chart – You have 4 different types of charts (5.33) that you can insert into your Google Doc, plus insert from Sheets:

- Bar
- Column
- Line
- Pie

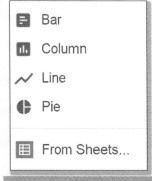

5.33 Chart insertion options

Generic data (5.34) will fill these charts linking to four generic teams. In the upper right corner of these generic charts, are two icons (5.35). The first icon gives you the option to unlink your chart from the Sheets. The second option lets you open up your chart in Sheets and than you can replace the generic data with your own information.

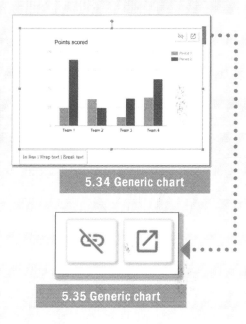

5.34 Generic chart

At the bottom of the CHART insert is the option to insert **From Sheets**. When you choose this option, you will be taken to your Sheets (5.36)and you can choose your existing file. If there is not a chart currently on that Sheet, you will get the message: *"This spreadsheet has no charts."*

5.35 Generic chart

If the Sheet that your are inserting from your own collection of Sheets has more than one chart within it, you can choose which chart you would like to insert into your Slides (5.37).

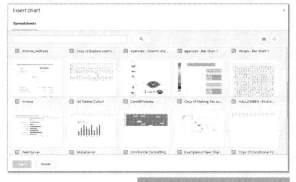

5.36 Sheet Chart Options

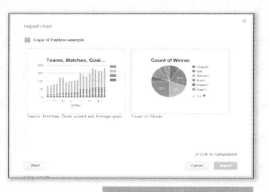

5.37 Multiple charts

5 **Link** – To insert a link:

1. Click on an item within your Slides presentation to select it. You can select a text box, an image, a word art image, a line or a shape. You can also highlight a section of text within a text box to turn that section of text into a hyperlink without editing the rest of the text.

2. Click "**Insert**" and select "**Link**".

3. Type the web address that you would like the link to open in the "URL for the Link" text area. Alternately, click "Email Address" and enter an email address to send a message to when the link is clicked. You can also click "Slide" and select a specific slide within your presentation for the link to open.

4. Click "OK" to close the dialog and create the hyperlink.

5. Click on the hyperlink while editing your slides to open the hyperlink pop-up menu. Click the link address to open the link. Click "**Change**" to change the hyperlink's destination. Click "Remove" to remove the link and return the linked object to its former state.

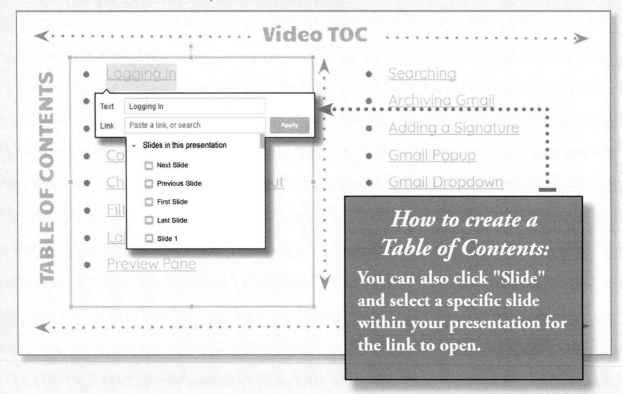

How to create a
Table of Contents:
You can also click "Slide"
and select a specific slide
within your presentation for
the link to open.

Video

To embed a YouTube video:

1. Click Insert on the menu bar.
2. Select Video.
3. A window will appear where you can search for:

A. YouTube video;
B. Select URL at the top of the window, and paste a URL for a specific YouTube video;
C. Insert from your drive.

4. Click Select.
5. Your video is now embedded in your slide.

Once your video is inserted into your Slide Deck and you select that video, up in the ICON MENU will appear the Text *Video Options*. Select this and a window will appear on the right side of your Slide Deck.

From here you can:

• Make full screen
• Add a start point
• Add an end point
• Autoplay when presenting
• Mute audio

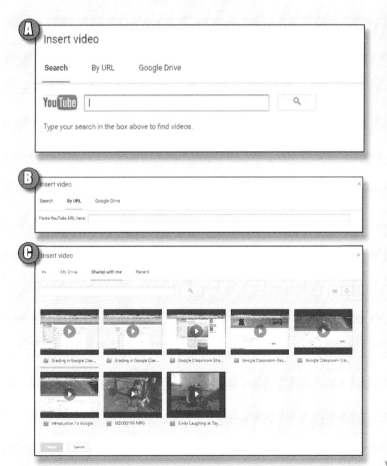

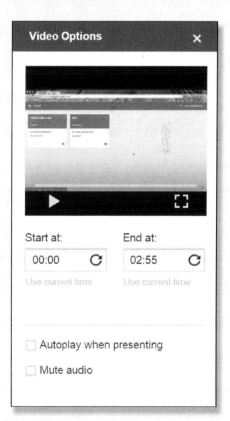

Word Art – When you select Insert > Word Art, popup box will appear and type your words in here (5.38).

Word Art|

Use Enter to save. Use Shift+Enter for multiple lines.

5.38 Insert Word Art

Use Enter to save your words gray filled words with a black stroke will appear and you can change the fill color and stroke color, weight, and style to what every you want it to be. (5.39)

5.39 Word Art Example

Line – There are seven line options (5.40). The lines and the shapes are good to combine together to make flowcharts and diagrams.

To create a flowchart, you can select the line tool and pick an arrow or connector to connect two shapes. You can place the shapes anywhere on the screen and the connectors would follow (5.41).

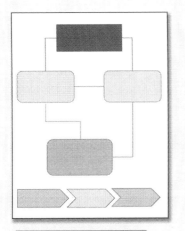

3.41 Flowchart

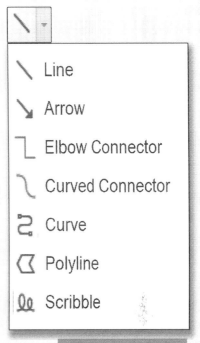

5.40 Line options

- Scale infinitely
- Colorize
- Change weight (5.42)
- Change style (5.43)
- Add endpoints (5.44)

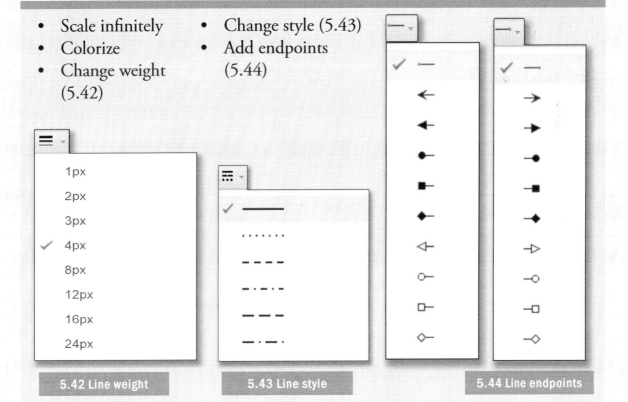

| 5.42 Line weight | 5.43 Line style | 5.44 Line endpoints |

9 **Shape** – There are four category of shapes (5.45). The shapes use mathematic equations and geometric primitives (points, lines, and shapes) to create art that is clean and can be scaled infinitely, without any loss of quality.

The things you can do with a text box are:

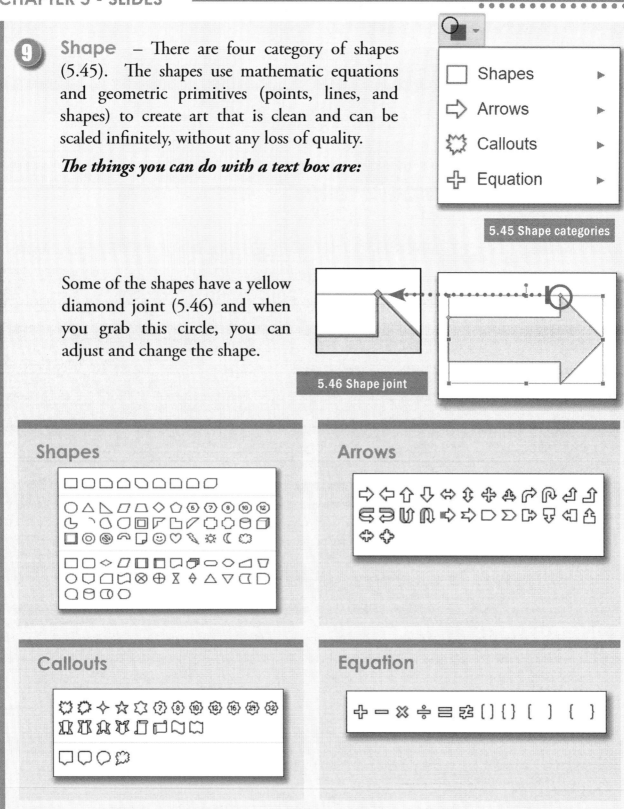

Shapes	►
Arrows	►
Callouts	►
Equation	►

5.45 Shape categories

Some of the shapes have a yellow diamond joint (5.46) and when you grab this circle, you can adjust and change the shape.

5.46 Shape joint

Shapes

Arrows

Callouts

Equation

10 Table – A table is a grid of cells arranged in rows and columns. It can be useful to present data in a table inside a word processing document because it is displayed in an organized and easy to read format. You can insert a table anywhere from 1x1 up to 20 x 20 and all equations in-between (5.47).

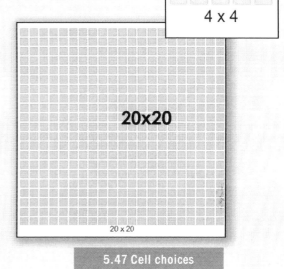

4 x 4

20x20

20 x 20

5.47 Cell choices

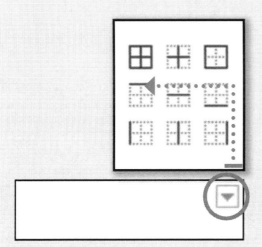

When you hover in the upper right corner of every cell, a dropdown carat appears.

Selecting this dropdown (figure above) will bring up a sub-menu giving you the option to customize and colorize individual lines within the cell (5.48).

5.48 Customize

Right-clicking within any cell (5.49) will bring up a sub-menu giving you the option to insert or delete rows or columns, and distribute them.

Table properties brings up the option to colorize background and borders and set specific sizes for cells, cell vertical alignment, table alignment, and padding.

5.49 Right click cell

Slide Numbers – Inserting Slide numbers will organize your slides in a numeric order, and you can skip the Title Slide.

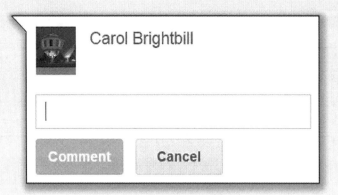

Comment – Select the cell where you would like to attach the comment and the comment box will appear for you to insert your comment. That cell will than have a triangle in the upper right corner to indicate that a comment is there.

Using this box, you can type in suggestions that you think would improve the file.

Special Characters – There are 24 categories (5.50) what spill down when you choose the first button when you select Insert > Special Characters.

A sub-menu appears (5.51) to even filter down your selection better.

Google makes it even easier for you if you can't exactly remember what you are looking for but have an idea. There is a track pad (5.52) and in the middle it states ***Draw a symbol here.*** As you start to draw, Google will show you symbols that resemble what you drew. If you insert the same characters frequently, they will show up in your recent characters. Find this list in the first drop-down menu.

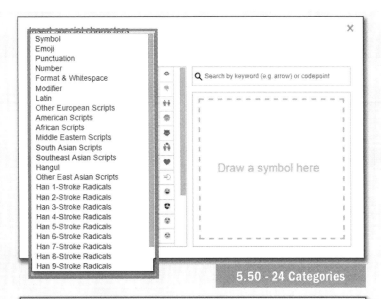

5.50 - 24 Categories

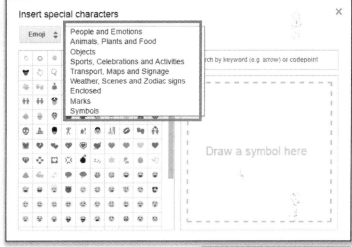

5.51 - Sub menu

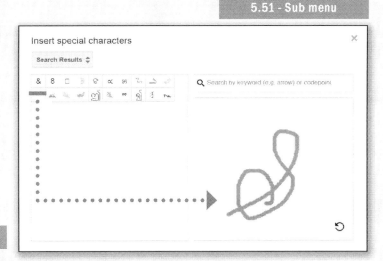

5.52 Track Pad

14 **New Slide (ctr M)** – Selecting the + will automatically add a new page based on the last page inserted.

Selecting the carat drop down (5.53) will open the choices of different sides that you can insert, color and layout is based on the theme that is selected but each choice of specific page i.e. Title slide; Section header - stays consistent in each theme.

5.53 Caret drop down

15 **Import Slides** – Choosing Import Slides, will present two options (5.54):

1. Presentation - An existing presentation housed in your Drive.

2. Upload - Upload from your computer.

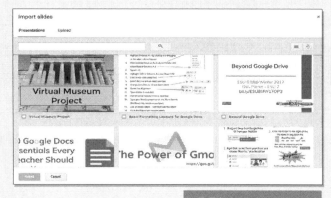

5.54 Import options

Once you have choose your option, click select. Now the second import window will open (5.55).

You can import the entire presentation that you are importing but you can also select certain slides that you want to place into your presentation.

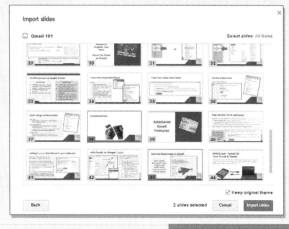

5.55 Import options

C-5 Text Menu - SLIDE

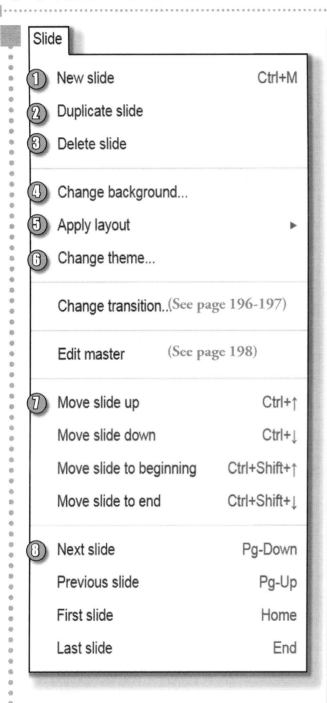

1. **New slide** – Adds a new slide to your presentation as explained on the previous page.

2. **Duplicate slide** – Makes an exact copy of the existing slide.

3. **Delete slide** – Removes the slide from your presentation.

Change background – You can change the color, reset the background, and reset the theme.

1. **Color** - You can change the color of the background to a solid color or a gradient color.

2. **Image** - Upload an image.

3. **Reset** - To reset the theme, you must choose a new color or background, and than select Reset.

⑤ Apply layout – If your slide is a Title slide and you want it to be a different slide in the Theme, just choose Layout and you can choose one of the eleven different slide layouts available. All choices are represented in the image on the right.

⑥ Change theme – Slides has eighteen different installed themes available. Selecting Change theme will open all themes that are available for you to use. Your current theme will be the top theme, and all the rest will be underneath it.

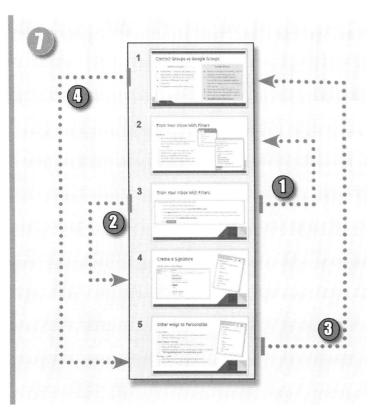

1. **Move slide up** – Moves the slide you are selecting up a position.

2. **Move slide down** – Moves the slide you are selecting down a position.

3. **Move slide to beginning** – Moves the slide you are selecting to be the first slide in the presentation.

4. **Move slide to end** – Moves the slide you are selecting to be the last slide in the presentation.

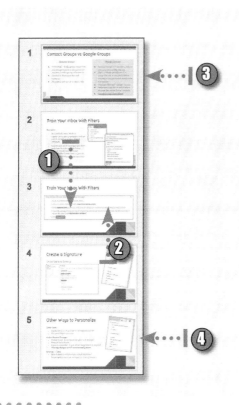

1. **Next slide** – Moves you down to the next slide.

2. **Previous slide** – Moves you up to the previous slide.

3. **First slide** – Takes you to the first slide in the presentation.

4. **Last slide** – Takes you to the last slide in the presentation.

C-6 Text Menu - FORMAT

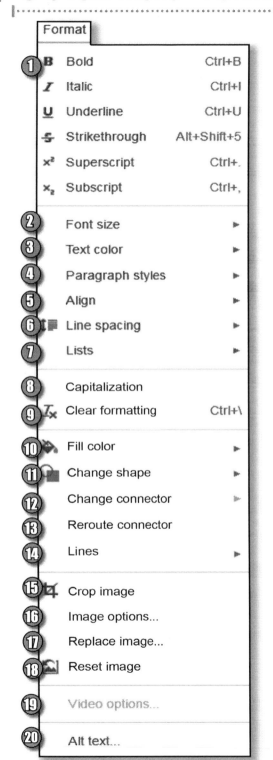

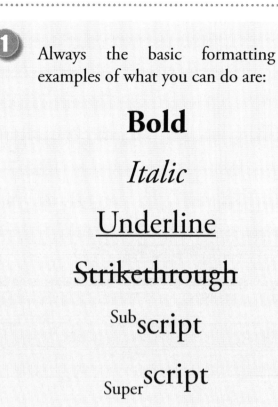

1 Always the basic formatting examples of what you can do are:

Bold

Italic

<u>Underline</u>

~~Strikethrough~~

_{Sub}script

^{Super}script

2 **Font size** – Starting with **Font size**, you can increase or reduce the size of your fonts.

Increase font size	Ctrl+Shift+.
Decrease font size	Ctrl+Shift+,

3 **Text color** – You have a wide variety of text and highlight colors to choose from. All the shades of the basic colors are offered by default (5.56).

When you select Custom at the bottom of the Default color window (5.56), a pop up window appears where you can move the slider to create a custom color or if you know a HEX color, enter at the top.

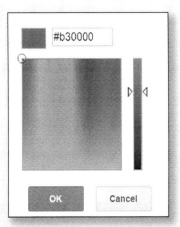

5.57 Custom colors

5.56 Default text colors

4 **Paragraph styles** – There are two choices with paragraph styles, to increase the text indent or decrease the text indent.

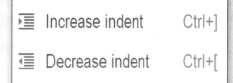

Increase indent   Ctrl+]

Decrease indent   Ctrl+[

5 **Align** – This is the placement of the text within the text box.

Left   Ctrl+Shift+L

Center   Ctrl+Shift+E

Right   Ctrl+Shift+R

Justified   Ctrl+Shift+J

↑ Top

↕ Middle

↓ Bottom

Text flushed left

Center text

Right text

When all words are justified their lines are even.

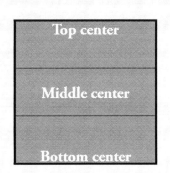

Top center

Middle center

Bottom center

Line spacing – Line spacing, in desktop publishing terms is called leading. So, as you add space, it can be (5.58):

- Single - distance equal to the depth of current line.
- 1.15 - distance equal to depth of current line plus .15% extra.
- 1.5 - distance equal to 1 and 1/2 times size of current line.
- Double - distance equal to two times current line depth.

Adding space before and after a paragraph creates a nice break between the paragraphs.

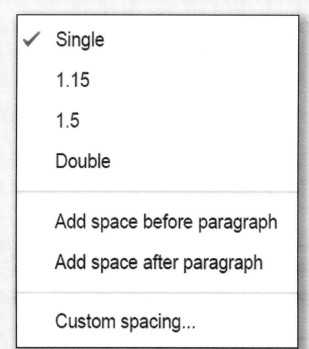

5.58 Line Spacing

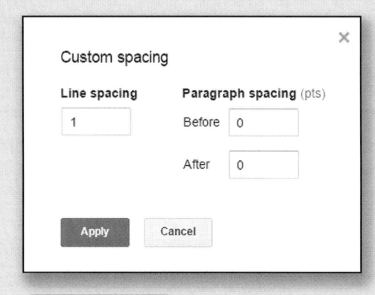

5.59 Custom Spacing

You can add your own custom spacing between lines and between paragraphs or after paragraphs (5.59)

7 **List** – Creating list items in your presentation is a way to help your items stand out or show important steps.

⅓≡	Numbered list	▶
≔	Bulleted list	▶
	List options	▶

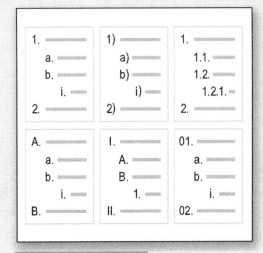

5.60 Numbered list

When choosing Numbered list (5.60) you can list out numerically and indents will be alphabetical, or list out alphabetical and indents will be numbered.

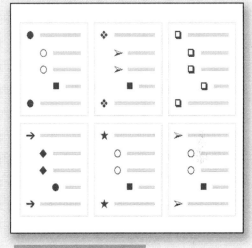

5.61 Bulleted list

When choosing Bulleted list (5.61) you can list out with a various shapes, arrows, circles, squares.

List options (5.62) gives you the option to restart numbering, edit prefix and suffix. If you choose More bullets, you will be taken to the number sections of Special Characters.

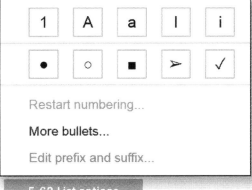

5.62 List options

8 Capitalization – Change the case of your text.

> lowercase
>
> UPPERCASE
>
> Title Case

9 Clear formatting – This will strip any styles and put your text back to the default font and style.

10 Fill color – You must first have an object selected, and when you choose Fill color will, a pop up box appears with your color fill options of Solid (5.63), Gradient (5.64), or Custom (5.65).

5.63 Solid color fill

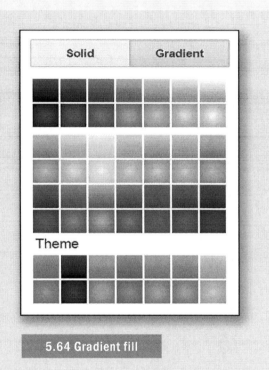

5.64 Gradient fill

With custom fill (5.65), you can slide the slider to choose a color or enter a hex number. You can also slide the slider on the far right to change the opacity of your fill.

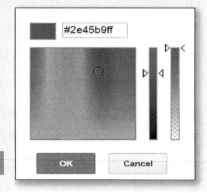

5.65 Custom fill

Change shape – You must first have a shape on the slide deck. Select the shape and than select Change shape. You can choose from any of the available shapes below.

Shapes

Arrows

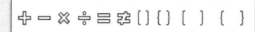

Callouts

Equation

 Change connector – This is an efficient way to update your diagram or flowchart. Select your connector, than select Format > Change connector and the box that will appear gives you three options.

Straight Connector

Elbow Connector

Curved Connector

Reroute connector – Select the connected shape or connector that you want to reroute. ...

In the Format tab, in the Insert Shapes group, click Edit Shape, and then click Reroute Connectors.

14 **Line** – There are six line options (5.6). Their flyout menu is shown below.

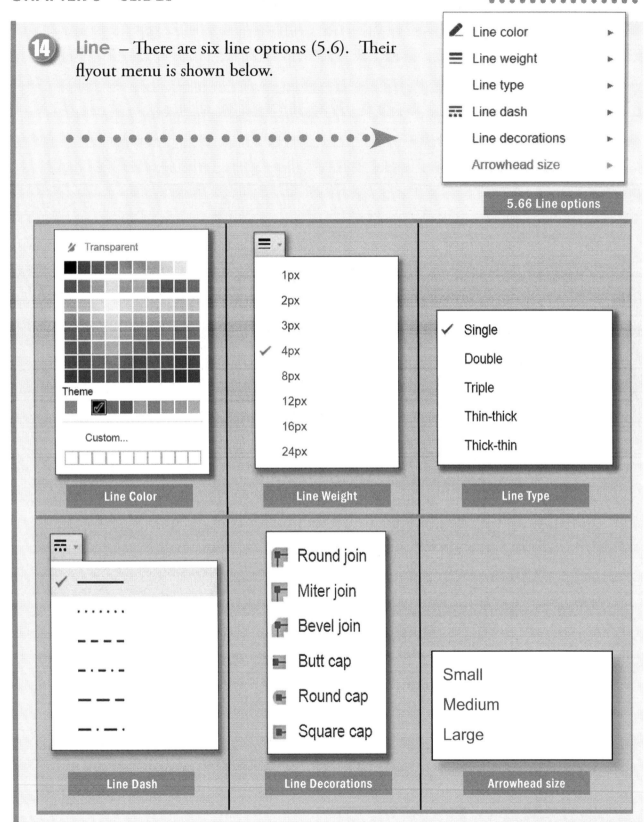

Line color	►
Line weight	►
Line type	►
Line dash	►
Line decorations	►
Arrowhead size	►

5.66 Line options

Line Color

Transparent

Theme

Custom...

Line Weight

1px
2px
3px
✓ 4px
8px
12px
16px
24px

Line Type

✓ Single
Double
Triple
Thin-thick
Thick-thin

Line Dash

Line Decorations

Round join
Miter join
Bevel join
Butt cap
Round cap
Square cap

Arrowhead size

Small
Medium
Large

15 **Crop image** – Cropping an image will remove parts of the image without scaling the size of the image.

The darker part of the image is what will show, where it is faded is the cropped part of the image.

16 **Image options** – You can adjust your image's Transparency, Brightness, and Contrast. If you don't like your adjustments, just choose Reset adjustments to put the image back to it's original state.

There are nineteen color options to apply to your image as show on the right.

17 Replace image – You have to first have your image selected, than go to Format > Replace image, and the box on the right will appear.

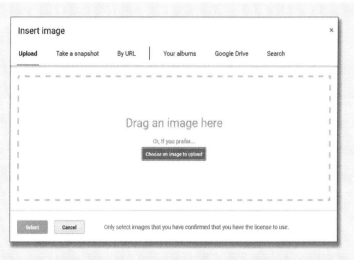

- Once you make your choice, the new image will appear in the box that the old image was but any of the formatting you had previously done will be stripped away.

18 Resetting image – Selecting to reset the image will strip away any adjustments you did from colorizing, transparency, contrast, even cropping and line styles will be removed. Your image will be set to it's original state when your first imported it.

19 Video options – Select your video and than select, Format > Video Options. A window will appear on the right side of your Slide Deck.

From here you can:
- Make full screen
- Add an end point presenting
- Mute audio

- Add a start point
- Autoplay when

20 Alt text – When you add Alt Text to an image, your are giving it a Title and a Description. This will help your Search Engine Optimization if you post your Slide Deck in a web browser. This was explained in the first chapter of this book.

C-7 Text Menu - ARRANGE

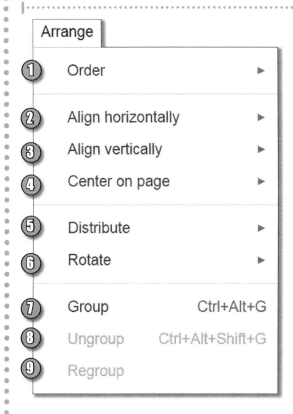

Arrange	
① Order	▶
② Align horizontally	▶
③ Align vertically	▶
④ Center on page	▶
⑤ Distribute	▶
⑥ Rotate	▶
⑦ Group	Ctrl+Alt+G
⑧ Ungroup	Ctrl+Alt+Shift+G
⑨ Regroup	

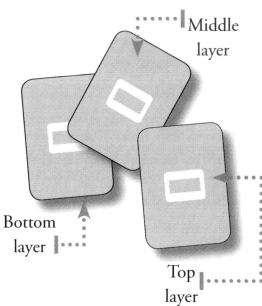

Middle layer

Bottom layer

Top layer

① Order – Ordering refers to the placement of objects on your slide deck. The first object, you put on the canvas is the bottom layer. Each subsequence item will layer on top.

Selecting order, allows you to rearrange the order of these objects, moving the bottom up or the top down.

> Bring to front
> Bring forward
> Send backward
> Send to back

- Click **"Bring to Front"** to bring the selected object to the front of the other objects.
- Click **"Bring Forward"** to bring the selected object in front of the object it was immediately behind.
- Click **"Send Backward"** to move the selected object behind the object it was immediately in front of.
- Click **"Send to Back"** to place the selected object at the back of the objects.

2 **Align horizontally** – There are three options when aligning horizontally:

Left
Center
Right

- Click "Left" and all selected objects will be moved to align with the object of the farthest left.

- Click "Center" and all selected objects will be moved to align with center most object.

- Click "Right" and all selected objects will be moved to align with the object of the farthest right.

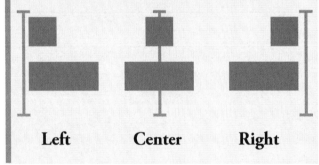

Left   Center   Right

3 **Align vertically** – There are three options when aligning vertically:

Top
Middle
Bottom

- Click "Top" and all selected objects will be moved to align with the object of the farthest to the top.

- Click "Middle" and all selected objects will align with the middle most object.

- Click "Bottom" and all selected objects will be moved to align with the object at the bottom.

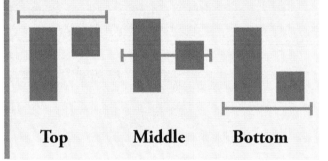

Top   Middle   Bottom

4 **Center on page** – There are two options when centering on page:

Horizontally
Vertically

- Click "Horizontally" and all selected objects will be moved to align to the very horizontal center of the page.

- Click "Vertically" and all selected objects will be moved to align to the very vertical center of the page.

5 Distribute – There are two options when distributing items on a page:

> Horizontally
>
> Vertically

- Click "Horizontally" and all selected objects will be moved to align horizontally with each other.
- Click "Vertically" and all selected objects will be moved to align vertically with each other.

7 Group – Grouping is like gluing your objects together, they become one.

8 Ungroup – After your items are grouped and you want to separate them, you ungroup them.

9 Regroup – After you have ungrouped you items and decide you want to regroup them.

6 Rotate – There are three options when aligning horizontally:

Rotate clockwise 90°
Rotate counter-clockwise 90°
Flip horizontally
Flip vertically

Flip horizontally

Rotate clockwise 90°
Rotate counter-clockwise 90°
Flip horizontally
Flip vertically

Flip vertically

Rotate clockwise 90°
Rotate counter-clockwise 90°
Flip horizontally
Flip vertically

Rotate Clockwise 90°

Rotate clockwise 90°
Rotate counter-clockwise 90°
Flip horizontally
Flip vertically

Rotate Counter-Clockwise 90°

C-8 Text Menu - TOOLS

	Tools	
①	Spelling...	
② ✦	Explore	Ctrl+Alt+Shift+I
③	Define	Ctrl+Shift+Y
④	Q&A history	
⑤ 🎤	Voice type speaker notes...	Ctrl+Shift+S
⑥	Preferences...	
⑦	Personal dictionary...	

① **Spelling** – It is always good to spell check your file for errors.

When you go to Tools>Spelling, a pop-up box will appear (5.67). It will have suggestions for the correct spelling and you can select Change or Ignore. You can also add a word to the system dictionary.

As you enter text, if Slides thinks it is misspelled, it will have a squiggly line under it.

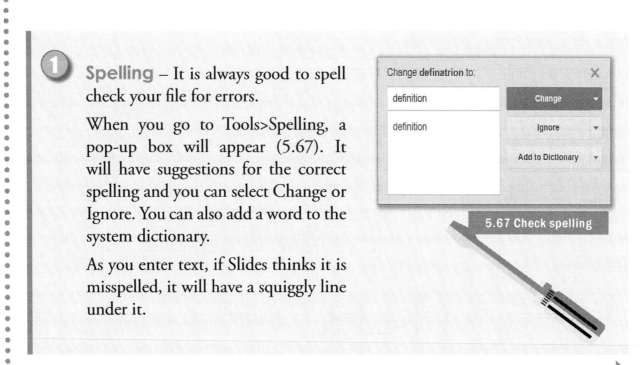

5.67 Check spelling

Explore – Explore in Slides is really a fun tool to use. It is also called Suggested Layouts.

1. Open a presentation in Google Slides.
2. At the bottom right, click Explore.
3. You might see images or information you can use to help finish your work.
   - **Layouts:** To choose a new layout for your slide, click the one you want.
   - **Web search:** Search the web for information related to your presentation.
   - **Images:** To preview an image, click Preview Zoom in. To use an image, click it. This will also add the link to the bottom of the image.
   - ***Google Drive:*** You can search Google Drive for content to use with your presentation.

If you don't see suggestions:

You may not always see suggested layouts in Explore. To help suggested layouts appear, you can:
   - Use a default Slides theme or default Slides layout.
   - Reduce the amount of text on your slides.
   - Remove any shapes on your slide.
   - Make sure all images are at least 100 x 100 pixels in size.

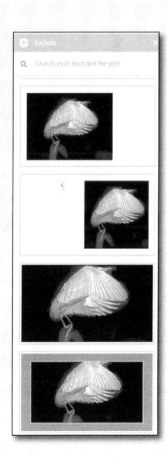

Define – When you select Insert > Define, a Dictionary panel opens. Type in the word that you want a definition for and the breakdown of the word, including it's pronunciation, uses, even synonyms appear.

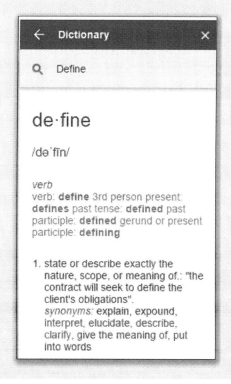

Q&A history – Accept and present audience questions. Presenters can start a live Q&A session with an audience during a presentation with Google Slides. You can present questions at any time, and people can ask questions from any device.

This feature really ties into the collaboration that the Google Apps offer. Within your presention, you can go to Slides QA Presenter view when you start your presentation.

A URL will be displayed that you can share with your audience. Within this URL is where your audience can ask their questions. They can type their question in the box at the top of the screen with the option to remain anonymous.

Their question will be at the top of your screen.

5 Voice type speaker notes – Type with your voice. You can type and edit by speaking in Google Docs or in Google Slides speaker notes.

6 Preferences – Preferences are auto settings that will work in Slides. Automatically capitalize words, Use smart quotes.

7 Personal Dictionary – Words, that aren't normally found in a standard online dictionary, are the words you want to add to your personal dictionary. If you business has a different type of name, add this.

C-9 Text Menu - TABLE

Table

① Insert table ▶

② Insert row above

Insert row below

Insert column left

Insert column right

③ Delete row

Delete column

④ Distribute rows

Distribute columns

⑤ Merge cells

⑥ Unmerge cells

① **Insert table** – A table is a grid of cells arranged in rows and columns. It can be useful to present data in a table inside a word processing document because it is displayed in an organized and easy to read format. You can insert a table anywhere from 1x1 up to 20 x 20 and all equations in-between.

② Inserting rows and columns will add additional rows or columns above, below, right or left in your table.

③ Deleting a row or column will remove that row or column.

④ Distribute rows or columns will give them even spacing.

⑤ Merge cells will combine the cells as one.

⑥ Unmerging cells will put the cells back in the original order.

C-10 Text Menu - KEYBOARD SHORTCUTS

Film strip	
New slide	Ctrl+M
Duplicate slide	Ctrl+D
Move slide up	Ctrl+↑ or Ctrl+←
Move slide down	Ctrl+↓ or Ctrl+→
Move slide to beginning	Ctrl+Shift+↑ or Ctrl+Shift+←
Move slide to end	Ctrl+Shift+↓ or Ctrl+Shift+→
Previous slide	Pg-Up or ←
Next slide	Pg-Down or →
First slide	Home
Last slide	End

With objects	
Duplicate	Ctrl+D
Group	Ctrl+Alt+G
Ungroup	Ctrl+Alt+Shift+G
Bring forward	Ctrl+↑
Send backward	Ctrl+↓
Bring to front	Ctrl+Shift+↑
Send to back	Ctrl+Shift+↓
Rotate clockwise by 15°	Alt+→
Rotate counter-clockwise by 15°	Alt+←
Resize larger	Ctrl+Alt+K
Resize larger horizontally	Ctrl+Alt+B
Resize larger vertically	Ctrl+Alt+I
Resize smaller	Ctrl+Alt+J
Resize smaller horizontally	Ctrl+Alt+W
Resize smaller vertically	Ctrl+Alt+Q
Select next shape	Tab
Select previous shape	Shift+Tab

Suppress guides (with mouse)	Alt+Drag
Duplicate (with mouse)	Ctrl+Drag
Only move vertically or horizontally (with mouse)	Shift+Drag
Rotate by 15° increments (with mouse)	Shift+Rotate
Keep object's aspect ratio (with mouse)	Shift+Resize
Resize from center (with mouse)	Ctrl+Resize

Selection	
Add to selection	Shift+Click
Select only completely enclosed shapes	Alt+Click

Text formatting	
Bold	Ctrl+B
Italic	Ctrl+I
Underline	Ctrl+U
Strikethrough	Alt+Shift+5
Superscript	Ctrl+.
Subscript	Ctrl+,
Clear formatting	Ctrl+\ or Ctrl+Space

Paragraph formatting	
Left align text	Ctrl+Shift+L
Justify text	Ctrl+Shift+J
Right align text	Ctrl+Shift+R
Toggle numbered list	Ctrl+Shift+7
Toggle bulleted list	Ctrl+Shift+8

Editing	
Insert link...	Ctrl+K
Define word	Ctrl+Shift+Y

Navigation	
Chat	Shift+Esc

Move to next misspelling	Ctrl+'
Move to previous misspelling	Ctrl+;
Zoom in	Ctrl+Alt++ or Ctrl+Alt+=
Zoom out	Ctrl+Alt+- or Ctrl+Alt+-
Explore	Ctrl+Alt+Shift+I

Menus	
File menu	Alt+Shift+F or Alt+F
Edit menu	Alt+Shift+E or Alt+E
View menu	Alt+Shift+V or Alt+V
Insert menu	Alt+Shift+I or Alt+I
Slide menu	Alt+Shift+S
Format menu	Alt+Shift+O or Alt+O
Arrange menu	Alt+Shift+R
Tools menu	Alt+Shift+T or Alt+T
Table menu	Alt+Shift+B or Alt+B
Help menu	Alt+Shift+H or Alt+H
Context menu	Ctrl+Shift+\ or Ctrl+Shift+X

Comments	
Add comment	Ctrl+Alt+M
Open comments thread...	Ctrl+Alt+Shift+A
Enter current comment	Ctrl+Alt+E Ctrl+Alt+C
Move to next comment	Ctrl+Alt+N Ctrl+Alt+C
Move to previous comment	Ctrl+Alt+P Ctrl+Alt+C

⑥ FORMS
Created, Edited And Stored Online

Plan events, make a survey or poll, give students a quiz, or collect other information in an easy, streamlined way with Google Forms.

Google Forms can make use of a variety of question types to gather information in an organized manner. Forms can also be customized and personalized. All responses are automatically collected in a Google Sheet, which makes data analysis easier. Some teachers even use Google Forms to quiz their students.

A. HOW TO GET TO YOUR FORMS

1

After your have logged into your Chrome account, type in

https://forms.google. com

2

Go to the waffle and select the yellow rectangle icon.

3

From your Drive, select **BLUE NEW** button and go down to MORE, and than go to Forms.

Survey

'ser,vā/

noun

- examine and record the area and features of (an area of land) so as to construct a map, plan, or description

verb

- (of a person or their eyes) look carefully and thoroughly at (someone or something), especially so as to appraise them.

  "her green eyes surveyed him coolly"

- synonyms: look at, look over, observe, view, contemplate, regard, gaze at, stare at, eye; More

Selecting the Waffle Icon or typing into the omnibox forms.google.com, will take you to the repository of all your forms.

Templates . . similar to Docs and Sheets, Forms has ready made templates for your usage to help save your time.

B. FEATURES OVERVIEW - SETTINGS

Google Forms is now a full-featured forms tool that comes free with your Google account.

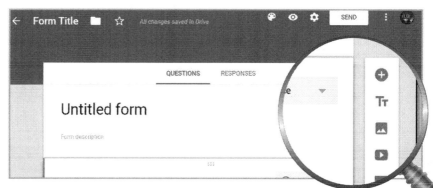

Running across the top menu gives you the action items that you can change the form's color scheme, preview it, use the Send button to share the form, and access other extra options, such as installing add-ons.

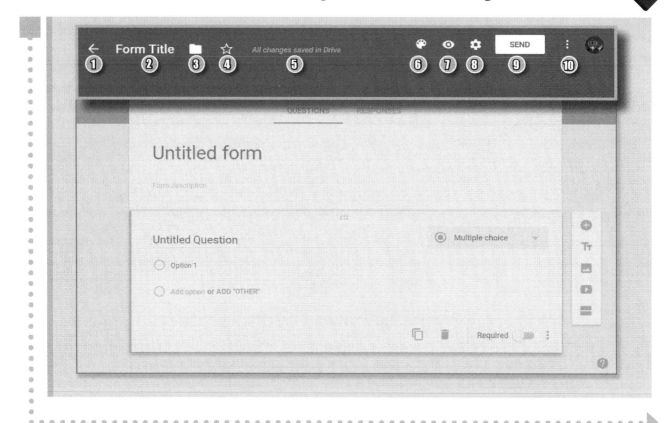

Home – Selecting the left facing arrow will take you back to the Forms repository where you will find the Forms templates and any of your existing forms.

Untitled Form – Make sure to give your form a name that you will remember. If you don't title it, you will have a lot of Untitled forms in your Forms repository.

Move to – Selecting the folder icon will give you the option to move your document to another location.

Star – Starring a document gives it importance and makes your file easier to search for.

All changes saved in drive – Every change you make is automatically saved in your drive.

Color palette – Clicking the color palette in the top right corner gives you the option to customize your form. There are 15 colors, which provide a dark color for the top section and a complimentary shade for the bottom (6.1).

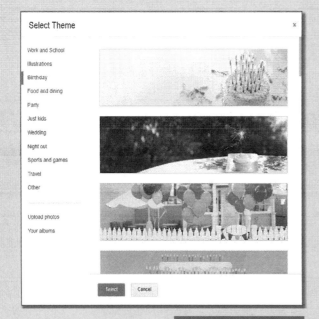

6.3 Google's library

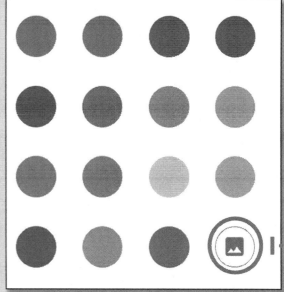

6.1 Colors choices

6.2 Photo icon

Click the photo icon (6.2) to select a photo or one of Google's style headers from Google's library (6.3) as your form's header photo. Or, you can also upload on of your photos, crop it to fit in as a form header. Forms will then automatically select a background color that matches your photo.

Some header images are animated GIFs such as burning candles, moving balls, and more, but if you add them to your form, they appear as a standard still image.

Preview – Clicking the eye icon will open a new tab in Chrome and give you a preview of what your for will look like. In this preview (6.4) is a pencil icon in the upper right corner which will take you back to editing your form.

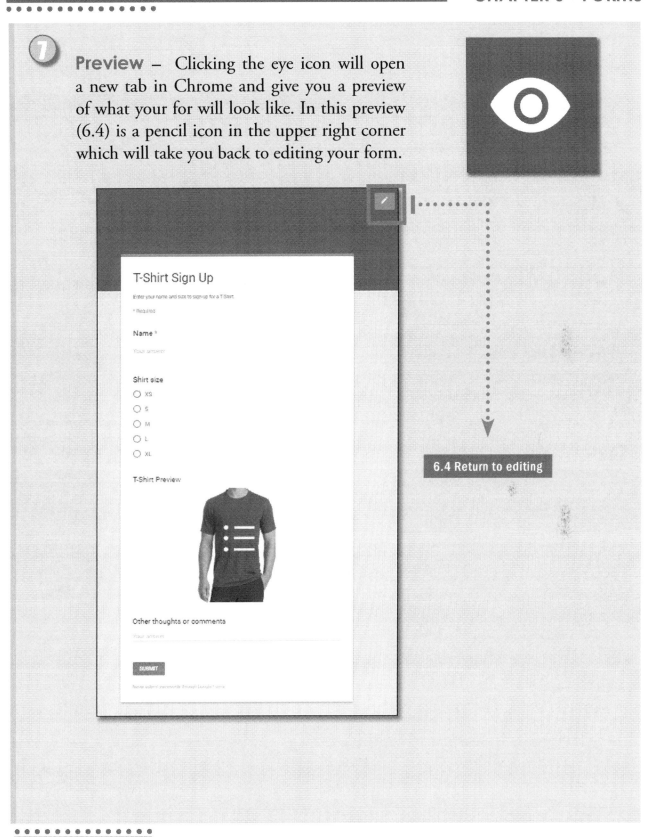

6.4 Return to editing

Settings – Clicking the gear icon will bring up the settings for your form.

General settings – Some of the things that will be present when you are in General (6.5) are:

- Collect email address.
- Response receipts - Respondents receive a copy of their answers.
- Limit to 1 response - respondent will have to sign into their Gmail account.

Respondents can:

- Edit after submit - change their answers.
- See summary charts and text responses - they will see other's answers.

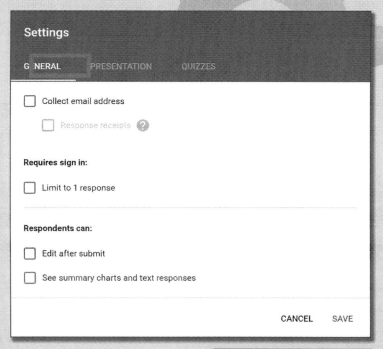

6.5 General Settings

Presentation settings – Some of the things that will be present when you are in Presentation (6.6) are:

- Show progress bar - a bar will appear showing amount finished and to go.
- Shuffle question order - Questions will randomly be moved.
- Show link to submit another response.
- Confirmation message: You can type in what you would like here i.e. *Thank your for your response.*

6.6 Presentation settings

Quizzes settings – Some of the things that will be present when you are in General (6.7) are:

- Make this a quiz - all will be grayed out if this is not turned on. Select the lever to turn on.

- Assign point values to questions and allow auto-grading.

Quiz options
Release Grade (two options):

- Immediately after each submission

- Later, after manual review - Turns on email collection

Respondent can see:

- Missed questions - Identify which questions were answered incorrectly.

- Correct answers - Show the correct answer for each question after grades are released.

- Point values - Show total points and points received for each question.

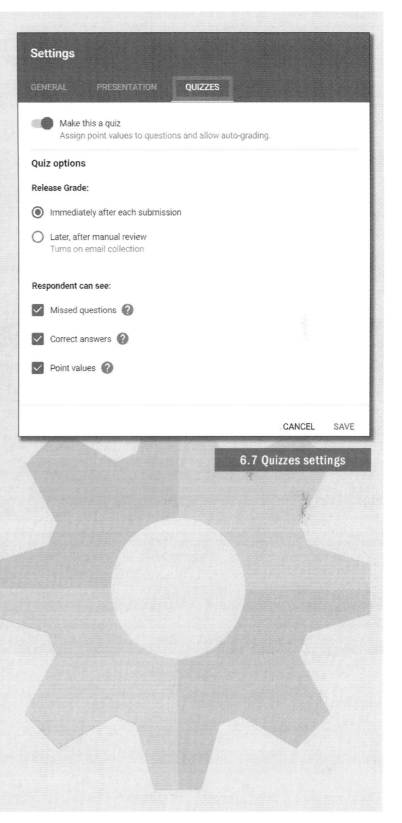

6.7 Quizzes settings

SEND

Send – You have created your form, now how are you going to deliver it to your recipients? Across the three standard ways and three social media avenues to send it.

Send via email – You can notify recipients via email (6.8). They can get a notice in their email with a button to click to Fill out form (6.9);

Put a check mark in the area to Include form in email and the entire form will be embedded and easily viewed right in the email to fill out and be submitted right there (6.10).

At the bottom of this section, you can Add collaborators. These collaborators can go into the form and have access to edit it.

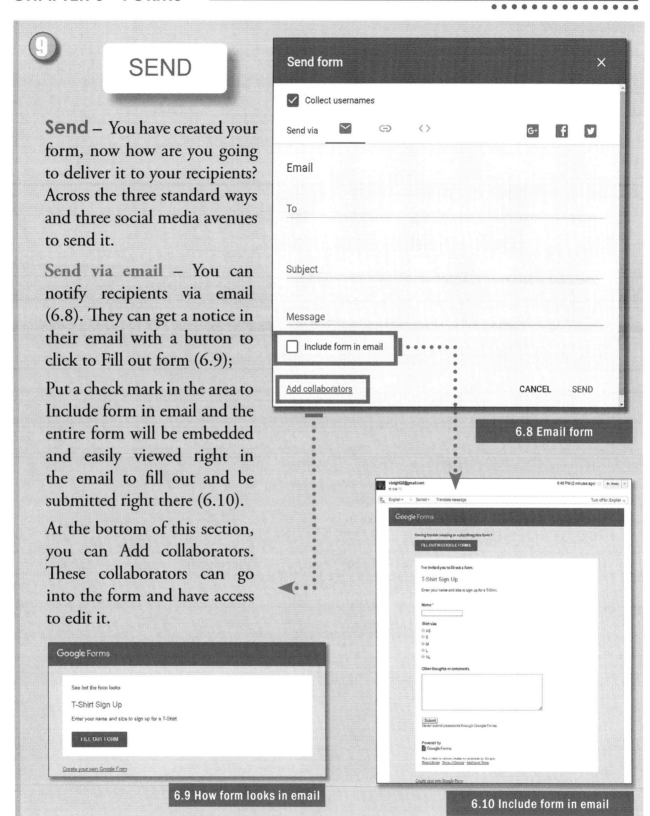

6.8 Email form

6.9 How form looks in email

6.10 Include form in email

Send via link – You can notify recipients via link (6.11). This link can be included in an email, add link on any of the other Google products such as Docs, Sheets, or Slides. The link can be added in navigation of a website.

At the bottom of this section gives you the option to Shorten the URL.

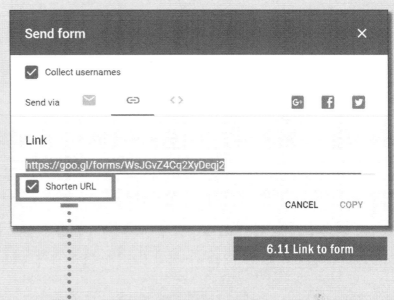

6.11 Link to form

Embed HTML – You embed the form in a webpage via an iFrame code (6.12). You are also given the option to change the width and height for you code.

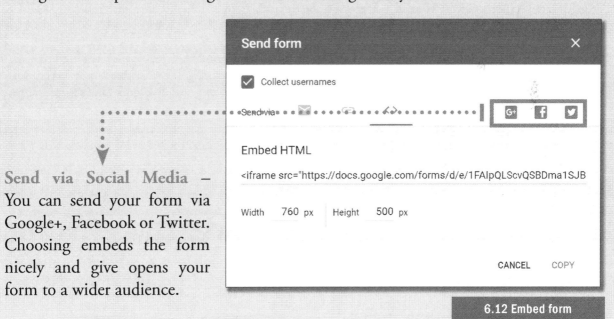

Send via Social Media – You can send your form via Google+, Facebook or Twitter. Choosing embeds the form nicely and give opens your form to a wider audience.

6.12 Embed form

More – Additional actions are under the three dot ellipse.

1. Preview - sames as on the previous number 7 of this section. You can see a preview of how your form will look to the recipients.

2. Settings - Full explanation in number 8 of this section.

3. Undo - Takes your form back one step in it's creation process.

4. Star - Adds importance to this form that is good for a filtering process.

5. Make a copy - You like your form and want to use it for another survey / quiz but you want to keep the original, so you can make a copy and edit it as you want to.

6. Move to folder - Keeping files in a folder is a good organizational skill to get in the habit of doing.

7. Move to trash - Moves to trash but does not completely delete it until you empty your trash.

8. Get pre-filled link - To send the pre-populated form to respondents, copy and send the link at the top of the form.

9. Print - Will give you a paper copy of your form.

10. Add collaborators - These collaborators can go into the form and have access to edit it

11. Help Center - Go to Help Center for any questions or issues you have.

12. Report a problem - Reports to Google any issues.

👁	Preview
⚙	Settings
↶	Undo
☆	Star
🗐	Make a copy
📁	Move to folder
🗑	Move to trash
⊖	Get pre-filled link
🖨	Print
+👥	Add collaborators...
❓	Help Center
📢	Report a problem

C. CREATING YOUR FORM - QUESTIONS

The Forms editor is very user friendly.

Your form lays in the center of the screen, beginning with a space for a title and description followed by form fields. Click a form field to edit it and add a question. Use the drop-down box next to the field to choose the field type, such as multiple choice, check boxes, short answer, and so on. The floating tool bar on the right lets you add more form fields. Switch between the Questions tab to the Responses tab in your form editor to see current responses to your form and link it to a spreadsheet.

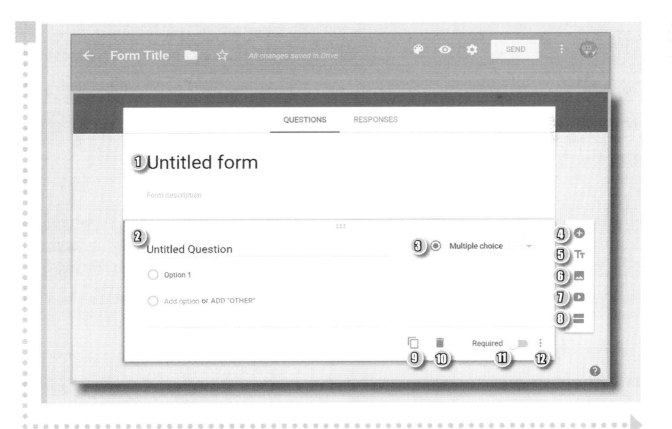

1 **Untitled Form** – As soon as you create a new form, a title and description fields are added automatically. You do not have the ability to add formatting to the title, description, or any of the form questions.

2 **Untitled Question** – By default, the Untitled Form will have one Untitled Question for you to start with. There are nine different question types that you can choose from, along with photo upload, text, and video.

3

Question types – Listed below are the nine question types and a description of each one.

☰	Short answer
☰	Paragraph
⊙	Multiple choice
☑	Checkboxes
⊙	Dropdown
••••	Linear scale
⊞	Multiple choice grid
📅	Date
🕐	Time

Short Answer – This field is used to gather names, email addresses, values, and more. You get one line of text to answer the question—though your users could actually enter as much text as they want.

There is validation that you can do with the Short Answer field (6.13). *You must select the 3 dots as shown in number 13 of this section.* Once you select the 3 dots, you can select to add a Description. also you can select Response Validation. Selecting one of the below fields will filter to a further selection field.

The Short Answer field can be:
    a. Number (6.14)
    b. Text (6.15)
    c. Length (6.16)
    d. Regular expression (6.17)

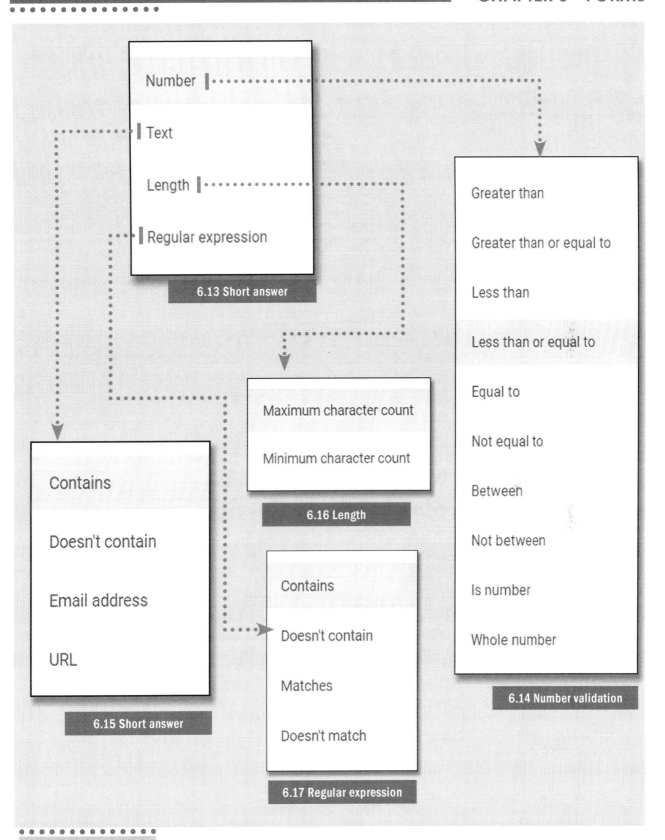

Number

Text

Length

Regular expression

6.13 Short answer

Greater than

Greater than or equal to

Less than

Less than or equal to

Equal to

Not equal to

Between

Not between

Is number

Whole number

6.14 Number validation

Maximum character count

Minimum character count

6.16 Length

Contains

Doesn't contain

Email address

URL

6.15 Short answer

Contains

Doesn't contain

Matches

Doesn't match

6.17 Regular expression

Paragraph Answer – Similar to the short answer field, this is a field for text—long-form text. Length and regular expression are the only data validations available here, so only use it when you want detailed feedback or longer notes in the answer.

Maximum Character Count

Minimum Character Count

Length

Regular Expression

Contains

Doesn't contain

Matches

Doesn't match

Multiple Choice – This is the default choice for a new questions Form. A respondent has the choices of what options you have listed. There is not Date Validation for a multiple choice but the respondent can jump to another section based on the answer.

Multiple Choice

What is your favorite color?

○ Red

○ Blue

○ Green

○ Other: _____

SUBMIT

Never submit passwords through Google Forms.

Checkboxes – This options is the same as multiple choice but instead you can list your answers and have them select as many as they want. You can have data validation that would require a users to select a specific number of options.

Select at least

Select at most

Select exactly

Dropdown – A dropdown create a type of menu, such as what is used in a website. Similar to multiple choice, with the same section jump and shuffle options, only in a menu. Good if you want to save space in your form.

Linear Scale – Have you ever gotten that survey where they want you to rank them on a scale of 0 to 10? This is a linear scale.

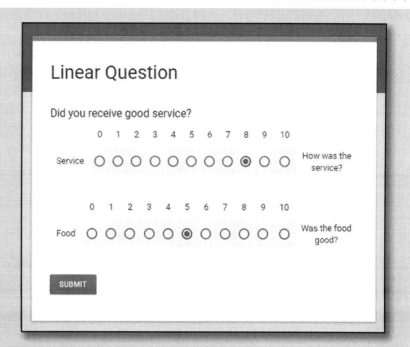

Multiple Choice Grid – This is a very confusing option. The entry fields are displayed in a list instead of a grid. You can include as man rows and columns as you would like.

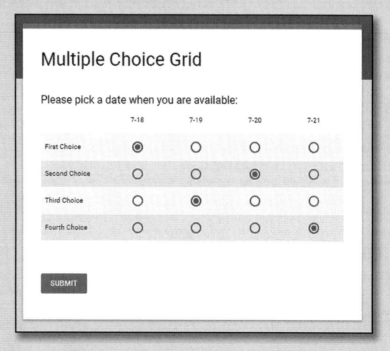

Date – To choose a date, a pop up calendar will appear and you can choose a date.

Time – To choose a time, you can enter it and choose AM or PM.

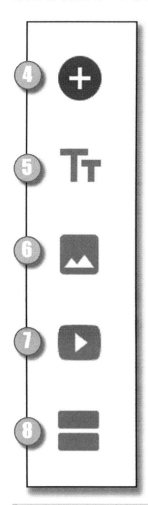

New question – Clicking the circle with the plus in the center will instantly add a new question to your form. The default question field type will be multiple choice.

Add title and description – You can have multiple titles and descriptions, not just at the top of your form. Good option to use if you have multiple sections.

Images – You upload an image, insert one from a link or Google Drive, or take a photo from your own webcam (as long as you have Flash installed). Or, you can search Google Images for photos, including royalty free stock photo and images from LIFE that are licensed to use inside Google Drive.

Video – The two choices for inserting a video are either a YouTube video or a URL.

Add Section – You can have as many sections as you like in your form. You can have your answer from your questions go to a different section in your form based on their answer.

Duplicate – Selecting the duplicate icon will create an exact copy of the last question. Great time saving feature!

Trash – Selecting the trashcan will delete and remove from your form the question you are on.

Required – If you take the button and slide it right, it will require an answer for the specific question. The respondent will not be able to submit the form if they do not answer that specific required question.

Not Required

Required

More – Selecting the three dots will change depending on which question type you have selected.

Some of the choices will be the data validation as talked about in the questions plus the option to add a new section.

D. CREATING YOUR FORM - RESPONSES

Your Form Responses

The whole reason your are creating a form, survey, or quiz is to obtain the responses. Google Forms breaks down the responses by offering charts and graphs so you can analyze the data, or grade the test.

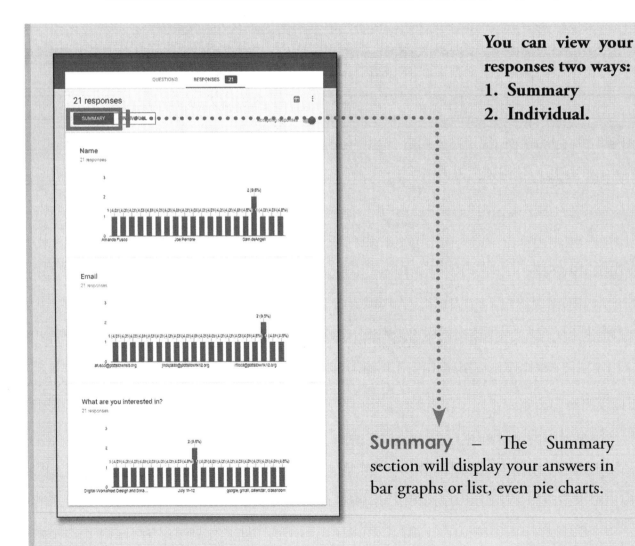

You can view your responses two ways:
1. **Summary**
2. **Individual.**

Summary – The Summary section will display your answers in bar graphs or list, even pie charts.

Individual – You can scroll through the individual answers to your form in the Individual tab (6.18).

Clicking on the forward arrows will take you to each individual answer (6.19). You can also print and trash each response separately.

6.18 Individual Summary

6.19 Scroll navigation

Create Spreadsheet – When you send a form, you can gather the responses inside the form or separately in Google Sheets.

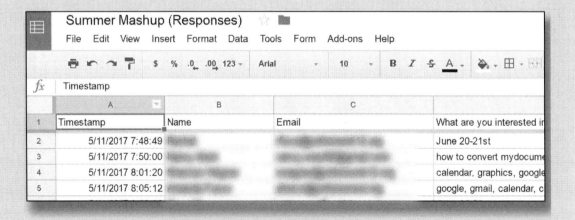

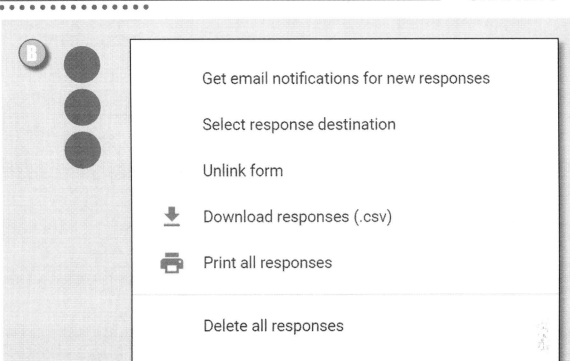

More – Selecting the three dots will give you more actions items that you can do as listed in the image above.

Accepting responses – If you turn this off, your form will no longer accept responses. Good if you are giving a quiz and you want to limit and give a time frame.

7 DRAWINGS

Web-based diagramming

Create charts, flowcharts, website wireframes, and picture annotation

Create vector drawings . . .

. . . in real time to create graphic organization, infographs, annotations of images, timelines and share for real time collaboration with your team! A fun, easy to use tool with a low learning curve!

A. HOW TO GET TO YOUR FORMS

1

After your have logged into your Chrome account, type in

https://drawings.google.com

2

From your Drive, select **BLUE NEW** button and go down to MORE, and than go to Drawings.

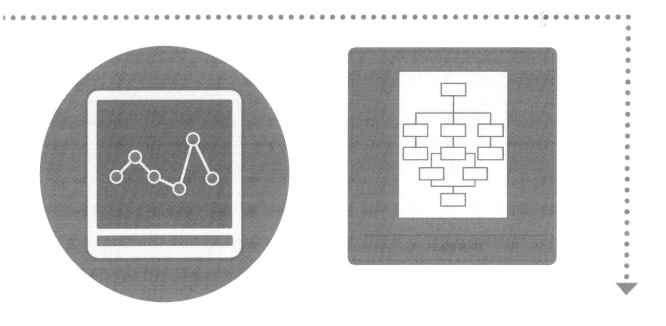

B. FEATURES OVERVIEW

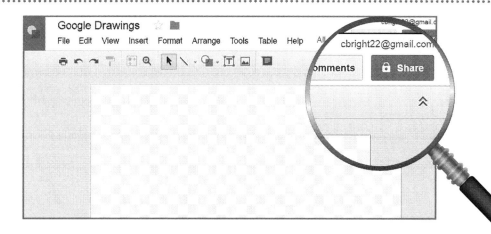

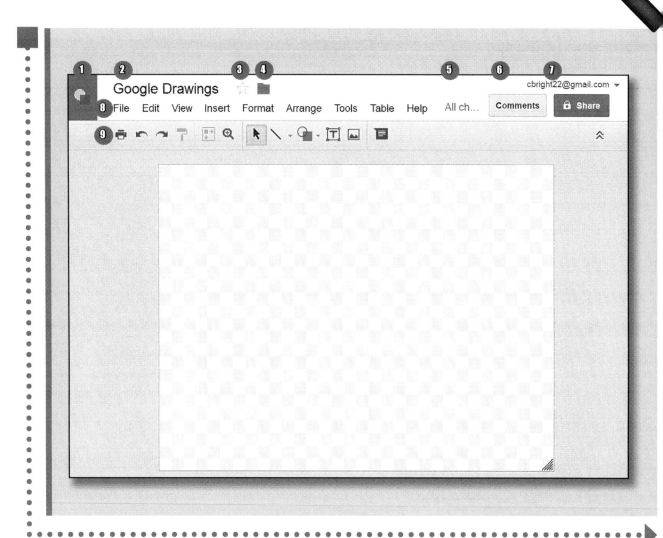

1

Open Google Drive – When you hover over the rectangle, a message appears stating "Open Google Drive", and clicking here will take you to your Drive.

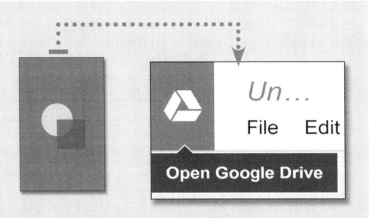

2

Title – Your drawing will default to say "Untitled". Good file management entails naming your files.

3

Star – Adding a star to your drawing will give it importance and easier to find in a search.

4

Folder – Selecting the folder, will take you to your Drive and you can place your Drawing in a new folder, in an existing folder, or just in your drive.

5

All changes saved – This message informs you that your changes are saved and if you click here, you will be taken to your revision history.

6

Comment – Select this icon and a comment box will appear for you to insert your comment. Using this box, you can type in suggestions that you think would improve the file.

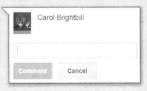

7

Share – The first thing under the file menu is one of the most important things about Google Apps, the ability to **Share** your file. I covered this intensively in the Drive section, pages 40-49.

8   **Text Menu** – Part C of this chapter will cover the Text Menu fully.

9   **Icon Menu –**

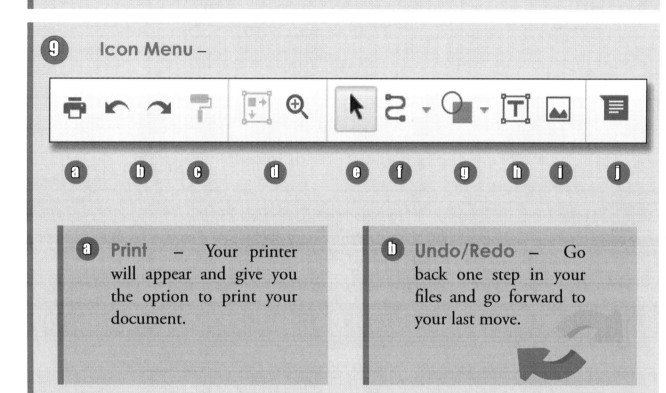

   a   **b**   **c**   **d**   **e**   **f**   **g**   **h**   **i**   **j**

a **Print** – Your printer will appear and give you the option to print your document.

b **Undo/Redo** – Go back one step in your files and go forward to your last move.

c **Paint Format** – This handy tool will copy the formatting of text, cells, or an object with the paint format tool.

1. Open a Google file.
2. Select the text, range of cells, or object you want to copy the format of.
3. In the toolbar, click Paint format .
4. Select what you want to paste the formatting onto.

d **Fit / Zoom** – You first select the magnifying glass icon (7.1) and touch the screen slide will increase size each time you touch it. You select the Fit to view (7.2) icon to fit the screen back to normal size.

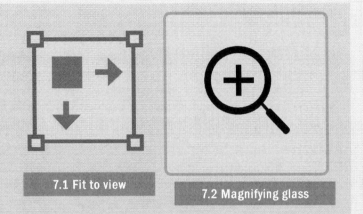

7.1 Fit to view

7.2 Magnifying glass

e **Select** – When you place any object on the Drawing canvas, you must first select if for any formatting or moving that you want to do it it.

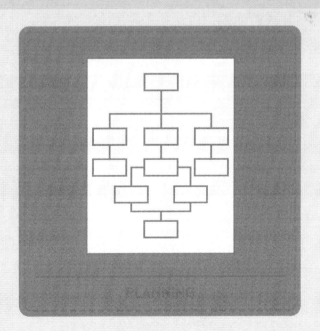

Line – There are seven line options (7.3). The lines and the shapes are good to combine together to make flowcharts and diagrams.

To create a flowchart, you can select the line tool and pick an arrow or connector to connect two shapes. You can place the shapes anywhere on the screen and the connectors would follow (7.4).

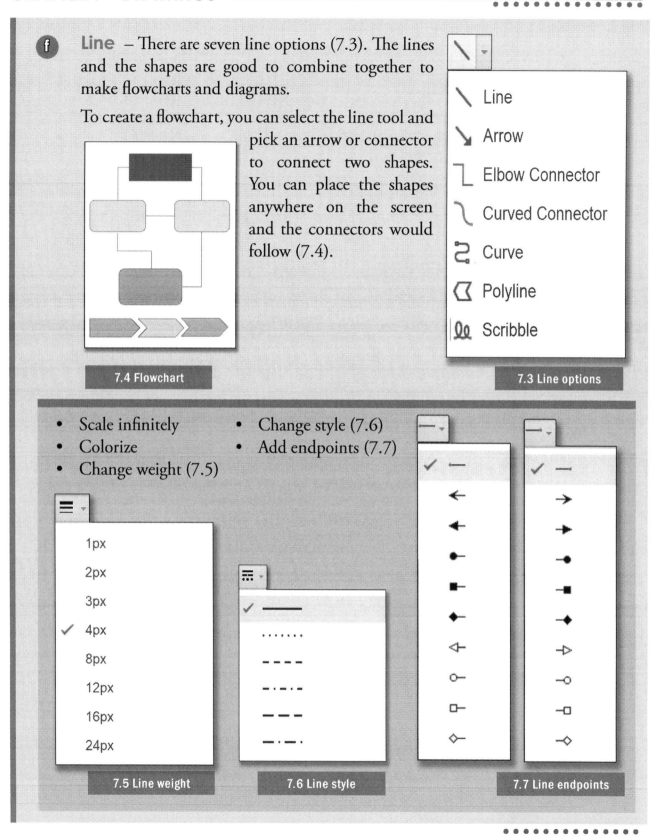

7.4 Flowchart

\	Line
\	Arrow
⌐	Elbow Connector
(	Curved Connector
ꙅ	Curve
《	Polyline
ℓℓ	Scribble

7.3 Line options

- Scale infinitely
- Colorize
- Change weight (7.5)
- Change style (7.6)
- Add endpoints (7.7)

1px
2px
3px
✓ 4px
8px
12px
16px
24px

7.5 Line weight

7.6 Line style

7.7 Line endpoints

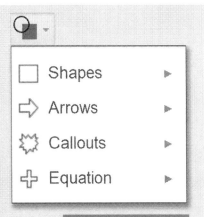

Shape – There are four category of shapes (7.8). The shapes use mathematic equations and geometric primitives (points, lines, and shapes) to create art that is clean and can be scaled infinitely, without any loss of quality.

The things you can do with a text box are:

7.8 Shape categories

Some of the shapes have a yellow diamond joint (7.9) and when you grab this circle, you can adjust and change the shape.

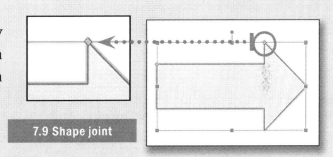

7.9 Shape joint

Shapes

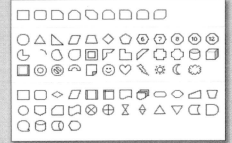

Arrows

Callouts

Equation

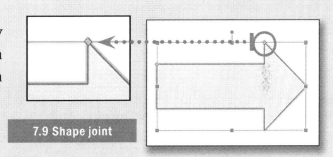

h **Text Box** – The text box is an entry field where the user can enter the information that they want to present.

The things you can do with a text box are:

- Resize it to whatever size you want.
- Enter verbiage.
- Rotate it.
- Add a stroke.
- Add a background fill.
- Change the text color.

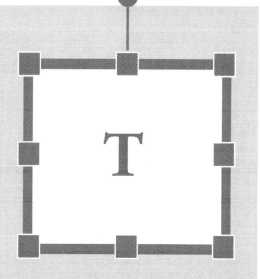

i **Image**– You can take your slides to the next level and go from boring to quite interesting by just adding a picture. As the saying goes, "A picture is worth a thousand words". There are six different ways to add an image. Images must be less than 50 MB and be one of the following file types: .gif; .jpg; or.png.

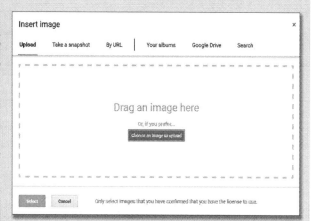

1. **Upload** – Selecting to upload will take your to your computer's hard drive and select Open.
2. **Take a snapshot** – If your device has a camera, you can take a snapshot and insert it directly into the document.
3. **By URL** – Paste the URL of an image from the web and click Select.
4. **Your albums** – Choose an image from one of your photos albums stored on the web and click Select.
5. **Google Drive** – Choose an image stored in Google Drive and click Select.
6. **Search** – Choose an image from the stock photography archive, or the Google and Life archives, and click Select.

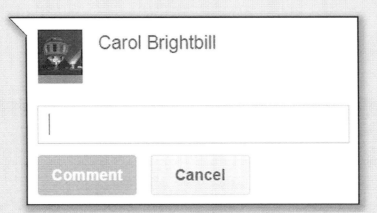

Comment – Select the cell where you would like to attach the comment and the comment box will appear for you to insert your comment. That cell will than have a triangle in the upper right corner to indicate that a comment is there.

Using this box, you can type in suggestions that you think would improve the file.

C. TEXT MENU

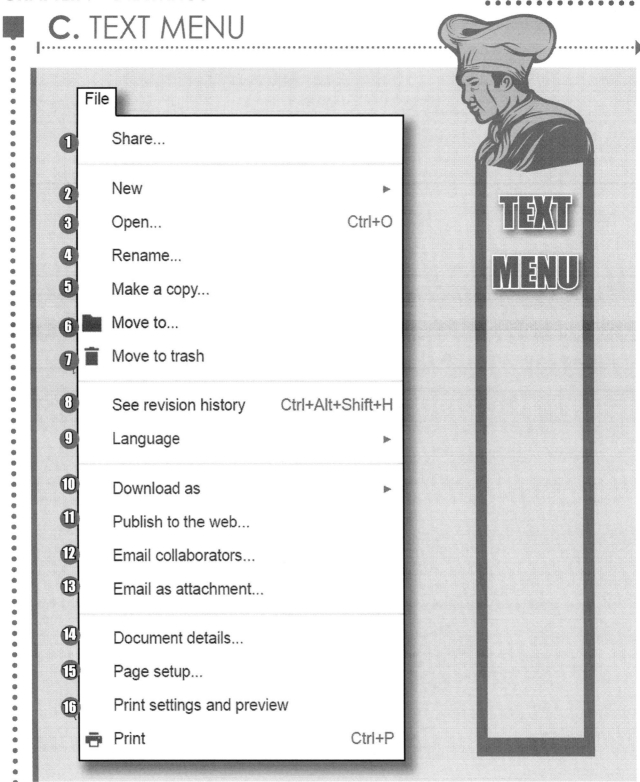

File

1. Share...

2. New ▶

3. Open... Ctrl+O

4. Rename...

5. Make a copy...

6. Move to...

7. Move to trash

8. See revision history Ctrl+Alt+Shift+H

9. Language ▶

10. Download as ▶

11. Publish to the web...

12. Email collaborators...

13. Email as attachment...

14. Document details...

15. Page setup...

16. Print settings and preview

Print Ctrl+P

TEXT MENU

C-1 TEXT MENU - FILE

1 **Share** – The first thing under the file menu is one of the most important things about Google Apps, the ability to **Share** your file. I covered this intensively in the Drive section, pages 40-49.

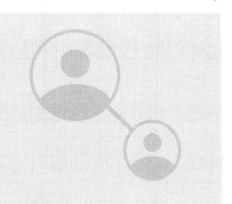

2 **New** – Clicking the New will show how dynamic the Google Apps are. From the New, you can create any one of the Google core apps. Additionally, you can select to create a new Doc from a template.

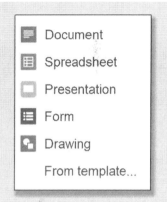

3 **Open** – Selecting **Open** gives you the choices of going to:

- My Drive
- Shared with Me
- Starred
- Recent
- Upload

Selecting dropdown arrow will let you open by file type.

4 Rename – When you select Rename, your cursor will instantly pop up to where your file has it's existing name and it will be highlighted. Renaming does not make an additional file, it just gives your existing file a new name.

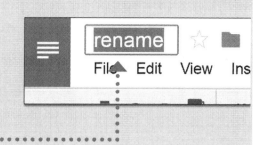

5 Make A Copy – There are two reasons to make a copy of your file:

1. When a file is shared and the rights are **View Only**, you can not edit the file. This is a smart practice to maintain the integrity of your file. If you select **Make a Copy**, you can rename it, now it is yours to go into and edit.

2. You want to update a file with new information but you want to keep the original file. This is another reason to make a copy of your original, so you can have a different version with the new information and keep your old version.

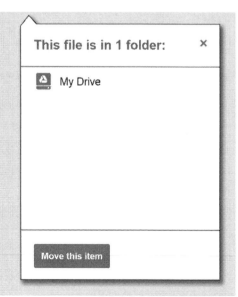

6 Move to – Selecting the folder icon will give you the option to move your document to another location. Especially if you created your file in the drive, it is better than just hanging loose with in your Drive folder.

This file is in 1 folder: ✕

My Drive

Move this item

7 **Move to trash** – This will delete your file from your drive but it is not permanently deleted until you delete it from your trash.

8 **See Revision History** – Gone are the days of paper drafts that teachers reviewed to see the thought process of their student. This is where Revision History comes in handy. It is also a great way to keep students, working on teams collaborating honest! You can see who has done what in the file.

When you choose **File > See Revision History**, another window opens showing the document, and a side bar will appear that details all the changes within the document.

You can select various dates or times and see the changes that occurred. You can also restore a previous version from this area.

When you restore a previous version, you do not loose any of the other versions, the restored version just jumps to the top.

Revision history

March

▼ **March 22, 7:43 AM**
■ Carol Brightbill

   March 22, 7:42 AM
   ■ Carol Brightbill

▶ March 20, 2:01 PM
■ Carol Brightbill

   March 20, 12:53 PM
   ■ Carol Brightbill

▶ March 17, 8:44 PM
■ Carol Brightbill

   March 17, 8:26 PM
   ■ Carol Brightbill

☑ Show changes

9

Language – To change your typing language.

Step 1:
1. Open a document in Google Drawing
2. Go to the top menu
3. Click File
4. Then Language and then the language you need.

7.10 Choose Keyboard icon

Step 2:
1. Choose keyboard icon at far right of icon menu (7.10)
2. Scroll down and choose the language keyboard you choose in Step 1.

Step 3:
1. Start typing and different language types will appear. (7.11)

7.11 Start typing

Language
1. Лангуаґе
2. Лангуаге
3. Ланґуаґе
4. Ланґуаге
5. Лангуахе
6. Language

10

Download As – You can downloading the file as a PDF, which will maintain the layout and embed the fonts enabling the file to be sent via email.

You also can download as a .jpg or .png.

If you download as a .svg, it is scalable.

PDF Document (.pdf)

JPG image (.jpg)

PNG image (.png)

Scalable Vector Graphics (.svg)

11 **Publish to the web** – Publishing to the web creates a webpage where anyone with the link can view your document.

A URL is created because it is a webpage.

With publishing settings, you can have a

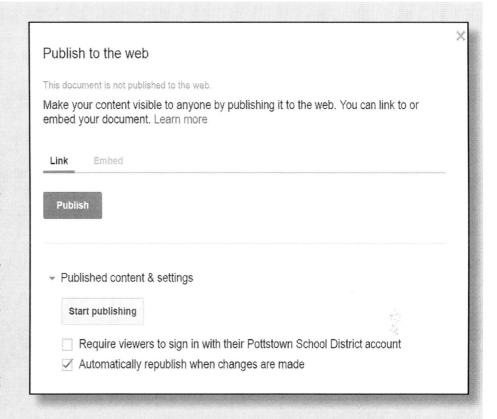

private document - a document in which you select who can edit - and still have it published to either the world or your domain (depending on the settings selected by your Apps administrator). Only users who you gave permission to will be able to view or edit the full original document.

When you publish, you can do the following:

- Create an embeddable HTML version of a doc. The HTML version can be embedded in blogs, Google Sites, and more.

- Show your doc to large web audiences. Only 50 people can view a shared doc at a time, but a lightweight webpage has much, much higher limits.

- Provide quick access to file downloads.

- Publish a one-time snapshot of a your document. To create such a snapshot, make sure you un-check "Automatically republish" when you publish your doc.

12

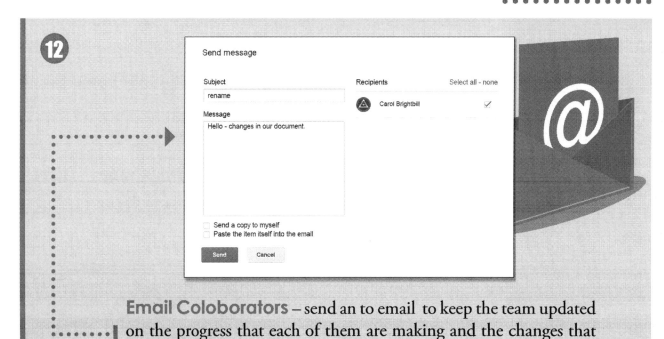

Email Coloborators – send an to email to keep the team updated on the progress that each of them are making and the changes that are happening to the file.

13

Email as Attachment – Not everyone has or uses Google Drawings so when you want to send the file to someone, you do have the option to attached it as a different file type.

PDF Document (.pdf)

JPG image (.jpg)

PNG image (.png)

Scalable Vector Graphics (.svg)

14

Document details – The details of the document provides useful information, especially if you don't know what folder your file is located or who the owner is.

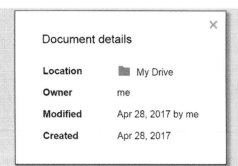

15 **Page Setup** – In page setup you can change the size of your page layout to be any size you want it to be.

This is why I think that Drawings is a great layout program that can be used similarly to the professional programs. You get there by choosing File > Page setup. In the middle of the box that appears will display Widescreen 16:9, and when you select this, you have 4 options:

- Standard 4:3
- Widescreen 16:10
- Widescreen 16:9
- Custom

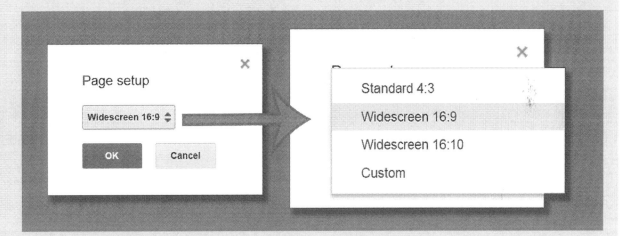

When you select Custom, you can choose 8.5 x 11" for letter size, 8.5 x 14" for legal, 11 x 17" for tabloid size. You can even choose 3.5 x 2" for business cards size and 24" x 36 poster size.

16 **Print Settings and Preview**– Open the drawing you want to print.

1. Click File and then Print settings and preview. A new window with a preview of your presentation and print options will open.

2. You can print from here.

C-2 TEXT MENU - **EDIT**

Edit	
1 Undo	Ctrl+Z
2 Redo	Ctrl+Y
3 Cut	Ctrl+X
4 Copy	Ctrl+C
5 Paste	Ctrl+V
6 Paste without formatting	Ctrl+Shift+V
7 Delete	Delete
8 Duplicate	Ctrl+D
9 Web clipboard	▶
10 Select all	Ctrl+A
11 Select none	Ctrl+Shift+A
12 Find and replace...	Ctrl+H

Where would word processing be without cut, copy, paste! And Control Z!! The best ever! Let's go down the menu:

1. **Undo** – action that takes you back one step in your editing.

2. **Redo** – action that jumps you back to where your were before your Undo.

3. **Cut** – places what you cut onto the computer clipboard and removes it from your file.

4. **Copy** – places what you copy onto the computer clipboard and leaves it in your file. Your computer clipboard only holds one item, the last thing you either copied or cut.

5. **Paste** – pasting will put whatever you cut or copied, from the computer's clipboard onto your file.

6. **Paste without formatting** – existing formatting from what your cut or copied will be stripped away when you paste and your content will take on the existing format where it is being pasted into.

7. **Delete** – whatever is selected will be removed from the page when you select delete.

8. **Duplicate** – an exact copy will be created from anything you have selected and you select duplicate.

9

Web clipboard – Copying to the Web clipboard is different than just copying to your computer's clipboard.

This clipboard can hold multiple items at once, across different apps. And since your are signed into your Google account, it is also syncs. Items will clear after 30 days.

7.12 Copy selection

 Copy selection to web clipboard

A "Google Docs How do I start ... ▸

Shapes

Clear all items

Web clipboard help

7.13 Existing clipboard

1. Select what you want to copy.
2. Choose Edit > scroll down to Web clipboard.
3. Choose Copy selection to web clipboard. (7.12)

Under where you select Copy selection to web clipboard, you items that are existing on the clipboard will list down (7.13). The next list item is Clear all items.

10

Select all – Depending on if you are in a text box, all your type will be selected, or if you are just on the page, all the items on the page will be selected.

11

Select none – This will deselect what your have selected.

12

Find and replace – Great time saving way to find specific words to replace.

C-3 TEXT MENU - **VIEW**

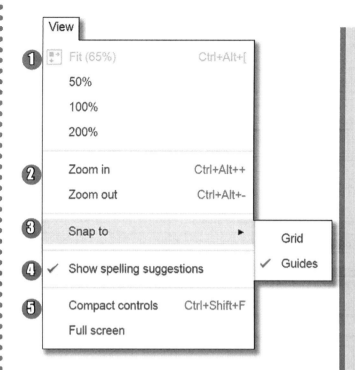

1. **View** – Fit to view, 50%, 100% and 200% viewing your canvas.

2. **Zoom in / Zoom out** – enlarges and reduces your view.

3. **Snap to** – Grid or Guides. When you are on Snap to Guides, a line will show, either horizontally or vertically, to guide you with your alignment.

4. **Show spelling suggestions** – Help with your spelling errors.

5. **Compact controls and Full screen** – Will remove the controls and than show them again.

C-4 TEXT MENU - **INSERT**

Insert

1. T Text box
2. Image...
3. Chart ▶
4. Link... Ctrl+K
5. A Word art
6. \ Line ▶
7. Shape ▶
8. Table ▶
9. Comment Ctrl+Alt+M
10. Ω Special characters...

1 **Text Box** – The text box is an entry field where the user can enter the information that they want to present.

The things you can do with a text box are:

- Resize it to whatever size you want.
- Enter verbiage.
- Rotate it 360.
- Change opacity from 0 to 100.
- Add a stroke from 1, 2, 3, 4, 8, 12, 16, and 24 pixels.
- Add a background fill.
- Change the text color.

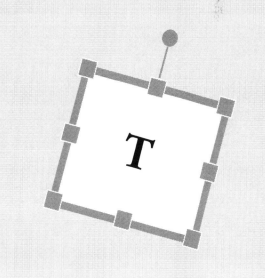

2 **Image**– Importing an image in drawings and adding annotations is one of the many uses for Drawings. There are six different ways to add an image. Images must be less than 50 MB and be one of the following file types: .gif; .jpg; or.png.

1. **Upload** – Selecting to upload will take your to your computer's hard drive and select Open.

2. **Take a snapshot** – If your device has a camera, you can take a snapshot and insert it directly into the document.

3. **By URL** – Paste the URL of an image from the web and click Select.

4. **Your albums** – Choose an image from one of your photos albums stored on the web and click Select.

5. **Google Drive** – Choose an image stored in Google Drive and click Select.

6. **Search** – Choose an image from the stock photography archive, or the Google and Life archives, and click Select.

When an image is inserted in a document, you can edit it in various ways. You must first select the image and than you will be able to either, crop it, recolor it. You will also have adjustments such as transparency, brightness, or contrast. You can also replace the image.

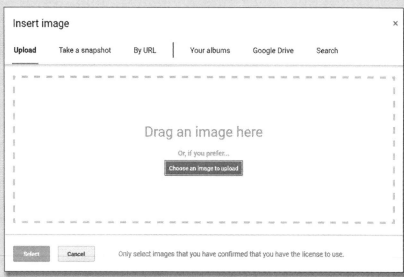

3 **Chart** – You have 4 different types of charts (7.14) that you can insert:

- Bar
- Column
- Line
- Pie

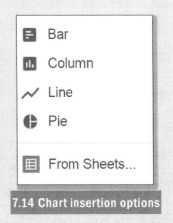

7.14 Chart insertion options

Generic data (7.15) will fill these charts linking to four generic teams. In the upper right corner of these generic charts, are two icons (7.16). The first icon gives you the option to unlink your chart from the Sheets. The second option lets you open up your chart in Sheets and than you can replace the generic data with your own information.

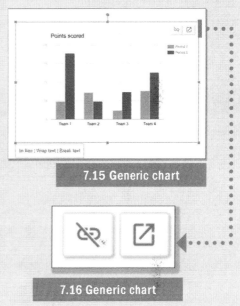

7.15 Generic chart

At the bottom of the CHART insert is the option to insert **From Sheets**. When you choose this option, you will be taken to your Sheets (7.17) and you can choose your existing file. If there is not a chart currently on that Sheet, you will get the message: *"This spreadsheet has no charts."*

7.16 Generic chart

If the Sheet that your are inserting from your own collection of Sheets has more than one chart within it, you can choose which chart you would like to insert into your Docs (7.18).

7.17 Sheet Chart Options

7.18 Multiple charts

4 Link– You can add a link to any object and it turns to a hotspot where the link can go to a web site.

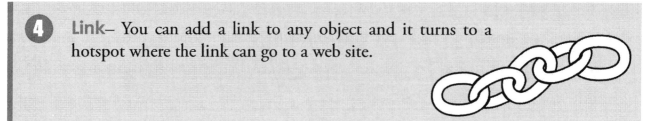

5 Word Art – When you select Insert > Word Art, popup box will appear and type your words in here (7.19).

Word Art|

Use Enter to save. Use Shift+Enter for multiple lines.

7.19 Insert Word Art

Use Enter to save your words gray filled words with a black stroke will appear and you can change the fill color and stroke color, weight, and style to what every you want it to be. (7.20)

7.20 Word Art Example

6 **Line** – There are seven line options (7.21). The lines and the shapes are good to combine together to make flowcharts and diagrams.

To create a flowchart, you can select the line tool and pick an arrow or connector to connect two shapes. You can place the shapes anywhere on the screen and the connectors would follow (7.22).

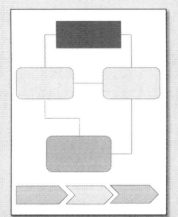

7.21 Flowchart

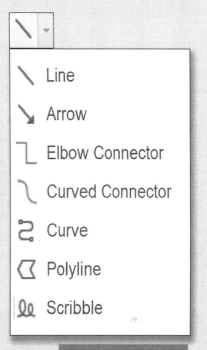

7.22 Line options

- Scale infinitely
- Colorize
- Change weight (7.23)
- Change style (7.24)
- Add endpoints (7.25)

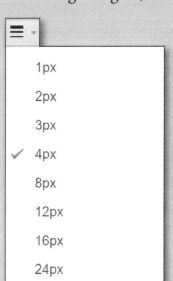

1px
2px
3px
✓ 4px
8px
12px
16px
24px

7.23 Line weight

7.24 Line style

7.25 Line endpoints

7 **Shape** – There are four category of shapes (7.26). The shapes use mathematic equations and geometric primitives (points, lines, and shapes) to create art that is clean and can be scaled infinitely, without any loss of quality.

The things you can do with a text box are:

7.26 Shape categories

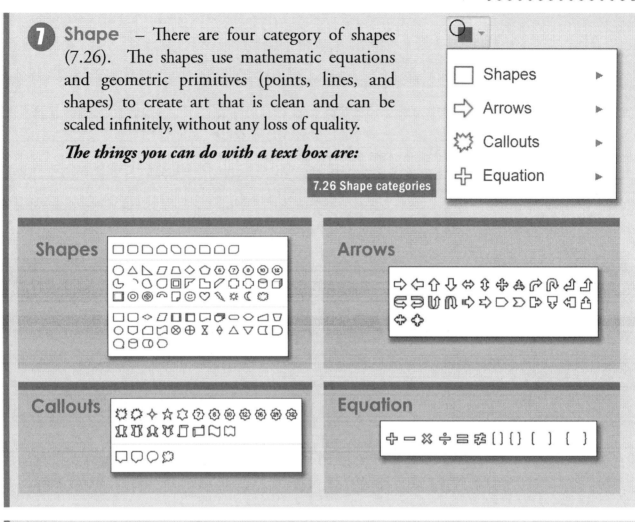

8 **Table** – A table is a grid of cells arranged in rows and columns. It can be useful to present data in a table inside a word processing document because it is displayed in an organized and easy to read format. You can insert a table anywhere from 1x1 up to 20 x 20 and all equations in-between.

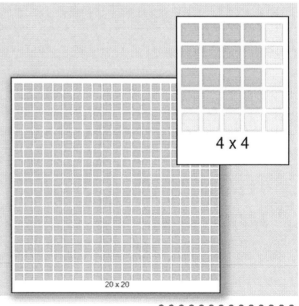

4 x 4

20 x 20

C-5 TEXT MENU - **FORMAT TOP**

Format		
① **B** Bold	Ctrl+B	
_I_ Italic	Ctrl+I	
U̲ Underline	Ctrl+U	
S̶ Strikethrough	Alt+Shift+5	
x² Superscript	Ctrl+.	
x₂ Subscript	Ctrl+,	
② Font size	►	
③ Text color	►	
④ Paragraph styles	►	
⑤ Align	►	
⑥ Line spacing	►	
⑦ Lists	►	

① Always the basic formatting examples of what you can do are:

Bold

Italic

<u>Underline</u>

~~Strikethrough~~

^{Sub}script

$_{Super}$script

②

Font size – Starting with **Font size**, you can increase or reduce the size of your fonts.

Increase font size	Ctrl+Shift+.
Decrease font size	Ctrl+Shift+,

3 **Text color** – You have a wide variety of text and highlight colors to choose from. All the shades of the basic colors are offered by default (7.27).

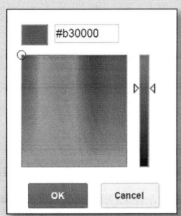

When you select Custom at the bottom of the Default color window (7.28), a pop up window appears where you can move the slider to create a custom color or if you know a HEX color, enter at the top.

7.27 Custom colors

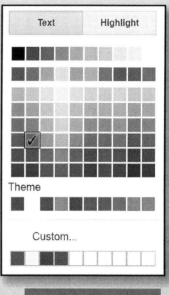

7.28 Default text colors

4 **Paragraph styles** – There are two choices with paragraph styles, to increase the text indent or decrease the text indent.

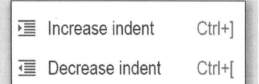

Increase indent   Ctrl+]

Decrease indent   Ctrl+[

5 **Align** – This is the placement of the text within the text box.

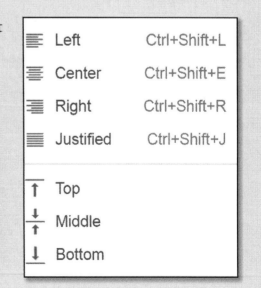

Left   Ctrl+Shift+L

Center   Ctrl+Shift+E

Right   Ctrl+Shift+R

Justified   Ctrl+Shift+J

Top

Middle

Bottom

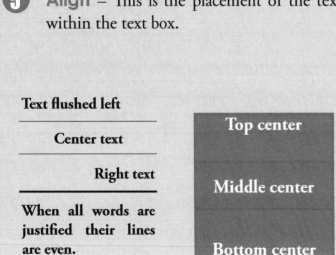

Text flushed left

Center text

Right text

When all words are justified their lines are even.

Top center

Middle center

Bottom center

6 **Line spacing** – Line spacing, in desktop publishing terms is called leading. So, as you add space, it can be (7.29):

- Single - distance equal to the depth of current line.
- 1.15 - distance equal to depth of current line plus .15% extra.
- 1.5 - distance equal to 1 and 1/2 times size of current line.
- Double - distance equal to two times current line depth.

Adding space before and after a paragraph creates a nice break between the paragraphs.

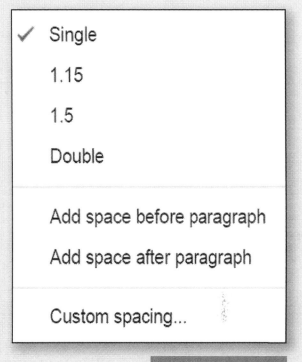

7.29 Line Spacing

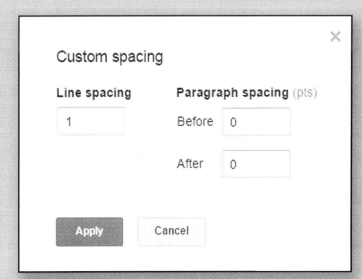

7.30 Custom Spacing

You can add your own custom spacing between lines and between paragraphs or after paragraphs (7.30).

7 **List** – Creating list items a way to help your items stand out or show important steps.

1⅔≡	Numbered list	▶
≔	Bulleted list	▶
	List options	▶

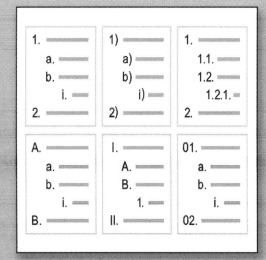

7.31 Numbered list

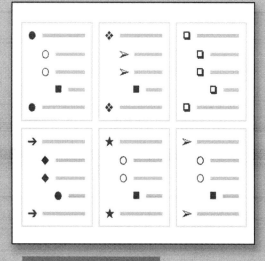

7.32 Bulleted list

When choosing Numbered list (7.31) you can list out numerically and indents will be alphabetical, or list out alphabetical and indents will be numbered.

When choosing Bulleted list (7.32) you can list out with a various shapes, arrows, circles, squares.

List options (7.33) gives you the option to restart numbering, edit prefix and suffix. If you choose More bullets, you will be taken to the number sections of Special Characters, see page 211.

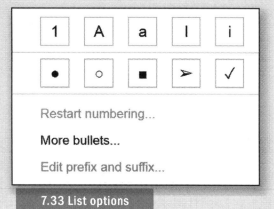

7.33 List options

C-6 TEXT MENU - **FORMAT BOTTOM**

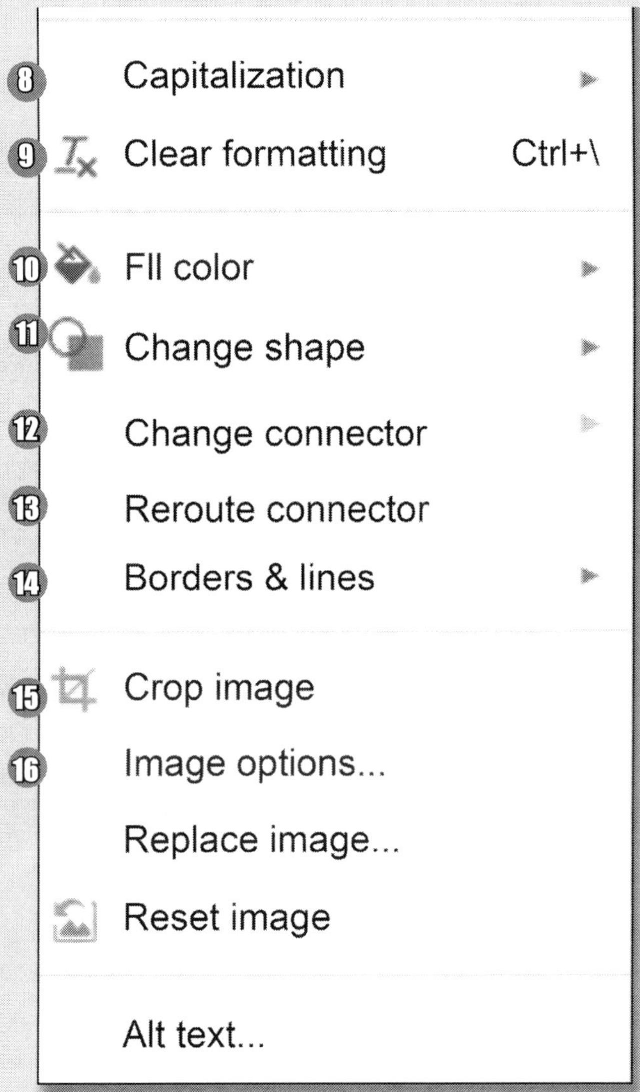

⑧   Capitalization   ▶

⑨ T_x Clear formatting   Ctrl+\

⑩   Fll color   ▶

⑪   Change shape   ▶

⑫   Change connector   ▶

⑬   Reroute connector

⑭   Borders & lines   ▶

⑮   Crop image

⑯   Image options...

     Replace image...

     Reset image

     Alt text...

8 **Capitalization** – Change the case of your text.

> lowercase
>
> UPPERCASE
>
> Title Case

9 **Clear formatting** – This will strip any styles and put your text back to the default font and style.

10 **Fill color** – You must first have an object selected, and when you choose Fill color will, a pop up box appears with your color fill options of Solid (7.34), Gradient (7.35), or Custom.

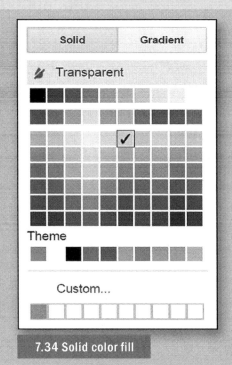

7.34 Solid color fill

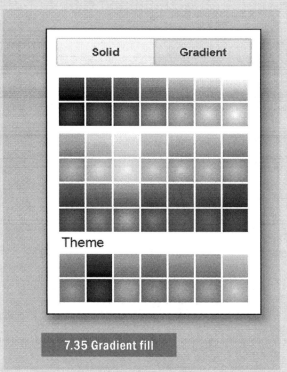

7.35 Gradient fill

With custom fill (7.36), you can slide the slider to choose a color or enter a hex number. You can also slide the slider on the far right to change the opacity of your fill.

7.36 Custom fill

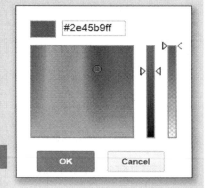

11 **Change shape** – You must first have a shape on the slide deck. Select the shape and than select Change shape. You can choose from any of the available shapes below.

Shapes

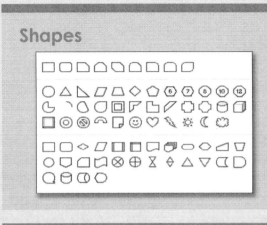

Arrows

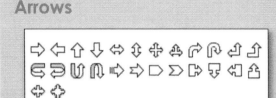

Callouts

Equation

12 **Change connector** – This is an efficient way to update your diagram or flowchart. Select your connector, than select Format > Change connector and the box that will appear gives you three options.

Straight Connector

Elbow Connector

Curved Connector

13 **Reroute connector** – Select the connected shape or connector that you want to reroute. ...

In the Format tab, in the Insert Shapes group, click Edit Shape, and then click Reroute Connectors.

14 **Borders and Lines** – There are six line options (7.36). Their flyout menu is shown below.

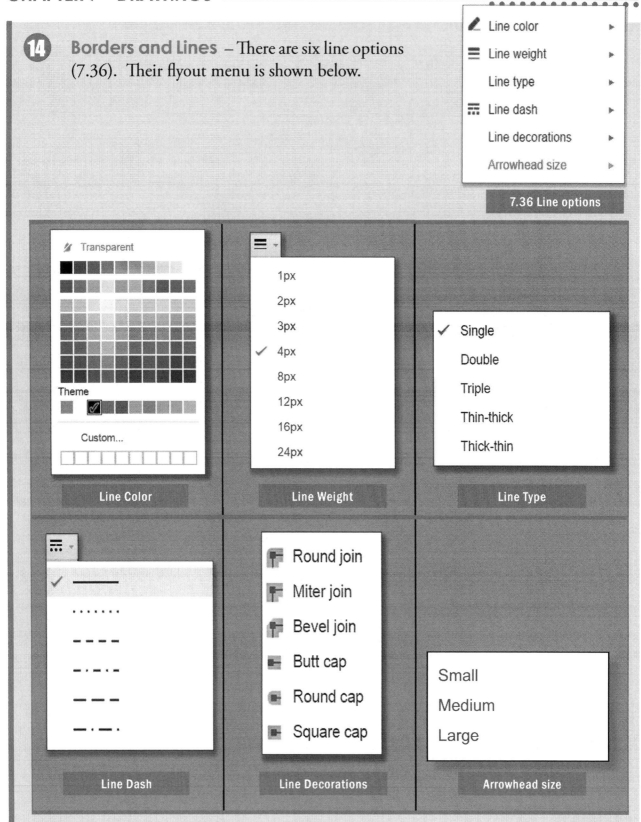

7.36 Line options

Line Color

Line Weight

Line Type

Line Dash

Line Decorations

Arrowhead size

15 **Crop image** – Cropping an image will remove parts of the image without scaling the size of the image.

The darker part of the image is what will show, where it is faded is the cropped part of the image.

16 **Image options** – You can adjust your image's Transparency, Brightness, and Contrast. If you don't like your adjustments, just choose Reset adjustments to put the image back to it's original state.

There are nineteen color options to apply to your image as show on the right.

C-7 Text Menu - ARRANGE

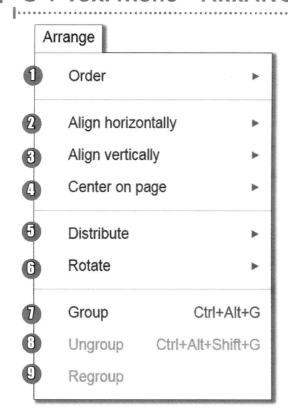

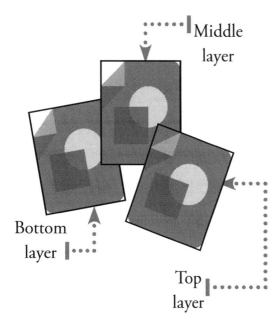

Middle layer

Bottom layer

Top layer

1 **Order** – Ordering refers to the placement of objects on your slide deck. The first object, you put on the canvas is the bottom layer. Each subsequence item will layer on top.

Selecting order, allows you to rearrange the order of these objects, moving the bottom up or the top down.

> Bring to front
> Bring forward
> Send backward
> Send to back

- Click **"Bring to Front"** to bring the selected object to the front of the other objects.

- Click **"Bring Forward"** to bring the selected object in front of the object it was immediately behind.

- Click **"Send Backward"** to move the selected object behind the object it was immediately in front of.

- Click **"Send to Back"** to place the selected object at the back of the objects.

② **Align horizontally** – There are three options when aligning horizontally:

> Left
>
> Center
>
> Right

- Click "Left" and all selected objects will be moved to align with the object of the farthest left.

- Click "Center" and all selected objects will be moved to align with center most object.

- Click "Right" and all selected objects will be moved to align with the object of the farthest right.

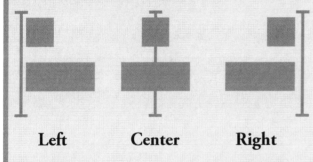

Left   Center   Right

③ **Align vertically** – There are three options when aligning vertically:

> Top
>
> Middle
>
> Bottom

- Click "Top" and all selected objects will be moved to align with the object of the farthest to the top.

- Click "Middle" and all selected objects will align with the middle most object.

- Click "Bottom" and all selected objects will be moved to align with the object at the bottom.

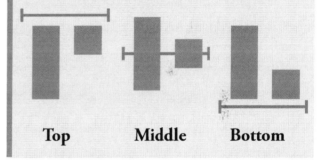

Top   Middle   Bottom

④ **Center on page** – There are two options when centering on page:

> Horizontally
>
> Vertically

- Click "Horizontally" and all selected objects will be moved to align to the very horizontal center of the page.

- Click "Vertically" and all selected objects will be moved to align to the very vertical center of the page.

5 **Distribute** – There are two options when distributing items on a page:

> Horizontally
>
> Vertically

- Click "Horizontally" and all selected objects will be moved to align horizontally with each other.
- Click "Vertically" and all selected objects will be moved to align vertically with each other.

7 **Group** – Grouping is like glueing your objects together, they become one.

8 **Ungroup** – After your items are grouped and you want to separate them, you ungroup them.

9 **Regroup** – After you have ungrouped your items and decide you want to regroup them.

6 **Rotate** – There are three options when aligning horizontally:

> Rotate clockwise 90°
> Rotate counter-clockwise 90°
> Flip horizontally
> Flip vertically

Rotate Clockwise 90°

> Rotate clockwise 90°
> Rotate counter-clockwise 90°
> Flip horizontally
> Flip vertically

Rotate Counter-Clockwise 90°

> Rotate clockwise 90°
> Rotate counter-clockwise 90°
> Flip horizontally
> Flip vertically

Flip horizontally

> Rotate clockwise 90°
> Rotate counter-clockwise 90°
> Flip horizontally
> Flip vertically

Flip vertically

C-8 Text Menu - TOOLS

Tools

① Spelling...

② Explore   Ctrl+Alt+Shift+I

③ Define   Ctrl+Shift+Y

④ Preferences...

⑤ Personal dictionary...

① **Spelling** – Alwasy goood to cheak your speling!!

Always good to check your spelling!

← Explore   ✕

🔍

WEB   IMAGES   DRIVE

② **Explore** – When you select **Tools**>Explore, without any words selected, the **artificial intelligence** of **Google** will scan your document and suggestions, from different words in the document, will appear in the Explore panel.

After your search, your results will filter into the 3 topics below:

1. Topics:

Features a number of suggested topics that are related to the content of your document. Click on any topic to access it's information.

2. Images:

The tab provides you with a set of images related to your content which you can add to your document. Added images come with a footnote at the bottom of the document.

3. Related research:

In this section you will be able to view research directly related to the topic of your document.

3 **Define** – When you select Insert > Define, a Dictionary panel opens. Type in the word that you want a definition for and the breakdown of the word, including it's pronunciation, uses, even synonyms appear.

4 **Preferences** – Preferences are auto settings that will work in Drawings. Automatically capitalize words, Use smart quotes.

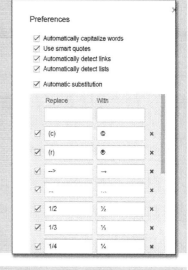

5 **Personal Dictionary** – Words, that aren't normally found in a standard online dictionary, are the words you want to add to your personal dictionary. If you business has a different type of name, add this.

C-9 Text Menu - TABLE

Table

1. **Insert table** ▶

2. Insert row above
   Insert row below
   Insert column left
   Insert column right

3. Delete row
   Delete column

4. **Distribute rows**
   Distribute columns

5. Merge cells

6. Unmerge cells

---

1 **Insert table** – A table is a grid of cells arranged in rows and columns. It can be useful to present data in a table inside a word processing document because it is displayed in an organized and easy to read format. You can insert a table anywhere from 1x1 up to 20 x 20 and all equations in-between.

2 Inserting rows and columns will add additional rows or columns above, below, right or left in your table.

3 Deleting a row or column will remove that row or column.

4 Distribute rows or columns will give them even spacing.

5 Merge cells will combine the cells as one.

6 Unmerging cells will put the cells back in the original order.

⑧ SITES

USER FRIENDLY WEB SITE DESIGN

Create a website for an easy portfolio, informational, or classroom site.

Drag and Drop . . .

. . . for easy placement onto you webpage. Insert images, your Docs, charts and so much more to have a web presence. Share your site with co-editors for easy collaboration.

A. HOW TO GET TO YOUR SITES

1

After your have logged into your Chrome account, type in

https://sites.google.com

2

From your Drive, select **BLUE NEW** button and go down to MORE, and than go to Sites.

Google revised their Sites in 2017, and in this chapter, I am only going to review the new Sites. The olds sites is supposed to be retired in 2018.

B. FEATURES OVERVIEW

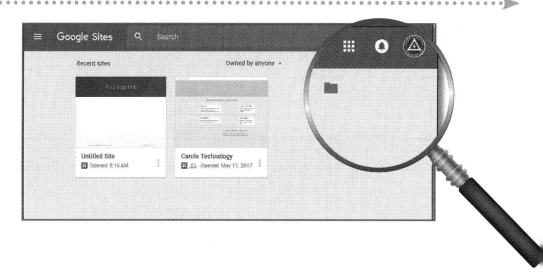

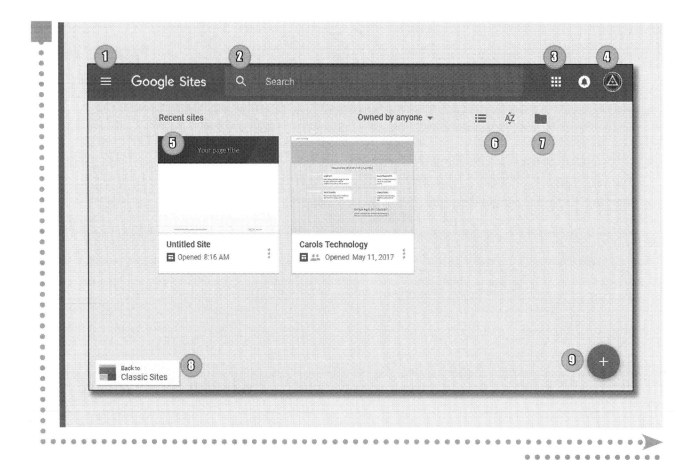

1 **Home** – Selecting the three lines will take you back to navigation where you can go to Classic Sites, Docs, Sheets, Slides, Feedback, Help and back to your Google Drive.

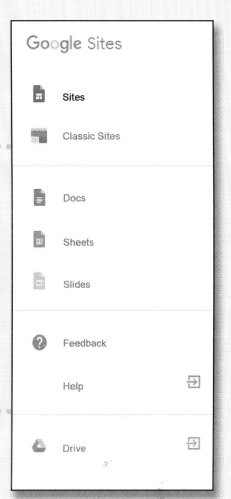

2 **Search** – Searching will take your to the files in your Google Drive. This makes adding a file to your Site easier to locate.

3 **Apps Grid** – This is another navigation tool, taking you to any app that is listed in the grid.

4 **Account** – Selecting your account icon will take you to where you can sign out, add account, or go to an account overview.

⑤ **Existing Sites –** Any sites you have created will either list down or be show as thumbnails in the center of the window.

⑥ **List or Thumbnail Grid** – You can switch back and from from list view (words) to grid view (thumbnails. The AZ will sort your list view alphabetically from A to Z or Z to A.

⑦ **Open** – Selecting the folder icon will take you to open from your Drive, Shared with me, Starred, Recent, or Upload.

⑧ **Classic Sites** – I will not review the Classic Sites. Google plans to phase out this feature and they encourage users to use the new Google Sites.

Migration options to transition your classic sites will be released in 2017. Both classic and new Sites will continue to be supported during this time.

Timelines and instructions regarding the gradual depreciation of classic Sites will be released in 2018. The specific deprecation date will be announced at least one year in advance.

⑨ **Create a new site** – Selecting the Red Circle with the plus in the center will instantly create a new Google Site. It is that simple !!

C. SITE CREATION OVERVIEW

① Home
Home – Selecting this icon (8.1) will take you back one step to your Sites home (8.2).

| 8.1 Home icon | 8.2 Sites Home |

② Title
Title – You always want to title your Docs, Sheets, Slides, and Sites. If you leave files untitled, you will now know the difference from one file to the other.

③ All changes saved in Drive
All changes saved in Drive – You can not see revision history with Sites but this notification tells you that your changes have been saved.

④ Undo/Redo
Undo/Redo – Go back one step in your files and go forward to your last move.

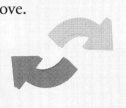

⑤ Preview

Preview – Selecting the eye will give you a preview of your site. You can change the preview of your site to reflect the device it will show on, from phone, to tablet, to monitor (8.3).

8.3 Phone / Tablet / Monitor

6. **Add editors** – As described in Sharing on page 36, to add editors is a way of collaboration. These editors can go into the Site and make changes, add pages, add documents.

7. **Publish** – Publishing your site allows people to view it on the web. You can allow anyone on the web to view it, or restrict access to people in your organization. This is the public version that you want others to see.

To publish your site:

1. Open a site in Google Sites.
2. From the top menu, click Publish. The "Publish your site" menu will open.
3. Type the site's URL under "Site address."

   Note: Terms that violate our Acceptable Use Policy will not be allowed.

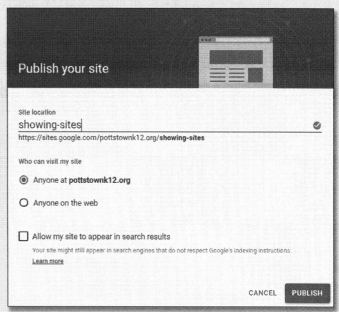

4. Under "Who can visit my site," choose who can see your site.
   - Anyone at your domain (only applies if you are a G Suite customer)
   - Anyone on the web (for G Suite customers, this is available only if enabled by your organization)
5. Under "Allow my site to appear in search results," choose how people can find your site.
6. Select this option if you want search engines to find your site.
7. Deselect this option if people must have the link (some search engines might still find your site).
8. When you're ready to publish your site, click PUBLISH. To confirm that your site published correctly, visit your site's URL.

8 **More** – The three dots takes you to the More menu (8.4).

Site analytics - You can monitor visitor traffic to your site with Google Analytics.

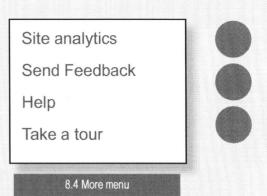

Site analytics

Send Feedback

Help

Take a tour

8.4 More menu

Step 1:

To register your site with analytics, go to:

https://analytics.google.com/analytics/web/?authuser=0#provision/SignUp/

1. Click Sign up.

2. Complete the sign-up form.

3. On the Analytics profile page, copy into your clipboard -- or otherwise note -- the Analytics account number listed after your site's name. It'll be in the format UA-XXXXXXXX-X.

Step 2: Turn on Google Analytics tracking for your site

1. Open your website in Google Sites.

2. Click More options More actions and then Manage site.

3. Under "Statistics," click the drop-down menu, then click Use Universal Analytics.

4. In the text box under "Analytics Web Property ID," paste in the copied, or otherwise type in, the Analytics account number for your Analytics account.

5. At the top of the screen, click Save.

It can take up to 24 hours for Analytics to track your site. To check if your site is being tracked, go to Google Analytics and check the Home screen.

D. EDITING MENU

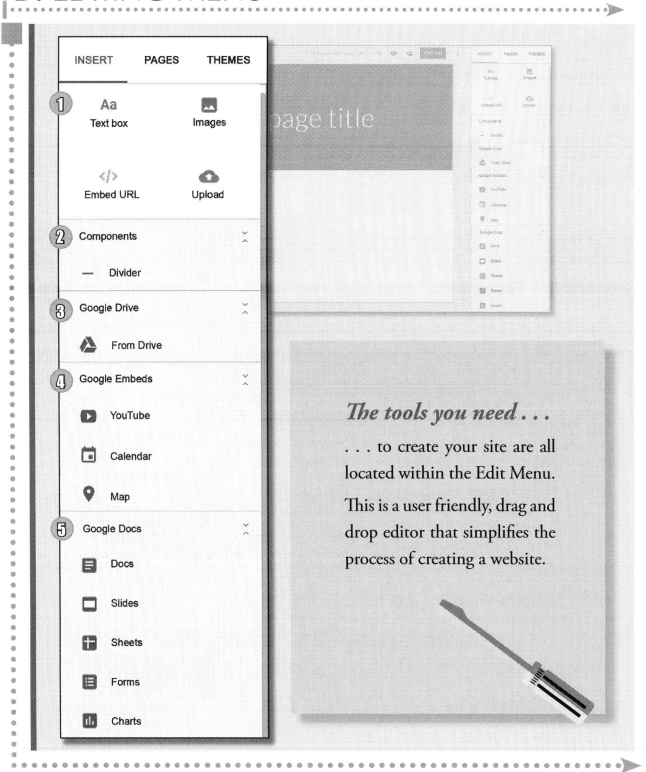

INSERT	PAGES	THEMES

1 Aa — Text box   Images

</> Embed URL   Upload

2 Components

— Divider

3 Google Drive

From Drive

4 Google Embeds

YouTube

Calendar

Map

5 Google Docs

Docs

Slides

Sheets

Forms

Charts

The tools you need . . .

. . . to create your site are all located within the Edit Menu.

This is a user friendly, drag and drop editor that simplifies the process of creating a website.

D-1 Insert

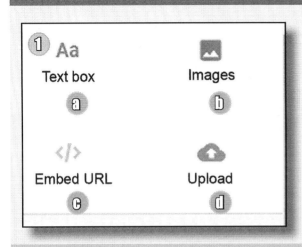

Insert – I'm going to work my way down the insert section of the Editing Menu, breaking it into sections to try and keep the flow easy and understandable.

a **Text box** – Text boxes are used to get your message out! You can have one word, a full sentence, or a paragraph. Selecting the Text box icon, shown above, a blue box, with pull round handles will appear on your page.

Your editing options will be at the top of this blue box (8.5).

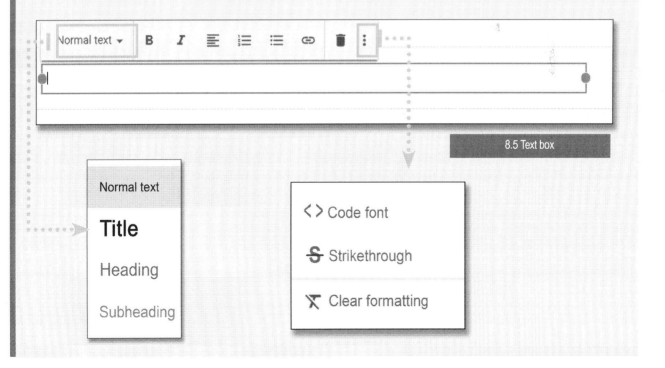

8.5 Text box

Text box (cont'd) –

A. **Style** - Normal text would is paragraph text. Title is used for the banner. Heading for the top of articles. Subheading for secondary emphasis.

B. **Bold** - used for emphasizing your words.

C. **Italic** - another means to highlight verbiage.

D. **Justification** - Either right, left, center, or full justification of your text.

E. **Numbered list** - 1, 2, 3, 4, how many as you want.

F. **Bulleted list** - A circular dot.

G. **Hyperlink** - used to link to either an external webpage or another page in your site.

H. **Trash** - To delete from your site.

I. **More** - Code Font - Code font just changes to font to a different format, it doesn't insert code. The other two choices are ~~Strikethrough~~ and to clear the format.

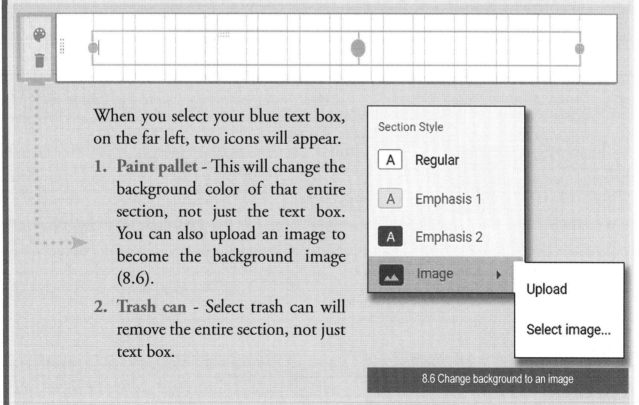

When you select your blue text box, on the far left, two icons will appear.

1. **Paint pallet** - This will change the background color of that entire section, not just the text box. You can also upload an image to become the background image (8.6).

2. **Trash can** - Select trash can will remove the entire section, not just text box.

Section Style

A Regular

A Emphasis 1

A Emphasis 2

Image ▶

Upload

Select image...

8.6 Change background to an image

Text box (cont'd) – When you select the text box, blue circle will be at each end. Grabbing one of these circles and dragging will change the background and you will see a grid in the background. This grid represents the columns in the background. Your webpage has 12 columns, as shown below (8.7).

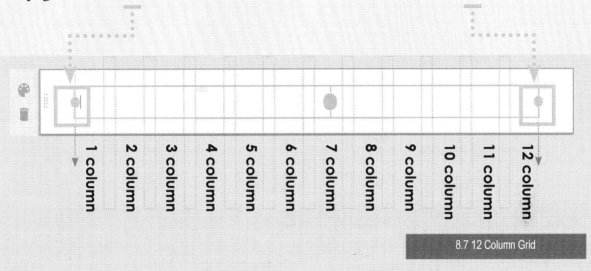

8.7 12 Column Grid

Below represents the different combinations you can do with this grid (8.8). There is a gutter between each column. This layout can give your overall page design consistency .

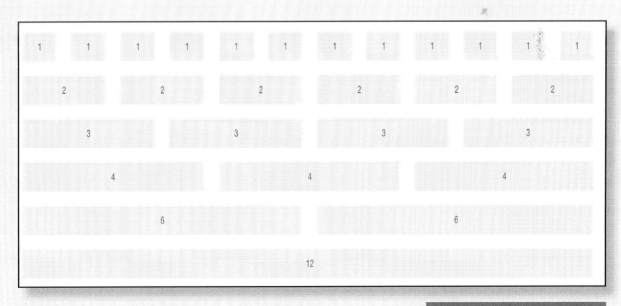

8.8 Column combinations

Image – Adding images to your Sites is easy. Your choices to import are:

> **By URL** - put a URL of an image and it will show on your page.
>
> **Search** - Type in your search and results will appear, but make sure that you go into Tools to filter your search for commercial resue with modification. You do not want to use an image that is copywrited.
>
> **Your albums** - This will take you take you to your Google Photos albums.
>
> **Google Drive** - This will take you to your Google Drive and you can insert an image by My Drive, Shared with me, and Recent.

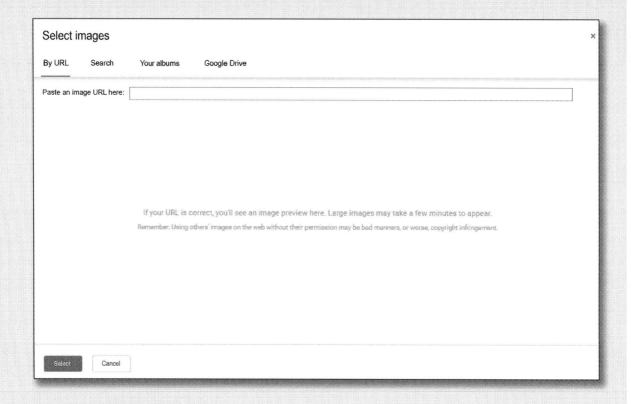

Image (cont'd) – When you have your image on your page, an actions toolbar will appear on top of it (8.9).

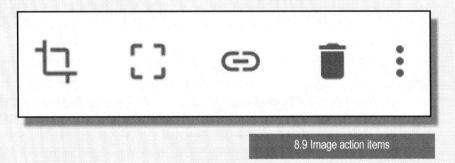

A. **Crop** - Cropping will remove parts of the image.

B. **Uncrop** - Restore the image to original state.

C. **Link** - Hyperlink your image to either another website or to another page in your site.

D. **Trash** - This will delete your image.

E. **More** - Selecting more:

- Replace image by either uploading or the options on the previous page.

- Add Alt Tag- Alt tags are accessed by screen readers who might have trouble seeing your content.

Embed URL – When you select this item, the message at the bottom of the pop-up box states "Paste a URL (link), and we will attempt to embed the content into your page" (8.10).

Embed from the web

URL
_____

Paste a URL (link), and we will attempt to embed the content into your page.

CANCEL   ADD

8.10 Embed URL

This is good to embed a URL from another website, but a powerful feature is to embed your Google Doc into your website. When you are in any of your Google products, you can share them via link. This link can be copied and pasted into this area and your Google Doc will now be embedded into your Sites. The below image is a row in Sites of Docs embedded (8.11)

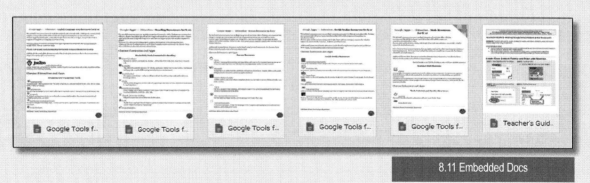

8.11 Embedded Docs

Upload – Selecting the Upload will take you instantly to your computer to upload an image.

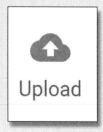

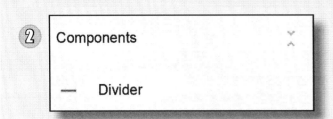

Components - Divider – A divider is a horizontal line used to create sections on your page.

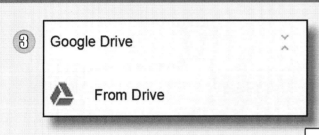

Google Drive - From Drive – Select Google Drive will take you to your Drive, to insert images from there.

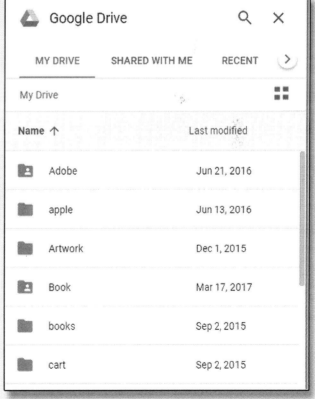

- My Drive
- Shared With Me
- Recent
- Starred

You can view by list view or grid view.

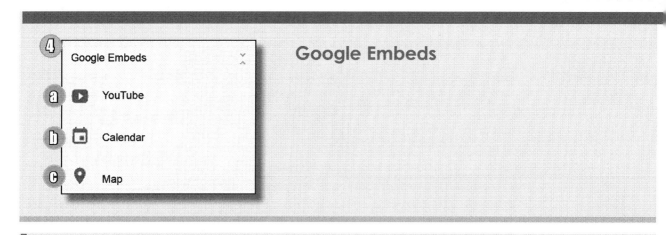

Google Embeds

④ Google Embeds

ⓐ ▶ YouTube

ⓑ 📅 Calendar

ⓒ 📍 Map

ⓐ **Embed YouTube** – When you select YouTube, a popup window will open. You can either search for a video on YouTube (8.12) or an Uploaded video.

After choosing YouTube, there is a search field where you can enter what you are looking for. After you select enter, a list will appear with the results (8.13). You can choose what you want and click Select. Your video will than be inserted on your page.

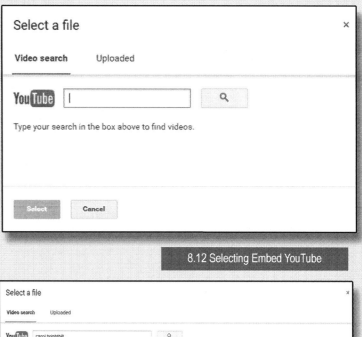

8.12 Selecting Embed YouTube

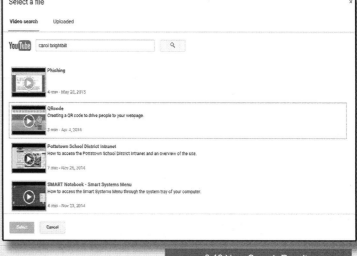

8.13 Your Search Results

Embed YouTube (cont'd) — With your video on your page (8.14), a toolbar will be located on top of it.

At the top are three icons:
- Fullscreen
- Settings (8.15)
- Trash

In the settings tab (8.15), you can:
- Change the Controls to Normal, Slide out of view, and Don't hide;
- Change the progress bar color from red to white;
- Allow Fullscreen

8.14 Embed on page

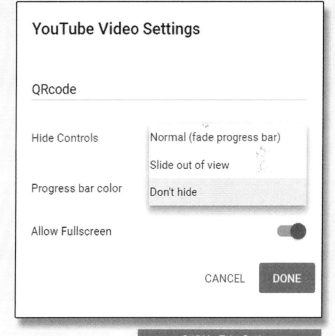

8.15 YouTube Settings

ⓑ **Embed Calendar** – With your Google account, you can have multiple calendars.

You have your default calendar, and you also have any calendar that is created when you create a Classroom. You can also have specialty calendars, such as Sunrise and Sunset, or your favorite sports team.

When you select to embed a calendar, all our your calendars will list down for you to choose from.

When the calendar is embedded, an action toolbar will be on top of it (8.16). From this toolbar you can:

- Fullscreen
- Settings (8.17); In settings you can change the View Mode to be Month, Week, or Agenda.
- Trash

8.16 Action toolbar

Calendar Settings

Beginner Readers

Show Title

Show Date

Navigation Buttons

Show Timezone

View Selection

View Mode   Month

Week

Agenda

8.17

Ⓒ **Embed Map** – As soon as you select Embed Map, a window will open where you can insert a Terrain Map or a Satellite Map (8.18). If you have created any maps, the second tab over will take you to them.

You can also insert a Placemark into your map.

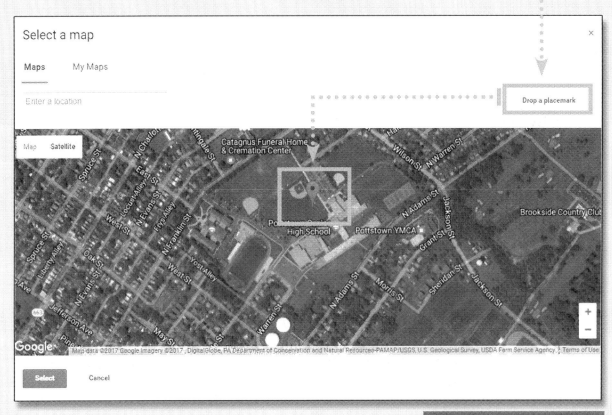

8.18 Satellite Map

⑤

Google Docs

▤ Docs

▢ Slides

▦ Sheets

▤ Forms

▥ Charts

Google Embeds – Your Google Apps embed seamlessly in your sites. You can scroll through the pages of your Docs, Slides or Sheets. Embedding a form is a great way to make it public.

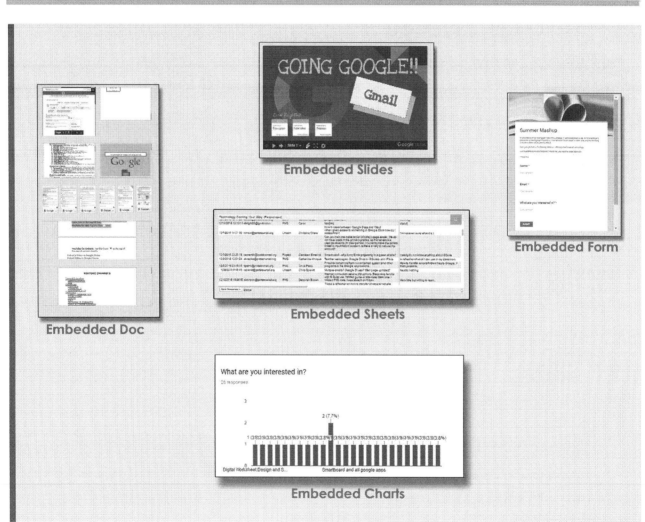

Embedded Slides

Embedded Form

Embedded Sheets

Embedded Doc

Embedded Charts

D-2 Pages

Pages – This will be the content of your Site. You will have a home page by default.

When you select this icon, a new page will be created. This is when you will give your page a name.

When you have multiple pages, they will stack on top of each other.

Selecting the 6 point grid at the far left of each page is a grab tool where you can move the pages up or down.

⠿   SHOWING   ⋮

- Set as home page - This option is not available on the Home page, just on all the others. And it gives you the option to make one of your other pages the Home page. The Home page is your top, first page. The one that is there by default.

- Rename page - will give your page a new title.

- Create sub page - this creates the dropdown navigational system common in websites.

- Remove page from site - this will delete the page.

- Hide from navigation - If a page is still in it's early stages and you do not want it to be seen.

Set as home page

Rename page

Create sub page

Remove page from site

Hide from navigation

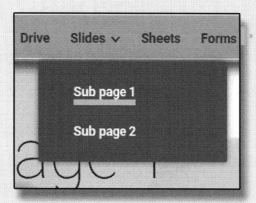

Creating a sub page will put a dropdown arrow beside the top page and than the sub page will list underneath it.

D-3 Themes

8.19 Six Sites themes

Themes – Google Sites comes with 6 Theme (8.19).

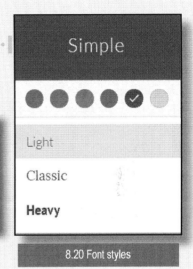

You can change the fonts from Light, Classic, or Heavy (8.20).

8.20 Font styles

There are six color choices but the last one, when clicked, displays a paint bucket which will turn into a color slider. You can also put a HEX color here.(8.21).

8.21 Color slider

D-4 Header

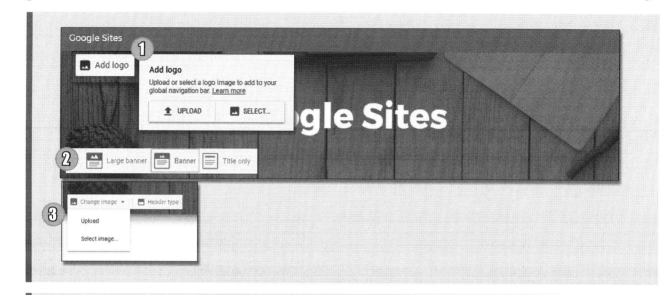

① **Add Logo** – Logos appear in the top global navigation bar, next to the site name. Sites intelligently detects the logo colors and uses them for your site's theme. Logo files can be in .jpg, .png, or .gif format. Tips: Remove any excess space around the image so the logo will resize properly. For best results, logos should be a minimum of 112 px tall.

② **Banner type** –

- A large banner will be about an inch deeper that the regular banner.
- Banner - Standard banner type.
- Title only - there will not be an image behind the page title.

③ **Change image** –

You can upload your own image for the banner or select an image from their gallery, by URL, Search, Your albums, or Your Drive.

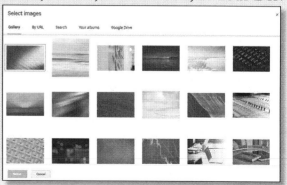

About The Author

Carol Brightbill is a Google Educator Level 1, Google Educator Level 2, and a Google for Education Certified Trainer. Her day job is as Technology Trainer for the Pottstown School District, in Pottstown, PA.

Carol also is a Graphic Designer and an award winning photographer. Her photography can be viewed at:

www.carolbrightbillphotography.com.

ACKNOWLEDGMENTS

Google Chrome Help Center:
https://support.google.com/chrome/?hl=en#topic=3227046

Google Drive Help Center:
https://support.google.com/drive/?hl=en#topic=14940

Google Docs Help Center:
https://support.google.com/docs?hl=en&authuser=0#topic=2811806

NOTES:

NOTES:

Made in the USA
San Bernardino, CA
24 May 2019